WHOSE HUMAN RIGHTS?

Margherita Rendel

Trentham Books

First published in 1997 by Trentham Books Limited

Trentham Books Limited
Westview House
734 London Road
Oakhill
Stoke on Trent
Staffordshire
England ST4 5NP

British Cataloguing in Publication Data
A catalogue record for this book is available from the British Library
ISBN: 1 85856 057 8

Designed and typeset by Trentham Print Design Ltd., Chester
and printed in Great Britain by BPC Wheatons Ltd, Exeter

WHOSE HUMAN RIGHTS?

CONTENTS

Acknowledgements

The first debt I wish to acknowledge is to the women who in earlier centuries and particularly in the last and this century have fought the battles for women's education, participation in the public domain of employment and public life and independence in the family and society, in short for women's emancipation and liberation, and who too often suffered physical danger, obloquy and social ostracism.

In relation to this book, I wish to thank Charlotte Mitra and Eileen Wormald for reading some chapters and for many helpful comments. I especially wish to thank Margaret Deyes for reading, commenting on and discussing the whole book. Her help has been most valuable. I also want to thank the staff of the London Offices of the United Nations and the International Labour Organisation and of the Institute of Advanced Legal Studies for finding references and materials not easily available; many other individuals and organisations have kindly sent me publications. Lastly, I want to thank Gillian Klein for her never-failing encouragement.

Margherita Rendel
December 1996
London

Introduction

This book is for those who are committed to human rights and for those who question whether human rights concepts and human rights procedures bring about any improvement in the conditions of life of people who are poor, weak, disadvantaged, excluded, have disabilities or are exploited. What effects do concepts and procedures of human rights have on the rhetoric of politics, law, economics and education and what effects on the practice of governments, administrators and bureaucracies, whether public or private? By what means do human rights achieve any results? What are the reasons for successes and failures?

The scope of human rights is vast; the number of intergovernmental institutions and organisations large. It is impossible to cover all aspects of the topics set out above within the pages of one book. I therefore decided to choose one disadvantaged group and one right and to examine the working of human rights primarily in relation to that group and that right, but not to the exclusion of other groups and other rights. Even so, it has proved impossible to provide anything like a complete account of these topics.

The group chosen is women, because they constitute at least half the population throughout the world, are everywhere disadvantaged in comparison with their male peers and exist in all other disadvantaged groups. In addition, for a variety of reasons, women have less access to physical force than some other disadvantaged groups. Furthermore, a person's sex is a given, not chosen, is visible and very difficult to escape from, change or hide. While all women share these characteristics, the specific situation and the specific needs of individual women and groups of women vary greatly and human rights must take account of these differences.

The right chosen is education, because access to education is usually essential for understanding the implementation of human rights and for enabling an individual or group to make effective use of human rights. Furthermore education can be important in creating and maintaining dominant ideologies, whether supportive of or hostile to human rights, but it should also provide the intellectual tools for decoding ideologies and understanding their implications. Education is a basic right in the modern world where a livelihood for many depends on literacy, access to 'book-learning' and the acquisition of intellectual, as well as practical, skills. For the disadvantaged, and especially the illiterate or semi-literate, education can provide a vital protection against exploitation; they will be able to read documents they are being asked to sign, they will have the means of seeking and of getting explanations of proposals being put to them.

It is not realistic to try to consider the rights of one group and one right in isolation. They have to be considered in context for several reasons. First, instruments on human rights contain non-discrimination articles applying them to virtually all groups of people. Secondly, developments in one institution or under one Convention are adapted for use in another. Thirdly, and most important, rights are interdependent. For these reasons, employment rights, trade union rights and refugees' rights are dealt with briefly.

The documents, institutions and organisations for human rights selected for examination have been determined by my choice of education and women. Emphasis has been given to the development of concepts and procedures within this framework. Despite the manifest and manifold violations of human rights we learn of every day, attitudes have changed. Abandoning cities to rape and pillage is no longer considered an ordinary incident of warfare, but a crime against humanity to be punished. Violence against women is no longer thought acceptable; governments have agreed internationally on the appointment of a Special Rapporteur for Violence against Women. The rhetoric has changed – and that is the first step to changing the practice. It is up to all people to use the rights we have to help to change the practice.

This book will, I hope, contribute to understanding the difficulties in making human rights effective and be a modest contribution towards making them more effective.

Chapter 1

Rights and power struggles

The first paradox of human rights is that the power of the State is used to curb the power of the State. The second paradox is that the power of the State is used to curb the power of those powerful enough to exercise some control over the State. How can the State control itself or those as powerful, and possibly richer, than itself?

It is possible because those who control the State believe that their continued authority and legitimacy depends on complying with the authorised demands of courts, tribunals, committees of investigation and so on, which the State could, if it wished, control or ignore. For the very powerful, submission to the rule of law is a voluntary act.

In contrast, for the weak, human rights provide a means of limiting or controlling the power and authority of the strong. The rule of law does not of itself necessarily provide such protection. Law can be an instrument of oppression as well as of protection and liberation; rights can be lost as well as won.

Let us begin by examining the conflicting pressures *within* the State. Most of the examples I use refer to Britain, but comparable examples could be found in virtually all States. The State is not one monolithic whole. It is notorious that organs of the State are in competition with each other: in competition for limited resources, for example in the annual budgetary round; in rivalry with each other for functions, for example MI5 and MI6[1], and MI5 and Special Branch of the Metropolitan Police[2]. It is notorious, and fills the media almost daily, that members of the Cabinet disagree with each other on policy, for example Gillian Shephard and her Cabinet colleagues on the funding of education[3]. Permanent Secretaries may demand written orders from Ministers wanting action which the former consider illegal[4];and lesser civil servants may resort to a variety of subterfuges or leaks to defeat or publicise what they consider to be improper policies or actions, for example Sarah Tisdall on the arrival of Cruise missiles[5], Clive Ponting on the sinking of the *General Belgrano*[6].

Other public servants take similar action, for example Nurse Pink on the treatment of elderly people in hospital[7]. Since whistleblowers are often victimised and lose their jobs despite acting to uphold proper and lawful standards, a charity has been set up to help and advise them[8]. And why else should there be so much anxiety in governing parties that civil servants might not implement the party's policy, but policies of their own, an anxiety that has led to the appointment of Special Advisers from outside the civil service sympathetic to a Minister's policies? It is known that what is even more bitter than an inter-departmental row is an intra-departmental row. Hierarchies, rules of procedure and disciplinary measures are intended to mitigate such disputes, but they depend for their effectiveness on individuals' willingness to observe them, that is on the belief that they are right. As the examples show, they do not always work.

It is therefore perfectly reasonable to expect organs of the State to monitor and exercise a control over other organs of the State. Indeed many powerful rulers have created organs of the State for this express purpose. For example, the mediaeval Lord Chancellor was the keeper of the King's conscience and it was his function to exercise the King's prerogative of mercy and to put right that which the administration or the common law courts had done wrongly or unfairly. The law of equity is based on this function. Napoleon I created the Conseil d'Etat for similar purposes. French administrative law rests on this foundation. Democratic governments and Parliaments (and other organisations)[9] have created Ombudspersons for comparable reasons.

Virtually all governments have to have regard to at least some interests. Governments in democratic countries have to pay attention to a wider range of interests whether they are represented through the electoral system or through interest or pressure groups. This is an important constraint; some interests however, are not adequately represented. When a government is able to manipulate the electoral system, legislative, administrative and judicial procedures, groups or even majorities may be excluded from the political process and exploited and oppressed. This was done in Northern Ireland by the gerrymandering of constituency boundaries in order to exclude Catholics from representation. And in

South Africa the National Party carried through a series of legal and constitutional manoeuvres supported by an overwhelmingly white electorate in order to implement the policy of apartheid (Dugard, 1985). Popular opinion can oppose as well as support human rights. These injustices brought to Northern Ireland 25 years of endemic terrorism and to South Africa some 40 years of strife, suffering and exclusion from the international community.

Furthermore, since the State is not monolithic, differences between members of the Cabinet, within the government, within the majority Party, between the government and the administration, or within the administration, may be exploited by or in favour of the weak in order to achieve the ends they desire. Thus it seems the Home Office was opposed to renewing the right of individual petition to the European Commission of Human Rights (discussed in chapter 5, Part 2), but the Foreign and Commonwealth Office was in favour because of the adverse effect on Britain's international standing if the right were not renewed. Some senior staff in the Home Office are known to have been hostile to the making of the Sex Discrimination Act 1975, but the Secretary of State, Roy Jenkins, was in favour and appointed a Special Adviser specifically to carry through this policy and that of more effective legislation on racial discrimination. In the latter case, the elected Minister was able to overcome the opposition of civil servants. It was the right of the people to vote that put the Secretary of State into office and into power, but that is not a complete explanation.

In addition, the dominant class in society is itself not monolithic. How important such divisions are can be seen in the struggle for women's suffrage. Because women were excluded from participation in Parliament, from political processes, and therefore from making or amending legislation, they were dependent on male legislators' agreeing to legislate in favour of women having the right to vote, to sit in Parliament and to hold public office. Without divisions within the male governing class, women would not have obtained the vote.

Some individuals or organisations are powerful enough to exercise a substantial measure of control over the State, because they control major industries, activities or resources. Some governments will see it as their function to assist such individuals or organisations. They may believe it is in their interest to do so in order to remain in power. Other governments may wish to limit this private power in order to improve the conditions of life of other less fortunate groups, people with disabilities, in poverty, or discriminated against – and may find themselves handicapped as a result of such private power.

Private power may be of one or more kinds. The following examples provide crude summaries of the arguments. The private power might be economic: 'If you impose a minimum wage and strictly enforce health and safety and environmental regulations, we'll move our factories to a country that has no such regulations where we'll make higher profits and you will face unemployment that will make the population hostile to you and cause you great expenditure in paying unemployment benefits so that you have to put up taxes and you will lose the next election'. But the government could join with other governments in supra-national and international organisations to develop and impose higher standards in all the countries concerned. National and supra-national legislation and inter-national Conventions could be enforced, and, in principle, property seized and assets frozen.

The private power may be financial: 'If you try to restrict our privileges and our freedom to make great profits, we'll organise a run on your currency, so that you lose reserves, have to devalue, put up interest rates and lose the support of the electorate'. Governments may use legislation to impose controls on the activities of financial institutions, and supra-national and international organisations can also impose rules and conditions.

Or the private power might exploit inadequacies in the law and 'inequality of arms': for example: 'O Local Authority, if you do not grant us, a rich international company, planning permission, we shall take you through public enquiries and the Courts at length; and your resources, as a small (or even a large) authority, are inadequate for the legal expense involved and you may lose and have to pay our costs as well as your own'. Again, national governments have means to prevent this type of threat if they wish to do so.

Or the private power may be ideological: 'If you pursue policies inimical to my interests, I shall use my media to misrepresent and rubbish your policies, your Ministers, your leaders and to persuade the electorate that what I want is what they want'. This threat is the most difficult to deal with, because controls over the media risk running counter to freedom of expression and the right to receive information, and could enable the government to suppress hostile or contrary opinion. But how far does freedom of expression in the face of private organisations and of fashion in fact exist at the present time?

The most telling example of the submission of force to the power of the State is the subordination of the military to the civil power, something we take for granted in Western democracies but which is too often an exception elsewhere in the world. It is obvious that the military are physically able to take over, seize whatever they want and do as they please, subject to officers giving and other ranks being willing to obey such orders, or to soldiers deciding to take such action on their own account. The military do not behave in such a way, not because civilians might be on the streets opposing such action – they could be shot down – but because the military accept the principle of their subordination to the civil power and to agreed constitutional arrangements, and because they are not prepared to shoot down civilians. The acceptance of these principles does not necessarily prevent individual soldiers from behaving wrongly or prevent individual serving or retired officers from plotting to overthrow a particular government, seeking a change of government or even of regime.

If this analysis is valid, then it is the ideological configuration, the system of beliefs and values which is crucial to the control of force or power. The corollary is that education, media and other forms of moral and intellectual influence are crucial to the winning of rights, and to the maintenance of rights and of democracy. This is not to say that ideology alone is sufficient. It must be supported by institutions, legislation, practices and procedures; and these are necessarily the responsibility of the State because only the State has the power and authority to provide and enforce national rules, institutions and procedures for this purpose.

The Development of Human Rights

The history of human rights is an account of how legislation has been obtained, often by force, institutions formed and developed, and practices and procedures elaborated. In the process, both the scope of human rights and the range of potential beneficiaries has been enlarged. It is an irregular process of gradualism, but it is no tale of rights 'broadening down from precedent to precedent'[10]. It is instead an account of struggle – struggle to gain rights, struggle to retain rights and struggle to regain rights. It is possible to note only a few of the more important arguments and developments here.

Concepts of human rights are intimately linked with concepts of fair treatment and of equality. It is clear that human beings want to be treated 'fairly' and will rebel or resist when treated too unfairly. They want their essential humanity to be recognised, that is, both their similarity with other humans, and their own individuality, their own specific character and characteristics. These are demands for equality and for freedom. As Tawney showed, equality and liberty are not incompatible (1931). On the contrary, equality is a pre-condition for freedom, both formal legal equality, equality before the law and substantive equality, the ability, resources and actual opportunities needed to make formal equality effective.

Resistance and Rebellion. What form resistance or rebellion will take depends on circumstances. For the very weak and isolated, it may be suicide, as when Chinese women threw themselves down the family well and so brought a curse upon the household (Croll, 1978: 37). For those who are strong, it may mean military action, or the threat of it, as when, to take an obvious example, the Barons extorted Magna Carta from King John at Runnymede in order to restore rights which they believed were their due. These are two extreme forms of resistance. Others are mass rebellion, terrorist attacks, the refusal of soldiers to obey officers, conspiracies. Still others are civil disobedience, hunger-strikes, sit-ins, marches, street demonstrations, strikes, go-slows, lobbying by individuals or groups, activity by pressure groups, publicity stunts such as hiding in an organ-loft to shout 'Votes for Women' at an important political meeting (Strachey, 1928/1978: 311), and the woman who showed her naked body covered with slogans protesting against the celebration of the motor industry in Coventry Cathedral in January 1996, fly-posting, leafleting, writing letters, signing, collecting signatures for and presenting petitions, and so on. Most of these forms of resistance are dependent on the classic civil and political liberties of freedom of assembly, freedom of association, freedom of expression and the franchise.

It is because oppression and inequality can breed revolution, as was noted two and a half millennia ago by Aristotle (*Politics*), that the threat of resistance and of rebellion often induces the powerful to accept curbs on their power.

Widening Concepts. Notions of equality and freedom have a long and honourable history. We find them in ancient Greek democracies, although rights were limited to the adult free male citizens, who alone were both entitled and required to participate in the government of their city-state, thereby incurring obligations as well as enjoying rights. Later, Christianity introduced an element of equality through the concept of all being equal in the sight of God (Vallat, 1971: 11; Madiot, 1991: 7). In the Middle Ages, rights were highly specific and particularistic. They were limited to particular groups: freemen, knights, holders of land, the Church, chartered towns and cities. The rights conferred were also specific: for individuals the right to use the King's rather than manorial courts, to protection from attack, to be free from labour services, not to be tied to the land; for selected towns and cities, the right to administer themselves, to levy tolls, to hold markets; and for guilds the right to control entry to training and advancement in their trade or occupation. Economic and social rights were therefore included, perhaps even dominant. Unger (1976: 66-86) suggests that the particular way in which post-feudal society developed in Europe required the supremacy of the rule of law, a notion developed in modern Europe from canon law and Roman law. These elements came together in the early modern period and laid foundations on which modern systems of human rights could be built.

Concepts of democracy were expressed in seventeenth century England, for example by Rainsborough on 20 October 1647 in the Putney Debates[11]:

> I think that the poorest He that is in England hath a life to live as the greatest He, and therefore truly, sirs, I think every man that is to live under a government ought first by his own consent to put himself under that government.

Ideas expressed in the Putney Debates recur and are developed in various forms during subsequent years. Locke develops the idea of consent to government by those of the governed who are property-owners. Tom Paine in *The Rights of Man*, Parts I and II, presents a far more revolutionary prospect, including measures of social security for the aged and for others, a prospect taken for granted in this century. In *A Vindication of the Rights of Woman*, 1792, Mary Wollstonecraft, one of a long line of feminist writers[12], castigated the frivolous education of such girls as received any education, which, she claimed with some justification, tended to make women foolish and vicious. She stressed the importance of education founded on knowledge and understanding to enable women to be useful members of society.

Towards the close of the eighteenth century, the shift to a universalist conception of rights was expressed in official documents such as the American Declaration of Independence in 1776 and the French Declaration of the Rights of Man and of the Citizen in 1789. It was an ideological shift that prepared the way for claims of rights and to equality for all classes, for racial, ethnic and religious minorities, for women and ultimately for children, animals and the environment. A nice example of such an application can be found in the Declaration of Sentiments adopted by feminists at the Seneca Falls Convention of 1848, that *annus mirabilis* of revolutions:

> ...We hold these truths to be self-evident: that all men and women are created equal; that they are endowed by the Creator with certain inalienable rights; that among these are life, liberty and the pursuit of happiness; that to secure these rights governments are instituted, deriving their just power from the consent of the governed...

> The history of mankind is a history of repeated injuries and usurpations on the part of man toward woman, having in direct object the establishment of an absolute tyranny over her. To prove this, let facts be submitted to a candid world.

> He has never permitted her to exercise her inalienable right to the elective franchise.

> He has compelled her to submit to laws, in the formation of which she had no voice...[13]

The fact that ideas of equality were not originally applied to women, any more than the phrases of the Declaration of Independence 1776 applied to black slaves, does not nullify the crucial importance of these ideas in the development of human rights. They were phrased in universalist terms, but their authors simply did not conceive of those excluded, the outsiders, as part of the 'universe' to whom such ideas could apply; more exactly, the former outsiders have since forced themselves into that universe.

Economic Change and Political Structure. The ideological change taking place was not accompanied by equivalent changes in legal, administrative and judicial practice, nor by changes in attitudes on the part of many in positions of local or national power. The seventeenth century struggles in England shifted power from the King to the aristocracy and gentry, power which was largely unchallenged until the end of the eighteenth century. Throughout this period, agricultural innovation and the consequent desire to enclose land led to the expulsion of the peasantry from whatever land and resources they had access to. The effect was to create a landless class deprived of any right to subsistence except on the most oppressive terms. The Hammonds (1911/48) have shown how ruthlessly the aristocracy and landed gentry were able to exploit their control of Parliament to pass private Enclosure Acts permitting them to seize common lands[14].

The increase in wealth of the developing middle class made it possible to develop scientific and technological inventions. But the lack of intervention by the State and the failure to implement both Christian ideology and philosophical universalism meant that factory workers were treated by many employers as a mere commodity, and appalling slums and atrocious factory conditions were the disastrous norm. Robert Owen and Sir Titus Salt, industrialists who sought to provide model workplaces, decent dwellings and other amenities for workers at New Lanark and Saltaire respectively, were exceptions to this norm.

Many of the new, wealthy factory-owners and manufacturers were excluded from a right to vote and the newly industrial cities were not represented in Parliament. Their interests were subjected to those of the landed classes, the landed interest. Hence the pressure for reform of the Parliamentary franchise, a process accomplished in Britain by stages between 1832 and 1928. The Great Reform Act 1832 abolished the 'rotten boroughs'[15], ensured representation for the great industrial cities, and created national criteria for middle-class men to have the right to vote. First urban and then rural working men were enfranchised (1867 and 1884 respectively), and the Ballot Act 1882, requiring secret ballots, was passed to provide some security for those who wished to vote against the party of their employer or landlord. The passing of the Ballot Act shows a recognition that a right by itself is not sufficient; further legislation and action is needed to make the exercise of that right effective. It has take·

from 1870 until after the Civil Rights Act of 1964 for Blacks in the Southern States of the USA to be able to exercise the franchise granted by Constitutional Amendment XV nearly a century earlier.

As more and more classes of men were admitted to the franchise, the demands of women became more insistent. The ferocity of the opposition to women's suffrage and the lengths to which women had to go to secure the right to vote in Parliamentary elections reflects first of all the extent to which women were conceived of as non-persons and secondly the importance attributed to the sovereign Parliament as opposed to local government bodies, creatures of Parliament, where women won the vote earlier, though with difficulty.

Using existing rights to secure more. The right to demonstrate, to fill the streets and to hold public meetings, the right of assembly, could not much longer be refused by the government, after the horror and condemnation aroused by the massacre of Peterloo in 1819 when unarmed and orderly demonstrators including women and children were fired upon in St Peter's Fields, Manchester, by the Manchester Yeomanry, composed of manufacturers, merchants, publicans and shopkeepers on horseback (Thompson, 1968, pp. 748-753 and 757). The massacre was followed by the passing of the notorious and repressive 'Six Acts', which restricted public meetings, publications, and certain rights in criminal cases. The policy of open constitutionalism pursued by working-class reformers before Peterloo, Thompson observed, was proving more revolutionary than the policy of conspiracy and insurrection (p. 749). But even now no formal right of assembly exists in English law, and indeed the *de facto* right is restricted in a number of ways by legislation, made more restrictive by the Criminal Justice Act 1994, and is subject largely to police discretion. The *de facto* right of assembly continues to be of great importance. This has been so, for example, in winning the Great Reform Bill, in women's struggle for the franchise and in the struggle for the abolition of the poll tax in 1990. It continues to be important for the protection of suckling calves from veal crates – animal rights –and in opposition to ever more roadbuilding, the M11, Batheaston, and Newbury – a struggle for a good environment for all of us.

Existing rights have provided the basis on which it has been possible to demand further rights. This is plainly the case in Britain. Civil disobedience and demonstrations had to be used to obtain the franchise

The importance of political rights was clearly recognised by many political protagonists. For the constitutional suffragists and the militant suffragettes, the franchise was needed to establish women's dignity as citizens, and, as Marion Phillips wrote, it was not simply to have, but to use (Rendel, 1977: 59). In particular, political rights have been used to win economic and social rights.

Economic and social rights. Such rights have sometimes been granted by despotic or authoritarian governments, for example, limited educational provision in France by Napoleon I, or measures of social security in Germany by Bismarck's government in the nineteenth century. In Britain, most economic and social rights have been won as a result of the use of civil and political rights to vote into government parties favouring such rights, as was the case with the Liberal Government of 1905 and the Labour Government of 1945. Economic and social rights have also appeared in constitutions, for example in the Preamble to the Constitution of the Fourth Republic in France, and re-enacted as part of the Constitution of the Fifth Republic. These provisions were clearly a post-war response to the demands of the *Front Populaire* led by Léon Blum in the 1930s[16].

Economic and social rights are no more likely than civil and political rights to stay put. If the self-interest of the powerful may on occasion assist directly or indirectly the protection of rights, that self-interest may equally, on other occasions, seek their restriction or destruction. Or the weak may have won these rights as the result of a fortunate combination of circumstances, coupled with good leadership and the mobilisation of supporters, but these are rarely permanent factors. How then may the weak retain and strengthen rights once they have been won?

Institutionalising rights. For rights to be made secure, they must be embedded or institutionalised in a web of institutions, rules of procedure and beliefs: in legislation, constitutions and international Conventions. The inclusion of provisions for implementation and enforcement is of crucial importance. Thus in order to make their victory permanent and to prevent a recurrence of past wrongs, the supporters of William III and Mary II required them to accept the Bill of Rights in 1688. A series of Habeas Corpus Acts, framed in increasingly rigorous terms, were passed to ensure that the legislation was in fact observed (Sharpe, 1976). Since in Britain such legislation has only the force of any other law, it is vulnerable to amendment by any subsequent legislation incompatible with it, as the effect of immigration legislation on *habeas corpus* has shown. Other countries make better provision for their human rights, both by giving them constitutional force and by phrasing them in more general terms than is usual in English law. Equally important is the creation of a hegemony or societal system of values, in favour of the effective enforcement of rights. This topic is discussed later in the book.

Let us consider institutionalisation through legislation with enforcement procedures. The reformers need to have control not only of the procedure in the legislature, but also of the bureaucratic and legal processes involved in drawing up legislation. Formulating legislation is a process which can take months or years, and when undertaken in a hurry without adequate consultation is most likely to lead to major problems in implementation, inconsistencies and confusion in application, and numerous subsequent amendments by regulations and amendments to amendments. Demands for reform of the law on abortion took some 30 years from the founding of the Abortion Law Reform Association (ALRA) in 1936 until legal abortion was obtained in the 1967 Act. Since then, at least four attempts to destroy the effect of the Act have had to be opposed (Private Member's Bills introduced by White in 1975, Benyon in 1977, Corrie in 1980, and in the Human Fertilisation and Embryology Bill in 1990) and there were two Ten-Minute Rule Bills,[17] one each in 1969 and 1978.

The Sex Discrimination Act was won surprisingly quickly in eight years from Joan Vickers' attempt to include sex within the scope of the Race Relations Bill in 1967 to the passage of the Sex Discrimination Act in 1975. In contrast, demands for equal pay were first expressed formally in a Resolution of the Trades Union Congress in 1888, but the Equal Pay Act was not passed until 1970 and was not due to come into effect until 1975 to give time for employers to adjust their wage rates to equal pay for the same or broadly similar work. Instead, too many employers used the time to segregate further men's and women's work. European legislation and a decision of the European Court of Justice (*Commission of the European Communities* v. *United Kingdom* 1982)[18] compelled an unwilling Government to produce amendments to the Equal Pay Act (the Equal Pay (Amendment) Regulations 1983)[19] in order to overcome the effects of the segregation and to provide equal pay for work of equal value but the Regulations were framed to make it as difficult as possible for equal value claims to be successful. The case of equal pay illustrates well the long time and technical difficulties of making effective reforms and the helpful part supranational organisations can play.

These are not exceptional examples. To expect major improvements to be achieved quickly and to be carried at once into 'the hearts and minds' of people is simply unrealistic. As accounts of winning rights show, success depends on careful thought, lobbying, publicity, strategic and tactical planning and persistence over many years.

Before the Second World War, rights which we should now call human rights were mostly confined to a few Western nation-states, some of which provided traditional civil and political liberties in specific laws with or without special status, or in their constitution. Most also provided some, usually limited, social and economic rights in the form of educational services, health insurance, unemployment insurance, public assistance in case of indigence, some Trade Union rights, some protective legislation and some very limited planning controls to protect the environment. In contrast, the Soviet Union provided much more extensive social and economic rights for much of the population, but the formal political and civil rights they provided were biased in favour of the regime. In the former case, the value of civil rights was largely undermined by poverty, unemployment, inadequate education, poor health and bad housing, although political rights remained intact. In the latter case, social and economic rights were denied to whole classes and were undermined by the weakness of civil rights and the purely formal nature of political rights. The winning and keeping of rights therefore depend on peaceful or violent direct action, political processes, such as legislation, administrative action, lobbying, and also on legal processes. But, as we shall see, there are difficulties in using legal processes.

Constitutions, Law and Legal Processes

Rights of various kinds are commonly written into national constitutions and are often enforceable through a Constitutional Court. The Constitution of the USA provides the oldest example. The US Supreme Court has used provisions on rights both to deny rights and equality, for example by upholding legal segregation as in *Plessy* v. *Ferguson* (1896)[20] and to strike it down, for example in holding that separate facilities wer inherently unequal, as in *Brown* v. *Board of Education of Topeka* (1954)[21]. The Supreme Court has also condemned indirect discrimination, the equal rule with unequal effect. This general principle, used in the 'grandfather' cases[22], was developed in *Griggs* v. *Duke Power Company* (1971) to end the practice by which Duke Power demanded higher qualifications than the job required in order to exclude Blacks. *Griggs* has been very influential in the formulation in Britain of S. 1(1)(b) of the Sex Discrimination Act 1975 and the Race Relations Act 1976, and has been much quoted in early cases under these Acts. Legal concepts can travel in time and place.

In some countries, although rights may be written into the Constitution, they may be protected by means short of a Constitutional Court which can test the constitutionality of actual or proposed legislation. This is the case in France, where constitutionality is monitored by a Constitutional Council. However in the UK, what we might call constitutional provisions, such as the right to vote, the composition and duration of Parliament, Magna Carta, the Bill of Rights, the composition and powers of the Courts, the rights of citizens of any kind, have no more standing than an Act on the licensing of dogs. Indeed, a married woman's right to her own legally separate property was taken away by Finance Acts which deemed the wife's income to be that of her husband, so that the Inland Revenue repaid to him excess tax paid by her. This anomaly has now been removed, but similar denials of rights could recur. Our unwritten Constitution consists of Acts we think of as constitutional together with conventions and practices normally observed. All are vulnerable to the whim of a government whenever it is able to use party discipline in support of its wishes. The nearest we come in the UK to enforceable rights are the European Convention on Human Rights and relevant Directives of the European Union.

Several levels of legislation lie in a 'hierarchy of texts', the number and forms varying in different countries. Broadly there are four major levels: (i) Constitutional or entrenched provisions, (ii) statute law, (iii) regulations and subordinate legislation, (iv) advisory circulars, statements by Ministers and so on, which are not legally binding. Some statutes are outlines for legislation with the details to be filled in by regulations. In the UK, statutes can confer on the Minister power to amend the statute itself by regulations[23], and regulations are not adequately scrutinised by

Parliament or by any other means. Thus our rights can be whittled away by regulations almost unseen and unchallenged.

Statutes may provide formal rights, but be deficient in effectiveness. For example the British Sex Disqualification (Removal) Act 1919 enabled women, including married women, to be eligible for most public offices, professions and occupations, but did little to prevent discrimination against women. Indeed advice to the Treasury in 1921 expressly pointed to this method of evading the Act:

> the woman is not under an inherent disability from holding certain posts because she is a woman or because she is married. In other words, the appointment of a woman, or a married woman to these posts, if made, would not be invalid. It is quite another thing to say that a woman is entitled to be appointed to or to hold any of the specified posts on exactly the same terms as if she were a man, and this in fact is precisely what the Act refrains from saying. (Martindale, 1938: 99-100)

Litigation based on the Act was uniformly unsuccessful until *Nagle* v. *Fielden*, the Jockey Club case in 1966[24]. Similarly while legislation may grant rights, as the Abortion Act 1967 does, the rights may be contingent on other individuals or bodies being willing to give effect to them; for example under S. 4 of the 1967 Act, doctors may refuse to give agreement to abortions on grounds of conscience.

Legislation may impose on government or other bodies an obligation to provide services, but for procedural reasons, the terms of the legislation or the effect of precedent, it may be impossible for the intended beneficiaries to obtain the service apparently guaranteed. There are many examples in Britain at present. Lawyers have agreed that it is impossible for individuals to secure an adequate education service through the Courts (Harlow and Rawlings, 1984: 296). On this, Wade observes: that a duty owed to the public generally rather than to a person individually cannot be enforced by an individual (1994, pp. 611-12 and 787). The most striking case examplifying this principle is *R.* v. *Inner London Education Authority* ex p. *Ali* in 1990. It is common knowledge that 'Care in the Community' and hospital services fail to provide adequate services because of lack of funding for which the Government, not they, is responsible. Indeed the Court of Appeal has held that the Department of Social Security is not obliged to reach a decision on the amount of income support to be given to a claimant within the 14 days required by the statute, if there are not sufficient staff to deal with cases. Thus the Court appears to think that inadequate resources resulting from government decisions are sufficient to deny legal rights.

It is however possible for legislation to include effective enforcement procedures. Legislation may impose stringent requirements, for example the last Habeas Corpus Act in 1679, S. 9 makes a judge who fails to comply with the requirement to issue a writ personally liable to a fine of £500 payable to the applicant[25]. Habeas Corpus is now of very little value in immigration cases as a result of the Immigration Acts since 1971 and British legislation may now be contrary to the requirements of Art. 6(1) of the European Convention on Human Rights (Feldman 1993: 337).

Procedural law, as lawyers know, can determine substantive law. The role of the 'Brandeis' brief[26], by which evidence of the economic, social or other implications of a possible judgement may be put before the Court, has been crucial in a series of human rights cases before the US Supreme Court. Procedural provisions in the US Federal Courts, especially class actions[27] and *amicus curiae* briefs[28], have been particularly helpful to human rights issues and have been used effectively not only by the National Association for the Advancement of Colored People, but also by environmentalists and for women's issues. Comparable scope for presenting a full range of arguments on an issue so as to challenge, re-interpret or support existing jurisprudence (case-law) and the values which it incorporates are seldom available to a comparable extent in other jurisdictions. However, these opportunities are equally available to opponents of people seeking human rights. And Supreme Court Justices, appointed by the President subject to the approval of the Senate, often reflect the bias of the President. Constitutional, substantive and procedural law cannot by themselves guarantee rights.

Legislation may be designed to achieve ends by promotional measures rather than by prohibiting undesired actions. Legislation may include provisions for research and educating public opinion in its purposes, as do the Sex Discrimination Act 1975 and the Race Relations Act 1976. The American Executive Order No. 11246 of 1965, as amended, requires all those holding federal contracts to make 'good faith' efforts to increase the number and proportion of women and minorities in their workforce.

Failure to comply can, and in some cases does, lead to the cancellation of contracts. This requirement of affirmative action, now under attack, has been the basis on which training organisations and employment agencies working specifically for women and minorities have been able to secure the interest of employers and to win advancement for their clients.

A few British local authorities used similar means to promote equal opportunities for women, ethnic minorities, gays, lesbians and persons with disabilities. This practice was made almost impossible by S. 17 of the Local Government Act 1988 which requires local authorities to award their contracts without reference to non-commercial considerations. Only very limited provisions, chiefly restricted to training where the number of one sex or ethnic group is under-represented in an occupation, exist for positive action under the Sex Discrimination and Race Relations Acts. However these Acts impose duties on the Equal Opportunities Commission and the Commission for Racial Equality to promote equality between the sexes and between ethnic groups respectively. European legislation does permit positive action at least in its programmes.

The enforceability of provisions may depend on the attitudes of courts to such provisions. The more general the provisions, the wider the scope a sympathetic judiciary may give them. However, provisions on rights are generally concerned with redressing the balance between the powerful and the weak, between rich and poor: therefore in changing the *status quo*. Since the law tends to be a conservative profession, and since law inevitably looks to the past for precedents, the likelihood of a broad interpretation for new and enlarged rights coming from radical judges is not usually high.

In practice, courts and tribunals are systematically biased towards the past, because they are either bound or influenced by precedent. By bias, I mean a leaning or uneven distribution of weight (as in bowls), not prejudice or prejudging. It is reasonable for judges to look to the past to see how a type of issue has been decided on previous occasions. It is reasonable to demand that there should be certainty in law, that similar disputes should be decided according to the same rules and principles. If there is too much uncertainty, there is an incentive for every dispute to be litigated. And it is notorious that hard cases make bad law. The literal interpretation of legislation that has been so dominant in Britain emphasises the bias to the *status quo* and, sometimes, the *status quo ante*.

Reforms are therefore difficult to accomplish because the inertia of the system will operate against them. This should have the effect of helping to protect reforms that governments wish to reverse, but may not do so. Rights may be better protected by detailed provisions that give judges little opportunity to slide back from legislators' more progressive intentions. An example lies in the Divorce Reform Act 1969 which removed from judges discretion in granting a divorce when the conditions specified in the Act were satisfied, the exception being the ground of 'grave hardship'. This may be seen as making legislation 'judge-proof', that is drafting legislation in such a way that judges cannot interpret it in a sense contrary to that intended by the Government and Parliament, or create an absurdity, because the words of the statute are plain. As Norman Marsh has observed (1973:96): 'The Westminster Parliament has never regarded the courts as junior partners with itself in the legislative task, as the authors of the great Continental codes saw the relationship between their work and that of the Courts'[29].

Both pro-rights and anti-rights legislators can try to make legislation judge-proof, so that natural inertia cannot always be relied upon to defend existing rights. The teleological method of interpretation favoured by the European Court of Justice (ECJ) and increasingly accepted in British courts helps to secure reform, but could also be used to defend less desirable changes expressed in legislation. The remedy in that case is a Bill or Declaration of Rights with overriding authority.

Secondly, in an adversarial, as opposed to an inquisitorial, system of litigation, and where those claiming rights have to prove their claim, the claimants will always be at a disadvantage because, in case of doubt, the balance of probability will weigh on the defendant's side. In this sense, law is never equal and parties are never equal before the law. The side which has to prove its case is disadvantaged, although it is true that the burden of proof may shift in the course of litigation. It is easier to make a decision or to take action than to get either changed, another cause of bias. The result is that those seeking to secure the undoing of an unjust action have both to prove their case and to secure a change in the decision. It is, in principle, possible to legislate for reversing the burden of proof. In practice, this is difficult as the attempt to include such a provision in the Sex Discrimination Act has shown, because such a change would run counter to long-established and revered principle. The opposition of the

British Government to proposals from the EU for such a change in equal opportunities legislation re-inforces this argument.

Nonetheless, legislation, when backed by monitoring, support for implementation and the threat of litigation, is not useless. The effect of legislation is normally to bring about changes in processes and institutions in the State. To carry those changes into effect, individuals will be required to review the processes and shift the bias of the institutions they control and the processes they operate in order to implement the reform. In doing so, they may also have to change their ideas, as in the case of equality legislation, which has led to the creation of 'equality committees' and to a review of procedures for appointments, promotions, and conditions of service in many organisations. The wonder is that reforms are implemented, not that they are not.

The growth of rights has been erratic. Law has provided an essential foundation for this growth, both as legislation in its many forms and as litigation. In the next chapter, I look at the international development of human rights. In chapter 3, I turn to the various ways in which education can be used.

Notes

1. Peter Wright with Paul Greengrass, 1987, *Spycatcher: the Candid Autobiography of a Senior Intelligence Officer*, New York: Viking, gives an account of this rivalry.

2. With the end of the Cold War and the ceasefire in Northern Ireland since 1994, MI5 is looking for new work, and seeks to participate in the work of Special Branch in relation to terrorism, drugs and 'serious crime'. Special Branch stresses that police officers are subject to rules and accountability unlike MI5 who decide their own work in secrecy reporting only to the Home Secretary (e. g. *The Guardian*, 29 January 1996).

3. Gillian Shephard, the Secretary of State for Education and Employment in 1995, is known to have sought more money for education and to have opposed the voucher scheme for nursery education supported by the Prime Minister, John Major.

4. For example the Permanent Secretary at the Overseas Development Agency asked for written instructions from the Minister to finance the Pergau Dam in Malaysia which was considered bad value for money and a misuse of aid funds. It was the subject of an enquiry in 1994, which criticised the Minister.

5. Sarah Tisdall, a junior clerk in the Foreign and Commonwealth Office, leaked to *The Guardian* in 1983 two secret memoranda from the Defence Secretary to the Prime Minister concerning the orchestration of the public presentation of the arrival of Cruise missiles, vehemently opposed by much of public opinion. No damage was caused and no embarrassment to allies, but Ms Tisdall was prosecuted and sentenced to six months imprisonment (Geoffrey Robertson, 1989, *Freedom, the Individual and the Law*, Harmondsworth: Penguin).

6. Clive Ponting, a senior official at the Ministry of Defence, leaked information to Tam Dalyell MP, enabling the latter to challenge the accuracy of the Government's account of the sinking of

the *General Belgrano* in the Falklands War in 1982. Ponting also was prosecuted but acquitted (Robertson, note 5; Clive Ponting, 1985, *The Right to Know: the Inside Story of the Belgrano Affair*, London: Sphere Books).

7. After he had repeatedly and without result reported the risks of the understaffing of wards, especially at night, leading to danger for the elderly patients, Nurse Pink published details. He was dismissed.

8. Public Concern at Work, Lincoln's Inn House, 42 Kingsway, London, WC2B 6EN.

9. The Swedish institution of the Ombudsman has been widely copied and adapted throughout the world since the 1950s both in national and local, public and private organisations.

10. Tennyson was inexact when he wrote: 'A Land of just and old renown,/ Where Freedom slowly broadens down,/ From precedent to precedent'. You Ask Me, Why, iii, 1833.

11. The Putney Debates of 1647, so-called because they took place in the parish church in Putney, were between the leaders of Cromwell's Army, the Grandees, and the Levellers, to whom many of the rank and file and civilians belonged, about the future constitution of the country. Rainsborough occurs in various spellings.

12. Alice S. Rossi, 1993, *The Feminist Papers from Adams to de Beauvoir*, New York: Columbia University Press, gives a valuable account of 23 feminists, their lives, work and long extracts from their writings.

13. The full text is printed in many sources, e. g. Alice Rossi, note 12; William L. O'Neill, 1969, *The Woman Movement: Feminism in the United States and England,* London, George Allen and Unwin; Miriam Schneir, 1972, *Feminism: The Essential Historical Writings*, New York: Vintage Books; Mari Jo and Paul Buhle, 1978, *The Concise History of Woman Suffrage: Selections from the Classic Work of Stanton, Anthony, Gage, and Harper*, Urbana: University of Illinois Press.

14. This was not a new problem. Sir Thomas More had complained early in the sixteenth century of the expulsion of peasants to make sheep-walks, creating the 'sturdy beggars' who were so harshly punished. (Marx, *Capital* I 672-693, in Maureen Cain and Ian Hunt, (eds) (1979) *Marx and Engels on Law*. London: Academic Press; Sir Thomas More (1516) *Utopia*, trans. Paul Turner, (1965) Harmondsworth: Penguin, Book 1, pp. 46-49.

15. 'Rotten boroughs' were often villages or even places that had lost all their inhabitants (like Old Sarum outside Salisbury) but which were nonetheless represented by two MPs. The seats were usually in the gift of the Crown or of a landowner.

16. Gordon Wright, 1950, *The Reshaping of French Democracy*, London: Methuen, p. 169. Women did not obtain the vote until it was granted under de Gaulle in 1944, owing to the opposition of the Radicals and Socialists who feared women's clericalism and support for the Catholic Church.

17. Backbench MPs may introduce a Bill with a very short speech, hence a Ten-Minute Rule Bill. It is most unlikely to receive further consideration and is simply a means of raising the issue in Parliament.

18. The European Commission took enforcement action against the British Government after due warnings because British legislation did not comply with the requirements of the Equal Pay Directive.

19. The Regulations set up a complex and lengthy process for assessing whether the work in question is of equal value. In this way, the Government sought to limit the effect of the EC Directive.

20. *Plessy* v. *Ferguson*, 163 US 537 (1896): a State law permitting segregation on inter-State transport was upheld.

21. *Brown v. Board of Education*, 347 US 483 (1954): this most important case applied to educational facilities. It was the culmination of a long series of cases brought by the National Association for the Advancement of Colored People to reverse Plessy and to end segregation. In the following year there was a sequel when the Supreme Court held that desegregation should take place 'with all deliberate speed' (349 US 294 (1955) at 301). Richard Kluger, 1976, *Simple Justice: The History of Brown v. Board of Education and Black America's Struggle for Equality*, New York: Alfred A. Knopf gives a detailed and fascinating account of this campaign.

22. The 'grandfather' cases arose from the attempts of some States of the USA to exclude Black voters by limiting the franchise to those lawfully descended from males who had the vote before the emancipation of the slaves. Clement E. Vose, (1972) *Constitutional Change: Amendment Politics and Supreme Court Litigation since 1900*, Lexington, Mass: Lexington Books, D. C. Heath and Co., gives an account of this litigation in Chapter 2.

23. This is an abuse which has recently been re-introduced.

24. *Nagle v. Fielden* [1966] 2 QB 633. Mrs Nagle, who had for many years trained racehorses under the name of her head lad, applied for a licence in her own right, but was refused. Lord Denning held that she had an arguable case, whereupon the Jockey Club allowed her a licence.

25. This provision is still in force, but the amounts have not been changed. Sharpe (1976: 19) discusses its implications.

26. So-called after Brandeis who, in *Muller v. Oregon* in 1908 (208 US 412) secured the constitutionality of an Oregon law limiting women's hours in laundries to ten hours a day. Brandeis submitted to the Supreme Court a brief of 113 pages including only two pages of strictly legal argument;the remaining 111 pages showed the evil effects of long hours of work on women.

27. Class actions are actions in the name of a few individuals and 'all similarly situated' which enable issues concerning large numbers of individuals to be dealt with in one case. All in the class obtain an appropriate remedy. American lawyers sometimes complain of difficulties in using class actions, but the American action is much broader than the narrow English representative action which requires all those represented to share an interest common to each of them, to have an independent cause of action and for the Court to be satisfied after discovery of all the evidence that it is in the interest of the class for the plaintiff to sue. The English action is declaratory only, so that the plaintiff and each member of the class must sue for damages (The Supreme Court Practice (1995) Vol. 1, O15/12/4).

28. Briefs *amicus curiae* are briefs submitted to the Court by any persons or organisations with an interest in the outcome of the litigation, expressing information and arguments which they consider relevant. How much attention the Supreme Court pays to these briefs is unclear. In England such briefs can usually be submitted only by official bodies.

29. I am grateful to Norman Marsh for this reference.

Chapter 2

Which human rights?

Nearly all sovereign States have bound themselves to observe at least some instruments on human rights, that is to accept limitations on their power and to submit to questioning on their practices not merely by their peers, that is representatives of other sovereign States, but by citizens of other States, and to act in accordance with their recommendations. Sovereign power has rarely been absolute in the past even for the most powerful States. Now States have themselves limited their internal sovereignty as well.

Humanitarian law

The first attempts to establish anything that might be called international human rights originated in the second half of the nineteenth century. These attempts led first to the formation of the International Committee of the Red Cross[1] in 1863 and in 1864 to the first Geneva Convention for the Amelioration of the Condition of the Wounded in Armies in the Field. The 1864 Convention was the first of two series of Conventions, the Geneva and the Hague Conventions[2], now known as humanitarian law. The most recent, the four Geneva Conventions of 1990 and their two Protocols (additions), provide for humane treatment of both armed combatants and civilians in international and civil struggle. Journalists are protected provided they do not act contrary to their civilian status, but mercenaries and spies are not covered. Freedom struggles against colonial and racist regimes are considered legitimate. The Conventions also ban the use of weapons of mass destruction and the gratuitous destruction of property and dwellings. Rape of women during civil or international warfare is now an international crime. We see in these developments that the scope of humanitarian law has very substantially increased, that both rights and obligations have been formulated, as have means of implementation, though scarcely of enforcement.

Civil and international wars always produce refugees, and the majority of refugees are women, children, the elderly and those with disabilities. The Convention relating to the Status of Refugees 1951 was restricted to those who had become refugees before 1951, but the 1967 Protocol extends the Convention to those who have become refugees since that date. The Convention applies to anyone who:

> (2) ... owing to a well-founded fear of being persecuted for reasons of race, religion, nationality, membership of a particular social group or political opinion, is outside the country of his nationality and is unable, or owing to such fear, is unwilling to avail himself of the protection of that country; or who, not having a nationality and being outside the country of his former habitual residence as a result of such events, is unable or, owing to such fear, is unwilling to return to it. (Art. 1A)

The phrase 'membership of a social group' could apply to women in danger from fundamentalist regimes, for example Taslimi Nasreen from Bangladesh now a refugee in Sweden, or honour crimes[3].

The League of Nations and the Peace Settlement after 1918

Ideas of rights developed in a further direction after the First World War. The League of Nations, created by the Treaty of Versailles in 1919, was intended to provide means for settling international disputes peacefully, but these high hopes were disappointed by the mid-thirties when the League ceased to work effectively, if at all.

The peace treaties of 1919 and 1920 between the Allies and the Central Powers dismembered the latters' Empires by recognising the right to self-determination of many national groups, but this recognition applied in Europe only. The peace treaties also made special provision to protect the rights of racial, religious and linguistic minorities included within the successor States to use their own language, have their own schools and, generally, to maintain their own culture. These rights had to be guaranteed in national law that could not be amended by ordinary legislation. The Council of the League of Nations examined alleged violations, and disputes were submitted to the compulsory jurisdiction of the Permanent Court of International Justice, (Davies 1988: 3) which was established under the Covenant of the League in 1920[4]. These provisions were the complement to the creation of nation-states nonetheless containing sizeable ethnic minorities. The operation of the provisions gave rise to cases before the Permanent Court of International Justice. In one of these cases, the Albanian Schools Case, the Court, following earlier jurisprudence in 1923, recognised the principle of indirect discrimination, the equal rule with unequal effect:

> Equality in law precludes discrimination of any kind; whereas equality in fact may involve the necessity of different treatment in order to attain a result which establishes an equilibrium between different situations. (Opinion, 6 April 1935, Series A/B No. 64, PCIJ)

These treaty provisions proved ineffective after 1933 in so far as they applied to Germany.

Throughout the inter-war period claims for the right to national self-determination, that is independence, continued to be made by many peoples still subject to colonial powers. After 1945, more and more colonies won their independence, sometimes because the colonial government was convinced of the necessity of granting independence, for example the Attlee Government's grant of independence to India, but more often by armed struggle. Most of those nations whose right to national self-determination was not recognised between the Wars have now become part of the 'universe' enjoying that right.

Progress towards human rights is a very uneven process. Women have played an important role in both the national movements of civil disobedience, as in India, and in warfare, as for example in Algeria. The men have been dependent on the women's contribution, welcomed and encouraged their activity, however contrary to traditional social mores, but too often have sought to reject it after the battle was won – happy to exploit women's courage and abilities during the struggle, yet denying women the right to participate actively in public life afterwards.

The United Nations

At the end of the Second World War, the victorious Allies tried to avoid what were perceived as the weaknesses of the League when they created the UN. The UN's aims are far-reaching and its structures far more complex. The Charter of the UN goes much further than the Covenant of the League in recognising both principles of human rights and the work of what are now the Specialised Agencies, such as the United Nations Educational, Scientific and Cultural Organisation (UNESCO) and the International Labour Organisation (ILO), in securing human rights[5]. Articles 61-72 deal with the composition, functions and procedures of the Economic and Social Council (ECOSOC) in relation to human rights and fundamental freedoms, relations with Specialised Agencies and the making of recommendations. These provisions are discussed in chapters 4 and 5. This expansion of internationally agreed concepts of human rights has led to the development of many organisations able to contribute to identifying needs, to collecting data for this purpose and to assisting governments in the implementation of higher standards. These institutions make up the UN family of organisations, in addition to which geopolitical regional bodies in Europe, the Americas and Africa have been created. Furthermore non-governmental organisations (NGOs) have been important in developing human rights, as we shall see below.

The Specialised Agencies

The Specialised Agencies are autonomous organisations with their own Governing Bodies and separate budgets, but part of the UN family of institutions. States may be members of one or more Specialised Agencies without being members of the UN and vice versa.

Some of the present UN Agencies existed before 1945, for example the Universal Postal Union founded in 1874[6], and the International Telegraphic Union (since 1932 the International Telecommunication Union), founded in Paris in 1865 and relevant to the right to life because its International Radiotelegraphic Convention of 1906 set the priority for assistance to ships in distress. Other precursors of UN organisations also existed before the founding of the League of Nations. The World Health Organisation (WHO) was preceded by the International Office of Public Hygiene founded in 1909 which was itself preceded by a series of international conferences on quarantine regulations initiated in 1851 and culminating in the International Sanitary Convention of 1903. A similar organisation, the Pan-American Sanitary Bureau, had been created in 1902. The Health Organisation was established under the League of Nations in 1923. The three bodies joined to form the WHO in 1948.

The International Labour Office, now Organisation, (ILO) was founded in 1919 in response to pressure from several international conferences of trade unionists held before and during the First World War. Trade unionists feared that improvements in pay and working conditions that they had won in their own countries by hard lobbying and negotiations with governments and employers and often by strikes would be undermined and destroyed by competition from countries where far worse conditions prevailed. *O tempora, o mores*. The Office was attached to the League of Nations by the Treaty of Versailles. In 1946, it became a Specialised Agency of the UN. Its aims were set out in the Declaration of Philadelphia 1944. The Declaration sets out four principles:

(a) labour is not a commodity;

(b) freedom of expression and of association are essential to sustained progress;

(c) poverty anywhere constitutes a danger to prosperity everywhere;

(d) the war against want must be carried on with unrelenting vigour within each nation, and by continuous and concerted international effort in which the representatives of workers and employers, enjoying equal status with those of Governments, join with them in free discussion and democratic decision with a view to the promotion of the common welfare. (Part I)

The Declaration goes on to list the aims in more detail. These include full employment and a rising standard of living, satisfying work, recognition of collective bargaining, social security, health and safety, welfare of children, protection of women, equality of educational and vocational opportunity. From its inception, the ILO has been unique in having tripartite representation of governments, employers and employees in its Assembly and on its Governing Body, thus recognising and endorsing the importance and value of representatives of workers.

Although the United Nations Educational Scientific and Cultural Organisation (UNESCO) was not created until after the Second World War, calls for an international organisation for education go back to the early years of the nineteenth century. Marc-Antoine Jullien of Paris published plans for a Commission on Education in 1817. Several more proposals for and attempts to create an international organisation were made during that century, but failed for various reasons. After the First World War, an attempt was made, led by the International Alliance of Women, to establish such a body under the aegis of the League of Nations, but this attempt also failed. Apparently one of the reasons was that governments feared intervention in their educational system and the imposition of a scheme of education by such a body – an excuse for which there was no foundation. The International Bureau of Education was finally established in 1925, and is now funded by UNESCO. Both the individuals and the groups arguing for an international body stressed the importance of education for peace, co-operation and international understanding.

UNESCO itself was founded in 1946. Its mandate is wide-ranging, including, in addition to education, the promotion of science and the protection of cultural monuments. It has been the subject of much criticism over, first, its management and, secondly, its policies, in particular the desire of some developing countries to establish a New International Information Order to counter or complement the domination of especially the United States and to a lesser extent Britain and France and other Western countries over media and the reporting of international events. The outcome of the criticism was the withdrawal of the US, Britain and Singapore from UNESCO with the consequent loss of a great deal of its funds; none of those States has yet rejoined UNESCO despite substantial changes in the management of UNESCO. The work of UNESCO and of the ILO is discussed in chapter 5, part 1.

These are only a very few of the many Specialised Agencies whose activities directly or indirectly affect human rights. The Food and Agriculture Organisation (FAO), the United Nations Development Programme (UNDP), have sought to work for human rights, but the International Monetary Fund (IMF) and the World Bank are among those whose policies have been most severely criticised.

The Council of Europe

The Council of Europe was set up in 1949 by the democratic States of Western and Northern Europe. In the years following, it has very substantially increased its membership, especially after the fall of the Berlin Wall, and now has 38 members including the States in Central and Eastern Europe and Russia. The Council's remit now stretches from Iceland in the West to Vladivostock in the East. Like the ILO and UNESCO, the Council undertakes many advisory and technical projects including the promotion of education in human rights. Seminars and conferences on human rights have been held already as far afield as Central Asia. The European Convention on Human Rights is the best known of a considerable number that have been agreed and is discussed in chapter 5, part 2. The Convention Against Torture 1987 permits representatives of the Council to inspect all places of detention including mental hospitals as well as prisons and police stations.

The European Union

The European Union has developed human rights particularly in relation to women's rights at work, and this work will be discussed in part 2 of chapter 5.

The Commonwealth

For many years the Commonwealth Heads of Government have declared their support for principles of human rights. In London in 1977, they agreed to give more attention to human rights, a decision leading to the creation of the Human Rights Unit in the Secretariat in 1985. The Unit has no investigative or enforcement functions and concentrates on programmes and especially training in human rights for government officials of all kinds. It works on the Commonwealth practice of consultation and consensus. Declarations at the meetings in Harare 1991 and Cyprus 1993 again asserted the principles of human rights, women's rights, the ending of racism, the rule of law, just and honest government, the need for development and for reducing poverty and environmental degradation.

The Women's Affairs Department is specifically concerned with improving the condition of women, with ensuring that women's interests are taken into account in all programmes supported by the Commonwealth

Secretariat and encouraging Commonwealth Governments to take comparable action. The process was advanced when the Commonwealth Human Rights Initiative was established in 1987 by five Commonwealth non-governmental organisations (NGOs): the Commonwealth Trade Union Council, the Journalists, the Lawyers, the Legal Education, and the Medical Associations. Two years later they appointed an Advisory Group to report on how to improve human rights in the fifty member States of the Commonwealth, more than half of whose members have not even signed either the International Covenant on Civil and Political Rights or the International Covenant on Economic, Social and Cultural Rights (discussed in chapters 4 and 5). Its report, *Put Our World To Rights*, 1991, contains many useful recommendations and gives particular emphasis to the importance of education in human rights and of the work undertaken by NGOs. This is one of many initiatives taken by non-governmental groups on behalf of human rights.

Non-Governmental Organisations

Human rights have not developed merely as a consequence of 'social forces' or other impersonal effects however important social, political or economic circumstances may have been in providing a favourable opportunity for such developments. Events do not occur untouched by human hand, nor are people mere flotsam and jetsam tossed on the stream of change. Because we owe our human rights to the courage and self-sacrifice of individuals, rarely acting alone, usually in concert with others, we all need to be able to share in the burden of maintaining our rights by exercising them. Nor is it adequate to say, as has sometimes been said, that improvements occur because it is convenient for those in power to grant them; apart from anything else, this begs the question of why an improvement desired by others suddenly becomes convenient.

Groups, pressure-groups, interest-groups, NGOs working for human rights have often begun as *ad hoc* bodies, have subsequently become permanent, and have created links with similar groups in other countries to form international federations or organisations: our modern international NGOs (INGOs).

International NGOs lobbied informally at the League of Nations. One example is the International Alliance of Women who lobbied both to secure the establishment of a Committee to work for women's interests and for a range of women's rights, among them the right of married women to retain their nationality of birth, a matter of great practical importance when a cross-national marriage broke down.

After the Second World War, NGOs that had been granted consultative status were accorded a recognised position by Article 71 of the UN Charter. The UN Secretary-General in 1994 in his General Review of Arrangements for Consultations with NGOs wrote that the NGOs provide 'the closest approximation to direct popular participation in the inter-governmental machinery' (Brett, 1995: 99). The Advisory Group of Commonwealth NGOs summed up the functions of NGOs:

(1) information gathering, evaluation and dissemination;

(2) advocacy to stop abuses and secure redress;

(3) provision of legal aid, scientific expertise and humanitarian assistance;

(4) lobbying national and international authorities;

(5) promotion of legislation to incorporate or develop human rights standards;

(6) education, consciousness-raising or empowerment;

(7) building solidarity;

(8) delivery of services, especially in the area of economic and social rights;

(9) keeping open the political system. (1991: 18-19)

Brett discusses the contribution made by NGOs in publicising human rights problems, putting them on the public agenda, providing expert information to human rights monitoring bodies and to government delegates on these issues, assisting in drafting new standards. She shows that UN organisations have recruited staff from NGOs, because these individuals are more expert than any others, and that the methods of NGOs have been adopted.

Brett also draws attention to the limits of what NGOs can do. Many NGOs are relatively small with limited resources and dependent on attracting sufficient publicity to win donations and subscriptions; and

NGOs are no more immune from infighting and competition than any other type of organisation. But however effective NGOs may be in identifying, documenting and publicising abuses of human rights, it is only governments that can end them. Oppressive governments are often in effect 'protected' by friendly powers for political, economic or strategic reasons. The most that NGOs can do is draw public attention to these abuses and mobilise public opinion to put pressure on governments to end them or to press other governments to put pressure on the oppressors.

The other major group of functions of NGOs is to educate their own publics about human rights and ways of enforcing them, and to provide help and assistance to individuals and groups seeking to enforce them. Nearly all NGOs therefore engage in publicity campaigns of various kinds: Greenpeace's peaceful direct action, Amnesty's letter-writing campaigns in support of prisoners of conscience; research, and publication of the results of research which can be used to attract attention in the media and inform and influence governments and other bodies, lobbies, demonstrations, events for members such as sponsored walks, local branches, newsletters and other publications, providing speakers for meetings.

All these activities and the possibility of their being effective depend on human rights: civil liberties such as freedom of expression, of association, of assembly, and political rights. The struggle for human rights in oppressed countries is likely to depend on human rights in free and democratic countries being used to support that struggle. A duty therefore falls on groups and individuals to be mindful of our neighbours. And who are our neighbours? Our neighbours are those who are affected by our actions, both by what we do and by what we do not do. We therefore have an obligation to refrain from enriching ourselves at the cost of impoverishing others and a duty to act on behalf of others who are exploited and who request our help.

Many NGOs have educational departments, largely staffed by teachers, engaged in preparing materials for use in schools. Many of these are excellent in setting out the formal human rights (although the texts are rarely included), in delineating some of the problems of abuse of power, of inequalities in development and in seeking to educate children and young people in tolerance. However, they often provide too little information about the methods of implementation and enforcement of human rights, either as set out in the instruments or as they work and have been developed. This omission must leave readers with the impression that human rights instruments are no more than printed paper, a problem discussed by Law and Rendel (1992). Nor is the complexity and difficulty of securing international agreements on human rights always indicated in these materials. There are explanations of varying weight for these omissions. It is claimed that the legal language of the instruments and the complexities of procedure are too difficult for children. Teachers also may find them difficult if they have no training in the subject, but such training scarcely exists in teacher-training courses in Britain. In Britain, unlike France, human rights is not an essential part of the National Curriculum, although there are ways in which human rights may be included in the curriculum. Strong lobbying when the Curriculum was first drawn up obtained a brief reference to human rights, subsequently lost when the Curriculum was simplified.

NGOs depend on subscriptions and donations and sometimes are able to obtain grants. Essential fund-raising is assisted by some trading activities, such as catalogues of goods for postal shopping and the sale of donated clothes and other goods in shops. Oxfam in particular uses both methods to sell goods produced by co-operatives in developing countries and has established a successful trading arm with shops in many towns. These fund-raising activities often do little to inform their customers about the NGO's activities. The fear of appearing 'political' or of putting off some customers may be the reason.

The Commonwealth Advisory Group of NGOs commented on the rather narrow understanding of human rights in the public mind:

> Few make the connection between the struggle for human rights and an association of doctors; between international standards and the local group of factory workers who are fighting their employer for basic standards of safety; between state obligations and the youth group carrying out a campaign of awareness about the pollution of its local waters, or social workers organising a literacy campaign among local mothers. (*Put Our World To Rights*, 1991: 18).

I turn now to a more detailed consideration of concepts of modern human rights.

Types of rights

The purpose of securing peace by disarmament and by resolving disputes between nations without recourse to war is prominent in the Charter of the United Nations, as it was in the Covenant of the League of Nations, and in the Covenants, Conventions and Declarations on human rights. Peace is now regarded as one of the 'third-generation' rights, or, more accurately, as a right of solidarity, along with the rights to development and to a good environment. The 'first generation' are civil and political rights, and the second economic, social and cultural rights. This nomenclature is largely historical, based on the development of rights over long periods in Western countries, especially Britain, the USA and France.

Civil and political rights include the right to life, freedom from arbitrary arrest, the right to a fair trial, freedom of conscience, of speech, of assembly, of association, civil legal capacity, the right to the peaceful enjoyment of possessions, the right to vote, to stand for and hold elective or other public office and so on. These rights are associated with a liberal perspective and were originally fought for and won by white middle- and upper-class males, but all men and women need to have these rights and to be able to enforce them. These rights are also important to children directly or indirectly. Even though white middle- and upper-class males won these rights for themselves and did not have others in mind, these rights are just as relevant for others – an obvious point, perhaps, but one which needs making. Economic, social and cultural rights include such claims as the rights to health services, to education, to work, to social security, to paid holidays, to an adequate livelihood or standard of living, to joint consultation and health and safety at work and so on. It has also been argued that claims to economic and social rights should not be called rights on the ground that they cannot be provided or enforced in many countries, because governments lack the necessary resources, whereas the traditional civil and political rights make no such demands.

The International Bill of Rights

Modern human rights in instruments of international law have developed since the Second World War. The most important impetus for drawing up instruments such as the Universal Declaration of Human Rights 1948 (the Universal Declaration) came from the evidence of Nazi atrocities in

Germany and occupied Europe, the genocide practised against Jews, Gypsies, Slav intellectuals and professionals, and the murder of socialists, homosexuals and many others. To this was added the belief that such evil practices destabilised peaceful relations between nations and that therefore it was necessary for the maintenance of peace to erect a barrier to oppression.

At the same time as it approved the Universal Declaration in 1948, the General Assembly of the United Nations decided that the rights contained in it should be given legal force. It took until 1966 to arrive at a suitable formulation in two Covenants (not one as originally intended), the International Covenant on Economic, Social and Cultural Rights (the Social Covenant) and the International Covenant on Civil and Political Rights (the Civil Covenant). There were practical, political and ideological reasons for the long gestation of the two Covenants. The practical reasons were that whereas civil and political rights could be implemented, it was thought, by any government and could therefore be made binding immediately, economic and social rights impose substantial costs on governments which many could not possibly meet immediately. The obligations under the Social Covenant were therefore phrased as rights to be achieved progressively.

The development of human rights was distorted by the political differences during the Cold War until it ended in the early 1990s. The ideological reasons reflected disagreement between the Western powers, especially the USA and the UK, on the one hand and the Soviet Union and Eastern bloc countries on the other.

The former held to liberal, individualistic, natural rights. In contrast the Soviet Union saw rights as arising from the structure of the State and gave priority to economic and social rights over civil and political rights (Kartashkin, 1982). Further, the Soviet Union argued that formal freedoms were of little or no value to workers in bourgeois societies because workers lacked the means to exercise such rights. In the phrase attributed to Vyshinski: 'What liberty does an unemployed American worker have?' The Soviet position was that rights existed to assist the building of a socialist society and the transition to communism, but not to hinder them. Therefore rights could not be used against the regime and in effect they were turned into duties. Thus a right to work became a duty to work (Robertson, 1982: 10; Donnelly, 1989: 55-57; Madiot, 1991: 58-63). The corollary of this position was that the implementation and enforcement of rights were entirely an internal matter for the State concerned. This had an effect, together with the caution of the USA and the UK, on the provisions for the implementation and enforcement of the Covenants.

Individual and collective rights

Another way to look at rights is to distinguish between individual rights and collective rights. Civil and political rights have been seen as individual, all others as collective rights. In fact virtually all rights depend on collective provision. The right to vote, to begin with a civil right, cannot be enjoyed without the intervention of public authorities or without cost: electoral registers have to be compiled, polls supervised, votes counted and so on. This work, undertaken by the public authorities, is a form of collective provision. Fair trials depend on the appointment of judges, magistrates and clerks, training for judicial work, the drawing up and publication of rules of procedure and, indeed, of the provisions of legislation itself, and the maintenance of buildings or other places where courts can meet.

Rights of association and rights of assembly, traditional civil liberties, are rights accorded both to individuals to join associations or assemblies, and accorded to groups to exist, to undertake collective action, to have a legal personality in the case of associations and, in the case of assemblies, to hear speakers or march through the streets. These rights are both individual and collective.

The right to education, usually seen as a social right, also demonstrates the interdependence between individual and collective rights. An effective right to education depends not only on the collective right to the provision of an education service, but also on an individual right to secure access to that education service on equal terms with others, with equal treatment and as far as possible equal outcomes. In this respect, education is similar to health services, social security, provision of housing and so on. There is also a collective interest in individuals receiving a good education, being healthy, having enough to live on and not having to sleep on the streets. From a different perspective, however, a right to education may be little better than a right to be indoctrinated, a state of affairs which could conflict with freedom of conscience and freedom of thought. I examine this conflict in the next chapter.

Rights are individual in another sense: that individuals need to take some action to ensure that they get them. This is true of all rights, whether civil, political, economic, or social; for example individuals have to apply for social security benefits; but if they are to apply, they need to know their rights. Therefore the State must have an obligation to inform and to provide the means by which individuals are able to enforce their rights, sometimes against the State, and sometimes against other individuals or organisations; for example legislation has imposed a duty on employers to post the requirements of the Factories Acts in every workplace; householders are legally required to enter the names of all qualified residents for the purpose of compiling the electoral register. I turn now to a closer consideration of social rights and rights of solidarity.

Economic, social and cultural rights

Economic, social and cultural rights are a very mixed group. Some, on examination, may be similar in kind to civil and political rights, requiring little from the State other than legislation and little expenditure. For example, the right to form trade unions, often classified as an economic and social right and appearing in instruments on economic and social rights, falls squarely within freedom of association, a traditional civil liberty. However many States regulate freedom of association, banning or imposing disabilities on certain types of association, as is the case in France. The right to form trade unions is included as an economic and social right because of its importance for enabling workers, individually so vulnerable, to obtain better conditions of employment through their own collective action.

Similarly, the right to paid holidays requires legislation, inspection and power to take legal action to ensure compliance, but does not require the State to provide any further service. The right to health and safety at work requires legislation and official inspection but also much more expert advice and support for the identification of dangerous conditions and the development of safe practices. It is not enough simply to tell employers to observe safe practices and to punish those who do not. Safe practices depend on research and knowledge spread across industries, not merely based on individual industries or employers. The right to health and safety at work is therefore much more heavily dependent on collective provision than is a right to holidays with pay.

Rights to education, to health services, to housing, to social security require the provision of services directly or indirectly by the State, impose substantial costs and must be provided collectively if all individuals are to benefit. Rights to education, as we shall see in chapter 4, are chiefly concerned with non-discrimination, access and personal development. Compulsion is needed to ensure that all make their fair contribution to the provision of these rights. It is only the State which has such power of compulsion, for example through taxation or through enforcement by the Courts. (Even private insurance and private pensions are forms of collective rather than individual provision.) However the services are provided to *individuals*, although the rights are provided collectively.

As nationally and internationally recognised *rights*, social and economic rights are of recent development. As claims upon charity, and as the responsibility of governments, they are very ancient. Cultural rights have usually been quite another matter, and have frequently not been seen as such, still less conceded either in the past or in the present.

By cultural rights are meant the right of individuals and groups to use their own language, to practise their own religion, to study their own history, literature, artistic and other heritage and for these rights to be recognised officially as of value. The implementation of cultural rights makes it possible for the cultural group to protect their cultural heritage of buildings and artefacts. These rights have been violated, for example in the north of Cyprus occupied by the Turks where ancient buildings and archaeological remains have been desecrated or destroyed, artefacts sold abroad, all contrary to UNESCO Conventions, and even place-names changed in an attempt to remove all evidence of the Greek occupation of the area over centuries. Similar violations have now been committed in Bosnia and other parts of former Yugoslavia. Cultural rights are essentially collective rights that cannot be effectively enjoyed on an individual basis.

Perhaps the most obvious collective right is the right to national self-determination: the right of a group who see themselves as a nation to govern themselves. This is a right which runs contrary to many historical developments. The Scots and the Welsh, for example, see themselves and are recognised as nations, but are largely, though not exclusively, governed from London within the framework of political and administrative structures and processes largely determined by the English. This right also clashes with the pragmatic need to draw practicable national boundaries. Some of the impetus for the demand for national self-determination may spring from the exclusion of members of the minority national group from political participation and economic benefits, the disregard of their political demands, and the repression of a separate cultural identity within the State of which they form part.

The complexity of defining national boundaries in Central and Eastern Europe and the Balkans vividly illustrates this problem. Many more examples could be cited from all parts of the world. This right is relevant also to tribal and indigenous groups located within the boundaries of modern States, for example in Brazil and Burma and of nations split between several States, for example Basques, Kurds and Armenians. Less has been heard of the right to self-determination, as opposed to de-colonisation, since the Second World War than in the first half of the century. (Are there fashions in human rights?)

Rights of solidarity

The 'third generation' rights, or rights of solidarity, to peace, development and a good environment (Vasak, 1979; Robertson, 1982), are less well articulated in human rights documents, although there is now plenty of international law on the environment. The right to peace is protected, some would argue, by defensive alliances and strong military forces. How far this is a valid argument, I shall not examine in this book. The right to development has been protected in national law by various tariffs, subsidies, expert or other assistance to new industries, to depressed or disadvantaged areas and so on, but the scope for such measures is now strictly limited as a result of the General Agreement on Tariffs and Trade (GATT). The right to a good environment is protected by various forms of restriction on the use of property, in land law by restrictive covenants and easements, in the law regarding nuisance, and in legislation concerning planning, zoning of land, emission of smoke and other pollutants, storage of dangerous materials and so on. As in the case of economic and social rights, the formulation of these claims as rights is new, but they have predecessors of considerable antiquity in private and public law.

Rights of solidarity, with few exceptions, are also rights that can be provided only by collective action and will be enjoyed collectively as well as individually[7]. Our present concern with the environment, with acid rain, the greenhouse effect, pollution of the air, the soil, the seas and the rivers requires the collective action of States. There is no way in which human beings individually or even within individual sovereign States can enjoy a right to a good environment without collective action by their own and other States. States must therefore accept limitations on their sovereignty and secure the enforcement of rules agreed internationally. Untrammelled national sovereignty is increasingly and necessarily restricted. Instead it is replaced by shared sovereignty.

The examples I have given also raise questions both about the relationship between the right to national self-determination and other rights, in particular, political and cultural rights, and about the relationship of national sovereignty to international regulation.

The interdependence of rights

Sometimes it is argued that some rights are more fundamental than others. Is a right to life (a traditional civil liberty) more important than a right to food, an economic and social right without which life could not be sustained, or than a right to social security? Or are they two sides of the same coin? Chafee (1963; vol. 2: 1) argued that the most fundamental right was that of freedom from arbitrary arrest. How, he asked, could a person enjoy freedom of conscience, or a right of assembly, while held unlawfully in prison? But how can Chafee's hypothetical prisoner obtain release without knowing her/his rights? And that knowledge may depend on education, access to legal advice or information provided by the State. Sieghart (1985:83) argued that no right could be considered fundamental to all others. If, for example, individuals are to assert their right to life, their right to freedom from arbitrary arrest and the right to a fair trial, they need to know they have these rights. This has implications for information and education. Furthermore, they need to have access to advice and help in defending themselves, which in practice means access to legal aid and advice, and the provision of some kind of legal and forensic services either by the State or by some other form of public provision. The provision of legal aid and advice and of forensic services can be seen as part of civil and political liberty, but is similar to economic and social rights in the demands it would make on the State. The right to health services in the Universal Declaration and the Social Covenant is supported by and requires a minimum age for marriage, a civil right of especial importance for girls. Good health is not possible in a polluted or unsafe environment, whether at work, at home or elsewhere. The virtual ban on forced labour is an affirmation of the human dignity of each person, regardless of race, sex, class or other characteristics. These examples illustrate two points which are sometimes overlooked: first, that there is no clear distinction between traditional civil and political liberties,economic and social rights, and rights of solidarity; and secondly, that rights are interdependent[8].

Conflicting rights

Rights may also conflict with each other. The right to property gives rise to such conflict in various ways. It can stand in the way of economic and social rights which depend on redistribution of resources from rich to poor, chiefly through taxation, for example by the provision of a 'social wage'. Taxation without the consent of each individual owner and other redistributive measures have been claimed by some to be a violation of the right to property, and it was argued by Bodin in the sixteenth century that the right to property was absolute[9]. Such views have not been upheld by, for example the European Court of Human Rights. In a series of cases, the Court has upheld legislation on the control of property in the general interest. Cases have included leasehold enfranchisement (*James and others* v. *UK*, 1986, the Duke of Westminster's case), compensation for nationalisation of British shipyards in 1977 (*Lithgow and others*, 1985), rent reductions to prevent speculation in property and to encourage the improvement of sub-standard property (*Mellacher and others* v. *Austria*, 1989) and failure to comply with planning regulations (*Venditelli,* 1994). In all cases, it was agreed that the right to property had been interfered with.

Others have seen property as a trust, for example the Early Christian Fathers[10]. This concept is particularly relevant to rights to a good environment and to development, since both these rights depend in large part on control over property, what may be done with it and what may be done on it in the case of land. Property and land include, for example personal property, artefacts, financial instruments, options, contracts, licences, buildings, leases, agricultural land, fishing and shooting rights, factories, power-stations, mines, quarries, fisheries, moorings, and so on. Protection for property-owners, rich and poor, depends on traditional civil and political liberties: civil liberties for the protection of individual property rights – the poor are entitled to the protection of their small property – and political liberties for influencing more generally and collectively the uses to which control over property and the redistribution of property are put. As the eighteenth century enclosure movement shows, civil rights unsupported by political rights, the foundation of political power, did not provide protection for the rights of village labourers to their own land or their rights in relation to common land. Landlords simply secured Enclosure Acts depriving the villagers of both (J. L. Hammond and Barbara Hammond, 1911).

These two rights, to a good environment and to development, themselves may conflict, since development may well threaten proper care for the environment, economic and social rights and the civil and political rights of individuals. Ogoniland in Nigeria provides a topical example. This conflict is all too familiar, not only in the South, the Third World, but in the Second World of former Socialist countries and in 'Enterprise' or 'Export-producing Zones' everywhere, and in the First World where the alleged benefit to the economy of building yet more roads conflicts with many other rights, as the events at Newbury and elsewhere show so clearly.

Beneficiaries of rights

Human rights are intended to be universal, to apply to everyone. It was at one time claimed that rights applying to particular groups, for example to women, people with disabilities or Blacks could not be *human* rights, since not all humans are women, have disabilities or are Black. Human rights should be defined as rights applicable to human beings, whether or not all human beings would be able to use any particular right. It is clear in any case that some rights are of more use to some individuals or groups than to others. The right to property is clearly more important to property-owners than to beggars. On the other hand, rights concerning the use of streets, parks and similar public places are probably of greater importance to beggars, the homeless and to ordinary people than to great landowners. A definition of human rights that excludes rights specifically concerned with particular groups is a negation of rights. It is in fact sometimes possible to redraft rights in broader terms to include, without specifying, particular classes of beneficiary, but this should not be necessary.

In fact, human rights instruments have dealt specifically with the rights of oppressed racial groups, of women, of people with disabilities, of children, of refugees and of stateless persons among others. These instruments are not concerned with giving these groups rights over and above those enjoyed by other groups[11], but rather, recognising that these are disadvantaged groups, these instruments seek to ensure that the beneficiaries are able to enjoy the rights that majority groups or dominant groups expect to enjoy; in other words to secure equality in fact, as the Permanent Court of International Justice held in 1923 and again in 1935.

The right to a good environment clearly has implications for the natural environment: animals and plants, for inanimate nature, and for the created environment: neighbourhoods, buildings and artefacts created by preceding generations. None of these is able to claim rights on its own behalf, although animals, and even plants, can be considered beneficiaries. In addition to ourselves and our own benefit, surely there is a claim that can be made by us on behalf of our children, our children's children, and future generations. Our obligations in relation to the environment must surely require that the environment we hand on is not impoverished or degraded. Edith Brown Weiss calls these intergenerational rights (1984, 1988, 1992). She argues that we are, as it were, trustees of the environment. This is an argument similar to that already referred to above of the ownership of property as a trust, our occupation of the earth constituting a temporary ownership.

By considering who are the beneficiaries of rights we are the better able to examine whether rights are achieving their ostensible purpose of helping to redress the balance between the weak and the powerful, the poor and the rich. Rights may appear to some as rhetoric of moral principles, serving as a means of social control, mystifying the weak, which by its hypocrisy further oppresses the disadvantaged. To other critics, rights are simply a means by which some individuals seek to avoid their obligations.

Two conclusions can be drawn so far from this review. First, the traditional classification of human rights into three generations is too simplistic. Secondly, rights can rarely be absolute. One person's or group's absolute right is too often another's oppression and denial of rights. In both the Civil Covenant and the European Convention and its Protocols, the only unqualified right is the right not to be tortured or to be subjected to inhuman or degrading treatment (Articles 7 and 3 respectively). But if rights are not absolute, if they can conflict with each other, and none is more fundamental than the others, how can they be measured against each other and what determines the priorities? To determine the priorities, we must, I think, begin from the principles of human dignity and equality set out in the instruments. In chapter 5 we shall see some of the ways in which these priorities have been decided.

In chapter 4 I shall examine the specific nature of the rights set out in the instruments, particularly as they affect women and education, and in chapter 5 I shall consider how far the ostensible beneficiaries benefit from human rights.

Human Rights and Non-Western Cultures

As we have seen, human rights originated within a particular economic, religious, political and social context in North-West Europe and the North-East of the Americas. It has been claimed that 'Western' human rights are based on individualistic concepts of human rights that are irrelevant and inappropriate to the values of other cultures. How far is this true? And are there local struggles for human rights in other regions?

It is to be expected that 'Western' affirmations and procedures of human rights should have been accepted in other parts of Europe, in Central and Latin America and Australasia because they share many characteristics of a common political, legal and social culture. That the Constitutions of new and decolonised States contain Bills of Rights and similar provisions can be explained by their having been drafted originally either in Europe or under European influence. In few of these new States have the Bills of Rights actually been observed or even maintained in existence[12].

Western countries have been criticised not only for imposing their values on other cultures but also for double standards in assessing the policies and practices of governments in other cultural regions. Human rights, the right to life, liberty, an adequate standard of living and the means of sustaining these rights are of value to *all* individuals. Cultural relativism, as many authorities have observed (for example Ramcharan 1989, Donnelly 1989, Halliday 1995), has no validity if the universal value of these rights is denied. Problems arise in the way in which some human rights have been formulated. For example the right to holidays with pay (so much mocked by some commentators, for example Cranston, (1967)) is of great importance to employees. It can also be interpreted to mean that peasants and the self-employed should have enough to live on so that they should not have to work so long and for such long hours that they have no respite throughout the years. Difficulties may also arise in the ways in which rights are observed, implemented and enforced – or are not respected. But the nub of the criticism of 'Western' human rights lies in how far individuals and their rights and needs should be sacrificed to the real or supposed greater good of a larger group, whether family, clan, district, State or nation.

Yamane (1982) attributes the lack of regional human rights instruments in Asia and the failure of Asian governments to ratify UN human rights Conventions to the unfamiliarity of concepts of human rights and to the diversity of cultures, and of legal and political traditions in Asia. She also points out the priority given to loyalty to the group over the demands of individuals. Christie (1995) has shown that South-East Asians have argued that Asians regard the security and well-being of the community as of greater importance than the freedom of individuals to pursue their self-interest – a reversal, it is claimed, of Western priorities in human rights. He maintains that these arguments are often mere excuses for the repression exercised by autocratic governments feeling themselves threatened and shows that pressure for human rights increases as economic growth leads to higher standards of living; and he argues that economic growth is not impeded by democratisation. Also, it could be added, economic growth is both a result of and a contributor to wider and more extensive education, which itself can encourage a demand both for democratisation, and the human rights on which democracy rests. Furthermore groups of lawyers in Asia and in the Pacific are working on developing regional instruments of human rights.

Non-Western cultures have however in some measure adopted human rights for reasons of their own. The Permanent Arab Commission on Human Rights was set up primarily to safeguard human rights in Arab territories occupied by Israel and worked hard at the end of the 1960s to secure international recognition of the problems of the Arab population (Boutros-Ghali, 1982). However Halliday (1995: 43) presents an illuminating examination of how far human rights can be accommodated within even a liberal interpretation of Islam, and suggests that greater secularism is needed.

The African Charter of Human and Peoples' Rights was allegedly drawn up as a consequence of the excesses of Idi Amin in Uganda. More important now is the mass demand for human rights and for democratisation that has been prompted by the distress caused by structural adjustment programmes, by pressure from donors and from the increasing number of local NGOs (Kaballo, 1995). Kaballo shows that multi-party democracy has not survived even after relatively free elections intended to bring it back, since governments have simply disregarded constitutional and legal provisions. He goes on to argue that adequate economic conditions are essential for democratisation to survive and develop. The implication is that adequate conditions, in the sense of meeting the essential needs of the people, human rights and democracy (which include the right to an adequate standard of living) are interdependent. Kuenyehia (1994) describes the programme the Government of Ghana has developed in order to mitigate the damage caused to women's lives by structural adjustment programmes which have marginalised women and failed to address gender inequalities, thereby excluding women from democratic participation and undermining their human rights. Further necessities include adequate public bureaucracies, honest public servants, trade unionists and political activists able to work democratic institutions. Kaballo (p. 203 quoting Diamond) reports that some organisations are devoting some resources to this work.

The problems of democratisation and human rights in Africa and the relationship between economic growth, development and human rights raise in acute form fundamental issues. Here I shall list only three. First, democracy is intended to be an expression of will, popular and majority will, which is by no means always responsive to the claims of minorities or unpopular or stigmatised groups. Human rights are rooted in concepts of constitutional processes which recognise the claims to rights and to dignity of all groups and individuals. Democracy and human rights may therefore come into conflict. Secondly, the concentration of economic power may vitiate the exercise of political rights, as was discussed in chapter 1. Beck (1992) discusses the ways in which techno-economic interests have largely emptied democratic processes of substance.

Thirdly, Galtung (1994) asks what leverage human rights have on systems in which individuals, governments and economic organisations and companies are trapped. He argues that development, as much as human rights, is a Western concept, and that the notion of 'development' should be replaced by that of meeting needs. O'Neill (1986) also is concerned with meeting needs as part of obligations of justice. In the last chapter, I return to these problems in the light of how human rights are working at present.

Conclusion

As we have seen, both international instruments and especially NGOs have stressed the importance of education in human rights. The underlying assumption is that education will be able to influence the attitudes of peoples and the conduct of officials. In the next chapter, I examine what uses individuals and groups can and do make of education.

Notes

1. The International Committee of the Red Cross is exclusively Swiss. National Red Cross and Red Crescent Societies formed the League of Red Cross and Red Crescent Societies in 1919.

2. The Geneva Conventions have dealt with the treatment of persons including civilians in situations of war and the Hague Conventions have banned certain weapons and methods of warfare.

3. An honour crime is the murder of a woman suspected by male relatives of having had some contact with a man outside the family. The murder is not punished. In one case a widow who wished to remarry was murdered. *Dead or Doomed to Die*, n.d., Lausanne: Sentinelles, provides evidence of such crimes and of unsuccessful approaches in 1980 to the Sub-Commission on Prevention of Discrimination and Protection of Minorities of the Commission on Human Rights. Reports of such crimes have also appeared in the Press within the last two or three years.

4. Although the Permanent Court of International Justice was not established until 1920 under Art. 14 of the Covenant of the League of Nations, proposals for a permanent court of international arbitration had been discussed at the Hague Peace Conference of 1898 and again at the Peace Conference at the Hague in 1907. The Court was re-established as the International Court of Justice by the Charter of the UN in 1945. All its work is concerned with inter-State disputes, and although some provisions exist for inter-State disputes about human rights to be referred to the Court, these provisions have never been used.

5. The Covenant of the League provided that member States would seek to ensure fair and humane conditions of work for men, women and children, secure just treatment of peoples in colonial territories, would allow the League to supervise agreements concerning the traffic in women and children, and in drugs, the arms trade, to secure freedom of communications, and to act for the prevention and control of disease of international concern (Art. 23). Art. 24 provided for establishing links between the Secretariat of the League and international bureaux regulating matters of international concern.

6. The founder was Dr Heinrich von Stephan. Information about the origins of the Universal Postal Union can be found in *UPU Specimen Stamps*, James Bendon, (1988) Limassol, Cyprus: James Bendon, PO Box 6484. I am grateful to Mr Derrick Page of the National Postal Museum for this information.

7. The exceptions relate to individual rights in relation, for example to easements of light. Some individual restrictive covenants applying to housing estates or blocks of flats and concerning the use made of the properties can be provided only collectively by being included in the title-deeds of the affected properties. The environment thus safeguarded is enjoyed both collectively and individually.

8. Sieghart (1985) also makes this point.

9. The notion that the right to property is absolute is of modern origin and associated by many writers with the rise of capitalism. Reeve Andrew (1986) *Property.* Basingstoke and London: Macmillan, discusses this association. An alternative or additional interpretation associates the notion with the rise of the concept of absolute monarchy. Jean Bodin in 1576 argued that property belonged to the family, that the family was under the absolute power of the paterfamilias, that the power of the State stopped at the threshold of the house and that the sovereign had supreme power, unrestrained by law (Sabine, George H. (1951), *A History of Political Theory.* London: George G. Harrap: 344-345). As Sabine observes, this theory is not entirely self-consistent.

10. The notion of the right to property as a 'trust', stemming from the Early Christian Fathers, treats the ownership and administration of property as being justified on pragmatic grounds by a duty on the owner to give alms and to share the enjoyment of property (Gray, Alexander (1946) *The Socialist Tradition: Moses to Lenin.* London: Longmans; Reeve, 1986).

11. In the course of the debates on the Disabled Persons (Employment) Bill in 1944, some Conservative MPs claimed that if assistance were given to disabled persons in finding employment, then they would be privileged over the able-bodied. For example 'Who comes first?' asked Ian Fraser, the war-blinded Conservative MP for Lonsdale, in Committee of the Whole House (Vol. 396: 93).

12. The Supreme Court of India has attempted to ensure that the Rights and Fundamental Principles of the Constitution are upheld. In an innovatory development it has allowed NGOs to bring cases on behalf of those too weak or poor to act on their own account. This does not mean that human rights are always observed in India; they are not, as for example impunity for dowry murders shows.

Chapter 3

The users and uses of education

What are the uses to which education is put? How may the users of education employ it to develop or discourage an understanding of human rights and the ways of safeguarding human rights?

Education has always been and remains a site of struggle and conflict, a struggle for the possession of women's and men's hearts and minds, a struggle to secure the internalising of subjection; and a struggle for and by women and men to gain knowledge and skills, to develop their abilities, and to escape from poverty and exploitation – in short, a struggle about human rights.

Since the beginning of the nineteenth century, industrial and technical change has made it ever more necessary for the work-force to receive an education, with the result that employers and governments have had an interest in raising the level of education of the whole population. In Britain, as the political system was democratised, politicians saw education as increasingly important: 'we must educate our masters'[1]. Workers themselves saw education as increasingly valuable not only for securing a livelihood, but also as a means of understanding the changes in society of which they bore the brunt, and as a means of winning some control over their lives. The movement for girls' and women's education and the achievements of working-class intellectuals bear eloquent testimony to the value attributed to education by disadvantaged groups.

For centuries the Church had in various ways dominated the provision of education. In Britain during the nineteenth century, the Church failed to offer the education needed; consequently governments made provision, resulting in conflict between State and Church for the control of education. Since education carries values and ideology as well as information and skills, it is a potent weapon for repression as well as for enlightenment. The dominant classes of the nineteenth century were therefore faced with a dilemma: how to obtain a work-force sufficiently educated for purposes of employment in the then new industrial and commercial processes, but a work-force which would remain subordinate. Education gives its beneficiaries access to a range of skills, at the very least the basic ones of reading, writing and numeracy, which are valuable in themselves. These skills open access to all that has been written: to the writings of philosophers, critics, scientists, and pamphleteers; to poetry and works of fiction; to the literature and history of different cultures; to the Press; and to technical manuals and thus to other skills. They are the gateway to freedom of information and to freedom of expression. What tools to put into the hands of the masses! No wonder education has been used as an ideological tool and its content controlled to limit knowledge, mould attitudes and inculcate habits thought desirable by those in power. It has been used for maintaining hegemony, the dominance of a particular set of ideas. The emphasis has often been laid on narrowly vocational and technical skills, on selection and exclusion, on authoritarian, repressive methods, or on structures which reproduce existing social inequalities, thus discouraging access to the benefits and pleasures that education can bring. A right to education may therefore be no better than a right to be indoctrinated in subordination.

In much philosophical and theoretical writing, it is contended that education is valuable for the personal development of the individual; also that disadvantaged groups are short-changed by the educational system, as we shall see. I shall argue that the effects of the educational system and the ways in which individuals use it are far more complicated and varied. It is possible for those who are taught to take the bait without the hook, that is to learn the skills and the information but to reject the indoctrination. Indeed, as Gramsci points out, such skills and knowledge, and the self-discipline that successful study requires, are essential for the working class and for a socialist society (1971: 36, 37, 40). We might add for a free and democratic society. Disadvantaged individuals and groups have particular need of the skills and information obtainable through education. An analysis of the right to education must include an analysis of education policies and practice which takes account both of the possibility of individuals taking the bait without the hook and of their need to do so.

In this chapter, I shall refer almost entirely to formal education; that is schooling, further and higher education, adult and continuing education and in-service training, all that goes on in educational centres and services, instruction in the basic skills of literacy and numeracy, teaching of more advanced skills of intellectual comprehension and analysis, both theoretical and empirical, conveying information on a wide range of topics, both academic and practical, and stimulating new intellectual and aesthetic interests. I include both the overt 'official' curriculum, and the 'hidden' curriculum, the content of what is taught and the implication that what is not taught is not important, or is not appropriate for particular students, that particular forms of knowledge or skill 'belong' to others and are not to be shared. What I have to say refers also to the systems by which educational policies are decided and implemented. It is not possible to include within this chapter the learning that goes on outside the formal educational system, the acquisition of knowledge and the learning of skills that occurs in many other ways, through the media, through participation in organisations, from family, friends, colleagues and work-mates. Much of what I have to say about the formal system of education is also relevant to those other forms of learning.

We can identify three major groups concerned with education. First, there are the *providers*. These are teachers, lecturers, instructors, those who are engaged in conveying information and skills; the politicians, administrators, governors of schools and colleges who decide the policy, and now determine much of the curriculum; and the inspectors and others who ensure that the policies are implemented. Secondly, there are the *recipients* of education, the pupils and students of all ages. Thirdly, there are many *other interested parties*, for want of a better term: parents, employers, clients, those using the services of professional workers and tradespeople[2], trade unions of teachers, associations of providers and, indeed, the population at large. This terminology avoids the difficulty faced by Harris (1993) and others of calling parents, pupils and students 'consumers' of education, or school-leavers and graduates 'products' of the educational system to be 'consumed' presumably by employers. As we shall see, each of these three diverse groups use, or fail to use, education in a variety of ways. It is to these uses of education and the way that different groups and individuals use them that I now turn.

To assist in this examination, I am proposing six principal categories of responses to education: (1) *denial* of the value of education; (2) *repression* of access to or satisfaction in education; (3) *instrumentalism*; (4) *meritocracy*; (5) *enabling* so as to enlarge the possibility of social participation; and (6) *enjoyment* or *sybaritism* in the excitement of research at whatever level, in the sheer pleasure of learning and in the interest in trying something new or different. These categories are not necessarily mutually exclusive. I shall begin by elaborating the categories with examples and then use them to examine some educational practices. Table 3.1 (pp. 54-55) summarises the main characteristics of the categories.

The Denyers

We may suppose that all people in developed societies now recognise the value of literacy at least. *Denyers* may think that education beyond that bare minimum has been of no value to them and that they would have got on just as well without any; they may well see no need for others to be educated. Some whose own education was minimal or deficient, may not realise what they lack and see no need for education for themselves or for others. Some *interested parties* may think that education and training are superfluous and that common sense and 'sitting next to Nellie' are all that are needed. *Denyers*, then, may be *providers, recipients* or other *interested parties*. The lamentable decay of the two English Universities and of many schools in the eighteenth and early nineteenth centuries, vividly described and denounced in the reports of Royal Commissions on Oxford and Cambridge Universities in 1852 and by the Clarendon Commission in 1864, support the view that the value of education was largely denied (Barnard, 1961) by the ruling groups. This view is further reinforced when we consider the hostility of the nineteenth century educational 'establishment' to natural science, and 'modern' subjects such as history, geography and modern languages[3]. Nor were the favoured classics taught well (Simon, 1960). The State failed to provide even elementary schools until after the Education Act 1870, although grants were payable to some schools by the Committee of the Privy Council on Education from 1839. The result was a population uneducated and insufficiently skilled, and thereby *denied* the right to personal development.

The Repressers

Some *repressers* will see education as a means of maintaining their own superior position in society and as a means of social control. They are likely to see their own education as having *instrumental* value and they may even have enjoyed it. They may be divided into two sub-categories. First there are those who value education for themselves and their own kind, but exclude others: *excluders*. The prohibition in the American South in the nineteenth century on teaching slaves to read and write is an extreme example. Other examples would be those who excluded girls and poor children from the charitable foundations which became the 'public' schools; who excluded or imposed a *numerus clausus* on the admission of women, Jews, racial or religious minorities to schools and universities, or saw the universities as appropriate only for the aristocracy and a few professional men[4]. It would include also those who so organise educational systems as to make it impossible in practice for any, or more than a very few, individuals from excluded groups to obtain the sort of education which dominant groups expect for themselves. In nineteenth century England, this view was associated with maintaining a class-segregated educational system (Delamont, 1978b) and was most clearly advocated by the Taunton Commission in 1868[5]. More recent examples include the higher pass level required from girls than from boys taking the 11+ examination in order to ensure equal numbers of girls and boys in grammar schools, thereby excluding qualified girls (Weiner, 1985: 2 and 13). Such a practice is one of many listed by the EOC as unlawful (1979:2-3), the hostility to increasing the number of university students – 'more means worse' – and the finding that the system for selecting medical students at St George's Hospital, London (and other medical schools) systematically discriminated against Black applicants and women (Commission for Racial Equality, 1988; *The Guardian* 30 July 1987).

There is a second and more sinister type of represser: the *deceivers*. They are those who, like the first group, value education for themselves and their own kind and recognise the importance of a certain minimum of knowledge and skills for outsiders. However they seek to control the content of what the outsiders are taught and the methods by which they are taught so that the pupils and students will be thoroughly discouraged from pursuing any educational activity for themselves or from making an independent use of such skills and knowledge as they acquire. This type

Table 3.1 Classification of educational policies and attitudes to education

	Belief	Intentions of supporters of Belief	Effect on Educational System	And on society	How implemented by policy makers	And by Teachers	Attitudes of Recipients	
							Those who Agree	And those who do not
1. DENYERS	Education of little value. Deny right to education	Don't waste time and resources	Little or no investment in ed., run down system. Don't get ed., or help others to get ed.	Ignorant, unskilled, prejudiced population	Restrictive, minimalistic	Get long holidays better pay don't bother	Waste of time and effort. Can make money without it	Demands for education and self-help
2. REPRESSERS Excluders (Self-denyers)	Ed. OK for us. Keep others out. Reduce competition. No use to others	Keep this valuable 'positional good' scarce	Creates elite, selective investment only	Limits ability. Creates outsiders who may become alternative leaders	*Numerus clausus.* Limited investment and selection	Only worth teaching a few with suitable background or very bright	I'm all right. I'll get it if I can. That's for others not for me	Want more education and more opportunities
Deceivers (Self-deceivers)	Ed. for us. Kid the rest into thinking it's no good for them. Right to education for us, very little for others	Keep others out and keep them quiet and subservient to us	Creates elite, subordinate mass, false consciousness	Mutes dissent, tends to rigidity and perhaps strong reaction	Selection, segregation, theories to support differential treatment	Teach up for the elite. Teach down for the rest.	I'm all right I'll get what I can I'm no good	It's all lies
3. INSTRUMENTALISTS	Ed. useful for jobs. Limited right to limited education	Produce more efficient labour force	Restricts what is taught and who are taught	Competent but narrow people. Does not maximise people's abilities. Creates future problems because of lack of wider understanding.	Emphasis on vocational training. No general education or cultural 'frills'	3 Rs discipline no 'frills' narrow	Relevant to jobs. Narrow interests ambition	Demands for broader education
4. LADDER-MAKERS CLIMBERS	Not many clever people. Ed. good for social and economic mobility for better job. Right to education for some.	Get good people into jobs where needed. Upward social and occupational mobility.	Competition. Selection.	Equality of opportunity, inequality of outcome. Could be deceiving. Some upward mobility.	Schools for the very bright and committed, selection, tends to vocational but cultural for some	Help the ablest, selection, competition. Both vocational (boys) and general (girls).	Upward social mobility, ambition	Should not/don't want to leave their class, family. Ed. for all not the few. Wider ed.

5. ENABLERS	Ed. good for people and for society and for democracy, political participation and enabling people generally. Right to broad education	Skilful population. Responsible democratic citizens, protection against tyranny	Open system, no segregation, greater investment, broad curriculum, compensatory education	Greater equality, less marked class differences politically, culturally etc. Informed population	Wide syllabus, equalisation measures, provision, policies for less able. Equal outcomes as far as possible, civic education	Treat all according to need. Encourage arts & music etc. Train for responsibility, political ed., general interest in world around	Wide interests, Responsible attitudes Participatory, develop abilities	Waste of time, not interested
6. SYBARITES Seekers	Ed. essential for search for truth and beauty	To search for truth or beauty. Research, scholarship etc.	Investment in research Autonomy for researchers, teachers	New knowledge and understanding. Greater adaptability and development	Promote research, scholarship, higher education	Encourage students, open up vistas through ed. Creativity intellectually vigorous	Get new ideas and pursue them Develop abilities and interests	Waste of resources Silly research topics, subversive
Hedonists	Education enjoyable	Pleasurable to pursue interests Give pleasure, enjoyment, satisfaction	Making full use of resources and people Enlarging the system	Happily, usefully occupied population	Provide wide-ranging adult education, wide curriculum at school, respond to demand	Encourage students' and people's interests, make learning enjoyable	Pursue own interests, learn more about non-vocational subject or activity, self-development	Should not subsidise other people's hobbies
Tasters	'Give it a whirl' Right to broad education	Pass the time Get them hooked	Making full use of resources, people Enlarging the system Increased demand	Some get interested and want more	Provide wide-ranging enjoyable classes or curriculum, attract potential students	Friendly, interesting teaching, warm atmosphere	Pass time, something interesting Somewhere warm, make friends	Should not subsidise other people's hobbies

of repression has been well analysed by feminists in relation to the education received by girls and women; they have found a curriculum which treats women as invisible and patronises and ignores girls and women in the classroom.

I include also within this category those who seek for others an education that is deficient or limited for reasons that can be shown to be false and which the *deceivers* know, or ought to know, are false. There is a difference between saying, as *excluders* have: 'we shall permit only ten per cent of our students to be women' and arguing, as *deceivers* have, that if a girl spent too much of her energy on intellectual work, her menstrual cycle would fail to establish itself, with a serious risk of permanent damage to the reproductive system, a view propagated in the last century (Dyhouse, 1981: 123, quoting Burstyn and Stanley Hall). A girl who worked hard might, it was said, get brain fever – a warning heard even in the 1930s. It is difficult to accept that *deceivers* honestly believe what they profess. But human beings easily deceive themselves, especially when it is in their own interest to do so, so it has been easy for men to believe that women are inferior or for Whites to believe that about Blacks; or as the Nazis believed that there was a world-wide conspiracy of Jews. We can say that people have a duty to be willing to open their minds to unwelcome ideas and must be trained to do so, just as they have a duty, and have to be taught, to be truthful and honest. If human rights are to be protected, we need to be less complaisant towards self-deception[6].

The *deceivers* are an important category and have been especially active in *repressing* women and racial groups. The cult of motherhood in the education of girls can be seen in this light. The notion of the inferiority of women, frequently associated with it, was given an extreme official statement in a Tsarist statute of 1845 concerned with State secondary education for girls (at a time when no such schooling existed in England and Wales):

> Woman, as a lower creation appointed by nature to be dependent on others, must know that she is not fated to rule but to submit herself to her husband and only through strict fulfilment of her responsibilities to her family can she assure her happiness and gain love and respect both within the family circle and without. (Quoted by Richard J. Evans, 1977: 114)

These sentiments would presumably win the approval of the present Government of Saudi Arabia whose education policy is specifically intended to reproduce the gender divisions of Saudi society (Nagat El-Sanabary, 1994). 'Maternal education' (Rendall, 1985) has been a common way of *repressing* women's demands for education. Scarcely less pernicious is the presentation of the domestic role as one of exceptional purity and virtue: the 'Angel-in-the-House' syndrome advocated most notably by Ruskin (1864) and Coventry Patmore. In late nineteenth century England, it attained the form of seeking to persuade middle-class women that they should sacrifice their intellectual development, and the activities to which it could lead, in order to propagate the race and to counter-balance the increase in the numbers of the working classes. (This argument has been heard at the present time in Singapore!) As Anna Davin has shown (1978), such policies were associated with the maintenance of imperialism in that period. It might almost have been a recipe for founding a caste society.

The cult of motherhood and of domesticity in the education of girls of all classes ignored the reality of the lives of many, now the majority of women. This cult was dominant in the past in the content of education. It is now most prominent in some of the media and in the rhetoric of some politicians. Throughout the nineteenth century, as subsequently, many women worked outside their home; the Poor Law Commission complained they were not at home to make supper for their husbands[7]. In the inter-war period especially, many women, unable to marry because of the slaughter of men in the First World War, had no choice but to earn their own living. Now many earn their own living and their children's as well because they are deserted, divorced or widowed, because the family needs two incomes, or because they wish to. Furthermore, as the debates of the 1950s and 1960s showed, home-making, care of husband and children are isolating and for most women insufficient as exclusive activities. The cult is especially pernicious in playing upon the very natural desire of most women to have children and in distorting the joy of bringing up children by denying women other satisfactions. This cult is *deceiving* in the false picture of adult life that it presents, and in its damaging influence on girls' educational chances and therefore on their opportunities for future employment, independence and autonomy. It is also *deceiving* in its emotional impact in seeking to foster an excessively tight and exclusive bond first between the wife and husband and subsequently between mother and child, raising expectations in the woman which are unlikely to be fulfilled and which may feel claustrophobic to the husband and child(ren). Perhaps this is a reason why some women prefer not to marry. At the same time, attitudes in the ambient culture, which are too often endorsed rather than corrected in education, encourage boys to perceive girls as inferior, weak, dependent, and material for future conquest and possession.

The *deceivers* had a dual purpose in their treatment of working-class girls: to accommodate them to their class as well as to their gender status. Thus in nineteenth century England, female candidates for the Normal School examinations, unlike their male counterparts, were not set examinations in mathematics, Euclid, mensuration, algebra, or a language which for the males might be Greek, or Latin or French[8]. In the Board schools, needlework and other forms of housework became for girls an increasingly important part of the curriculum to the exclusion of science and craft subjects. They were trained to be obedient servants and good wives and mothers. Anna Davin (1979) has shown how this was done through the content of the reading books in such schools; the reading books emphasised the duties of obedience, hard work, submission to social superiors and contentment with the social position in which the girls (and boys) found themselves. Some liberals even argued in the 1970s that 'middle-class culture should not be thrust down working-class children's throats' – presumably a reference to 'high' literary and artistic culture. To exclude working-class children from such culture or to limit their access to it would deny them knowledge of important aspects of human achievement – a policy implicitly attacked by Richard Hoggart (1957: 277-278)[9]. A right to education must surely include for all, irrespective of class, race or gender, some knowledge of high culture and of the culture (using culture here in the anthropological sense) of groups other than one's own, and access to the pleasures and rewards that such knowledge can bring.

The practice of indoctrinating young children in their gender, class and racial status continues, despite improvements, to the present time. Feminists have attacked not only the sexism and sex-stereotypes, but also the racism and classism in readers[10] (as have other scholars), and they have pointed out the discrimination that occurs throughout the hidden as well as the official curriculum. Similarly, scholars have documented the racism and prejudice that pervade the treatment of children of ethnic minorities and which is endemic in the content of the curriculum. The failure to represent people with disabilities has now, properly, come under attack. Improvements in the content of education now and in very recent years may help to create a more equal future. However, there are two countervailing forces: employers and others in positions of power may not be sympathetic to such improvements, and those young people who lose power, status and advantage may resent the changes and those who are intended to benefit from them. It is the traditional civil and political rights that make criticisms of inequality possible in the first place and at all effective in the second. These rights also helped to secure the equal opportunity legislation that legitimates and gives power to the criticisms.

Another form of *deceiving* is to assume that children must not be asked or expected to do anything that they find difficult, a charge sometimes levelled against 'progressive' teaching methods. Walkerdine (1992: 15-24) argues that progressive education can be as *repressive* to working class and Black children and to women teachers as any other kind, because by excluding any 'pain', reality is in effect excluded; furthermore the rules of what children are expected to do are not clear and women teachers are turned into nurturers and nothing else in order to create an environment in which the 'natural' child can develop. The effect is to deny children the opportunity to learn that difficulties can be overcome and the satisfaction of doing so. A similar effect may result from 'waiting until the child shows it is ready', a policy which has the further disadvantage of discriminating against children whose families have little interest in learning. As Rosenthal and Jacobsen showed (1971), children respond to what their teachers expect of them[11]. Recent reports from HMI and OFSTED have commented that a number of schools and teachers have expectations of their pupils that are too low.

The results of *excluders'* and *deceivers'* policies are harmful not only to those excluded, but also to society as a whole. Only a small elite is produced so that the pool of ability is unnecessarily restricted, the forms and range of educational facilities are limited and opportunities for development, improvement and change reduced.

Responses by *recipients* to repression may be of several kinds. First, some individuals may agree that secondary, further, higher or continuing education is for the minority and that they themselves do not belong to that minority however it should be defined. They may be called *self-excluders:* education beyond the minimum is not for them. Secondly, those who accept the arguments of the *deceivers* as true for themselves may be *self-deceivers*, that is they believe, wrongly, they are inferior. This is the difference between saying 'I'm all right, this is just not of interest to me', and saying 'I'm inferior, therefore I shouldn't/can't have access to that education'. If *self-deceivers* accept such arguments for others, they are colluding with the *deceivers.* Thirdly, opponents of *exclusion* may be angry or resentful that they themselves are not included in the select few, or more generally that education is restricted to so few. They may resist the education offered, refuse their attention out of sheer boredom and become disruptive and unmanageable at school.

A fourth form of response is to find a means of obtaining education in spite of the *exclusion.* There are many examples in English educational history; the self-education of working men, the establishment of Mechanics' Institutes, the founding of efficient girls' schools and women's colleges; and dissenters, excluded by their religion from the universities, in the eighteenth century set up their own academies which provided the principal useful and enabling education in England at that time. Some, but not all, of these responses depended on the assistance of other *interested parties*, such as the women and men who created the Girls' Public Day School Trust and fought for the admission of women to universities. This constructive response did not go unopposed. Many girls' schools in the second half of the nineteenth century were obliged to introduce medical examinations for their pupils which, in the event, showed that education improved girls' health (Dyhouse, 1981). Less happily the schools acceded to pressures and reduced girls' intellectual work at the slightest hint of 'strain', and introduced domestic science and housework instead.

The Instrumentalists

Nearly all education is likely to have some *instrumental* content. Illiterate adults who learn to read clearly have instrumental reasons, although they may also be influenced by *sybaritic* reasons: they might have friends who enjoy reading. *Instrumentalists* are concerned to teach people what they need to know for their jobs and nothing more. General education is seen as irrelevant, a waste of time and to be paid for by those who want it. The *instrumentalists* are narrow in their concept of education, rather than deliberately *repressive* or *exclusive*, although *exclusion* may be the consequence of their policy, as we shall see shortly. *Recipients* of education may take a similarly narrow view of the education that they seek. In this category, as in that of the *denyers*, the attitudes and beliefs of *providers* and *recipients* coincide. The Government's present policy towards adult education comes close to this category by concentrating grants on courses that are award-bearing.

Some of the *other interested parties* will support narrow *instrumentalism* because they do not see why they should pay for the education and training of other people or their children. They are satisfied as long as they themselves, and their children learn enough to earn a good living and they can employ such skilled workers as they think they need.

Another implication is that *instrumentalists* will seek to relate opportunities for education and training to the numbers and types of jobs likely to be available and to restrict opportunities for training for occupations thought not to be in demand. Hence this approach is likely to produce competition for a limited number of places. However, such planning attempts have been notoriously unsuccessful, for example in regard to the number of doctors required and the numbers and kinds of teachers required. Furthermore the narrow educational base of those taught under such a system is likely to impede retraining for other occupations and to prevent individuals from making appropriate and responsible use of their abilities. A narrowly *instrumental* education or training may be useful for training people to manufacture widgets at present, but may prevent them from adapting to demands for new kinds of widgets, for finding new uses for widgets or for adapting existing skills for making something entirely different. In this way, narrow *instrumentalism*, whether on the part of *providers, recipients* or other *interested parties* not only denies the value of education, but is also quite inappropriate when technology is changing fast – or will older experienced workers with out-dated skills be replaced by ever younger inexperienced workers with the latest skill, to be replaced in their turn by the next cohort?

Shortages of competent staff may be caused by poor pay and conditions, as well as by the inadequacies of education or educational planning, and by the failure of the State as well of employers to provide training for skilled occupations. The present remedy of opening professions such as teaching and probation work to untrained individuals or to those trained almost exclusively on the job is likely to produce 'professionals' lacking the ability to discern the wider implications of their work and its environment and the strengths and weaknesses of new methods and new research, and who will therefore be scarcely able to carry out their work effectively. Such training is scarcely even *instrumental.*

We can identify three levels of education and training. *Instrumentalism* requires at least a specialised training for a particular profession or trade, but a broad professional or technical education relevant to related professions or trades[12] is necessary as well. A broad general education covering a range of subjects should be available to all. Since *instrumentalism* excludes the last level and may exclude the second, it fails to satisfy the right to education and *instrumentalists* fail to meet their obligations to society of providing an adequately trained and educated population.

The Meritocrats

The *meritocrats,* in contrast to the *repressers*, believe that the higher levels of education and the careers and occupations to which that education gives access should be open to talent. They may be called *ladder-makers.* They are therefore willing, for example to provide scholarships or other means to enable those considered sufficiently able to climb the occupational scale. For those deemed able enough, a broad education, the best possible, should be available, without discrimination or prejudice in the selection of those who are to benefit; equality of opportunity rather than equality of outcome is the aim. Those who are able to take these opportunities, *climbers*, see education as a channel for upward social and occupational mobility for themselves and/or for others.

Such mobility implies a layered, hierarchical society. Hence *meritocracy* is closely associated with selection and with competition. Selection frequently serves a *repressive* or *deceiving* function in that it provides an illusion of equality of opportunity while maintaining a reality, for the majority, of exclusion. The post-war 11+, and selection for university places (rather than qualifying for entrance as in many other countries), are examples of *ladder-making.* In the inter-war period, the scholarship system leading to secondary education was intended, according to Lord Eustace Percy, the President of the Board of Education in 1933, to act as a 'lift or stairway to the higher storeys of the social structure', (Glass, 1959: 336). It was instead more successful in maintaining the hierarchy of classes than in providing a ladder, still less a lift or stairway, by which working-class girls and boys could climb. While the right to secondary education of the middle classes was increased by the establishment of State secondary schools, that of the working classes continued to be largely denied.

Meritocratic selection makes the further assumptions that there is a limited 'pool of ability', that selection methods, both for present and for future performance, are accurate and that different treatment of children and adults of different levels of supposed ability is appropriate. Further-more, selection does not, and in practice cannot, pay adequate regard to the educational and cultural capital the child receives from her/his home. The criticisms of these assumptions are well-known. We have no accurate knowledge of what pools of ability there are, but we do know that oppor-tunity and necessity call forth all sorts of unexpected ability. Selection is often a lottery, whether at 11+, 18+ or any other level. Children labelled less able, given easier and not sufficiently demanding work, are denied the opportunity to develop, so that their subsequent failure is a self-fulfilling prophecy. In short, *meritocracy* turns education from a right to a privilege, based to a certain extent on luck.

Schools that select children who appear quite exceptionally gifted would therefore appear to be examples of *meritocracy*. Their justification is that they provide for children whose gifts need to be or ought to be developed when they are young, such as in England the Royal Ballet School and the Yehudi Menuhin School for Young Musicians. Would these children's right to education be restricted if such schools did not exist? It is at least arguable that their future professional opportunities would be restricted without the specialised training, which could not in practice be provided in the majority of schools, and which is provided in addition to normal schooling. But provision should also be made either in schools with a particular bias or in groups of schools in order to give opportunities to children with talent. Examples of such provision are the Young Musicians' Courses and the London Schools Orchestra based on Pimlico School and run formerly by the Inner London Education

Authority. The school, which is now the responsibility of Westminster City Council, offers a special music course for musically gifted children and lets accommodation to the Centre for Young Musicians. What is needed to overcome the difficulties caused by meritocratic selection of the exceptionally gifted is a continuum of provision.

Sponsored, and contest mobility (based on competition) in selection (Turner's classification, discussed by Hopper, 1977) can be seen as *meritocratic* processes, but the selectivity involved also brings it into the categories of *repression* and *instrumentalism*. *Repressers*, both *excluders* and *deceivers*, are more likely to adopt processes of sponsored mobility, since this form gives the selectors a greater influence over the few to be selected and therefore a greater measure of social control. This danger can arise when employers fund the higher or further education and training of individual students. Despite equal opportunity legislation, women and ethnic minorities are less likely to be sponsored than white men. *Instrumentalists* may prefer contest mobility, where it now seems girls are more likely to be successful, as less concerned with social or personal characteristics. Hopper's refinement of Turner's typology suggests that particularistic ideologies looking for diffuse skills offer a far more restricted right to education than universalistic ideologies.

'*Meritocracy*' operates also at the other end of the scale of ability by selecting those children deemed unsuitable or incapable of a 'normal' education. These may be children with an obvious physical handicap such as blindness or deafness for whom special teaching at least to enable them to learn how to overcome the handicap is clearly necessary. Children with dyslexia, those whose mother-tongue is not English or who have learning difficulties are among those who may need temporary special help. In principle and in accordance with policies of integrated schooling, this help is expected to be provided in ordinary schools. How far this right to education is effectively provided we shall see in chapter 6.

What effect does *meritocratic* selection have on the *recipients*? Favourable selection may lead individuals to be unduly anxious to please the group into which they are admitted. Alternatively, they may feel exiled from the group into which they were born and guilt at leaving it. Those not selected or selected for less favourable education may well resent the exclusion or disadvantage they suffer, as may their parents. Other *interested parties* are likely to be satisfied with the selection and education of those found able, but will find that *meritocratic* selection has failed to educate all those with ability.

Meritocrats operate by creating grades, rather than addressing the right to education as an entitlement of all human beings. *Meritocracy* and selection, while ostensibly providing for differences, in fact create divisions.

The Enablers

The *enablers*, in contrast, see education not merely as a means to a job or channel for upward social mobility, but as a necessary tool for understanding and participating in political, community and social activity. Such understanding is seen as an essential precondition for individuals to obtain control over their lives, the conditions under which they live and work and their environment more generally. The attitudes of *providers* and *recipients* coincide, rather than being reciprocal as is the case with the *repressers*. The *enablers* are the category who come closest to the old liberal concept of an education which develops the whole person, but yet has a general *instrumental* value. Indeed, Randall Collins (1971) found that the socialising functions of education are more important for obtaining employment than the technical (or vocational) functions and that this socialising function is the more important the more prestigious the employer. This suggests that a broad socialising education is essential if education is to provide good opportunities for *climbing*. The expansion of higher education after the Robbins Report falls into this category, as did, earlier, the policy of a broad secondary education for all, and as the present expansion of higher education should do.

Enabling education may have *instrumental* purposes as did the education organised by working men in the socialist societies of the earliest years of this century, following a tradition going back to the study groups of the Corresponding Societies of the 1790s. The members of the socialist societies organised their own rigorous classes on Marx and other socialist writers so that the students might understand the economic system and struggle for another form of industrial and economic structure. After 1909, the Plebs League and the Central Labour Colleges followed similar political aims (Simon, 1974: 296-303, 330-342). Similar *enabling* education can be seen in the actions of those working people who developed Halls of Science in the nineteenth century.

Albert Mansbridge, a working man, R. H. Tawney, both an academic historian and committed to the education of working people, and others together developed the Workers' Educational Association (WEA), concerned with 'impartial' education and the culture of its students, in the early years of this century and in the inter-war years. The WEA is particularly interesting as a reversal of the common pattern of authority and decision in education, because it is the students who in principle decide what they want to learn and can influence the choice of tutor. In practice this means that the syllabus of a course proposed by local activists, is negotiated between students and tutor, and tutors must adapt teaching methods and style to accommodate the demands of the students. These are *par excellence* demand-led courses.

Women's Studies courses are infused with a similar ethos of students taking control of their own learning. In addition Women's Studies have been concerned with empowering women psychologically. This has meant giving women knowledge of female achievements and a sense of the value of the work, both unpaid as well as paid, which women do. By being encouraged to talk and to write about their own experiences, women have learnt that what they say and do is of interest to others and that they are able to talk and write effectively. This building of self-confidence and learning of the skills of assertiveness (not aggressiveness) has enabled many individual women to act politically. In a rather similar way, the policy of women's refuges of helping women to help themselves rather than of doing things for women has empowered women to establish their own independent lives.

Women's Studies have the further purpose of reconceptualising academic disciplines so that they provide an account not only of men, but of women and of gender-relations. As many authors have shown, 'adding women on' in an additional chapter or lecture is not sufficient; re-examination is required of the relationship between the public and the private (what happens in the home), of the boundaries of disciplines, of what is considered irrelevant, unscientific or political and therefore outside the legitimate concerns of a discipline (Spender, 1981; Aaron and Walby, 1991; and many, many others).

Gramsci, in discussing the education necessary for the working class, stresses the importance of the 'cognitive baggage of information', not as erudition, but as 'the organisation, discipline of one's inner self' and being able to put the cognitive baggage in order. He stresses the importance of children being initiated into the existing culture (Entwistle, 1979, p. 91; SPN, 26-43). He demanded a common humanistic culture for all without premature specialisation (Entwistle, p. 91) and was hostile to merely vocational schooling (SPN, p. 40). The curriculum should also teach the values of objectivity, pluralism, rationality and the disinterested pursuit of knowledge (Entwistle, p. 91). Democracy means, he argued, that every citizen can 'govern' and hence both knowledge and skills are needed. Both for children and for adults, Gramsci was critical of untutored spontaneity (Entwistle, p. 91). Knowledge and self-discipline were necessary.

Gramsci's views on education have been described by Entwistle as 'conservative schooling for radical politics' and at first sight appear remote from and more authoritarian than the ideas underlying Women's Studies and the WEA, all three concerned with education as a means of empowering an underclass. Both the pioneers of the WEA, the members of the socialist societies and Gramsci were concerned with knowledge as a means of understanding and therefore of exercising some power and control – knowledge is power. The Women's Studies movement has a similar concern, but begins one step further back, by using knowledge of women's activities as a means of convincing the students that individual ordinary women have the ability to acquire more specific 'political' knowledge. In practice, there can be conflict between the 'political' and the cultural or 'impartial' aims of education, between for example the demands of trade unionists anxious primarily to improve their understanding and negotiating skills, and the *providers* of education, who need or wish to be apolitical, uncontroversial, or to persuade their students of the value of contrary views, as happened at Ruskin College in 1907 and more recently in 1988 over David Selbourne[13].

Gramsci stresses the importance of counter-hegemonic education – and *enabling* or empowering education achieves this for the majority of people and for members of disadvantaged groups – and argues that it must come from adult education in politics and workers' associations, not from schooling. We have seen that that is what has happened in Britain at various times in the last century and this. Gramsci's views and the practice of working class self-education groups and feminist consciousness-raising groups are similar.

The Sybarites

'People get more happiness from learning something new than from sex or the lottery' *The Guardian*, 11 March 1996, reporting a survey by Gallup for North Yorkshire Training and Enterprise Council.

Like the *repressers*, the *sybarites* are of several kinds, but they are unlike in practically every other way. There are the *seekers*[14], those who pursue education and who are dedicated to the search for 'truth' or 'beauty'. We may also include in this sub-category those involved in artistic forms of expression; this is appropriate since the arts contribute to educating not only the senses and the emotions, but also the intellect and understanding. The *providers* are those who maintain libraries, offer research funds and facilities for the *seekers* and give them freedom to pursue and publish their work. In many ways *seekers* are concerned more with the right to freedom of expression than with the right to education; but without access to education, they would scarcely be able to become *seekers*. Furthermore, the work of some *seekers* contributes significantly to the improvement of education. *Interested parties* benefit directly and indirectly from their work in new knowledge, new methods and better understanding of our world.

Secondly, there are the *hedonists* who are using educational provision in order to pursue hobbies or activities for pleasure. Many will be adult students in evening institutes and on similar courses. Thirdly, there are those using educational facilities to fill time: 'I'll try an evening class instead of watching the telly'; to meet others; or to economise on fuel at home – a rather low level of *sybaritism* perhaps, at least initially. For want of a better term, I call them *tasters*. For both these groups, what begins as a hobby, curiosity or a desire for companionship may lead to more serious study or education, vocational or professional activity. *Tasters* discover their course is interesting and are thus led to try other courses out of curiosity, for variety, for hedonistic, instrumental and other reasons. The *providers* offer the *hedonists* and *tasters* a range of classes and courses on a very wide range of topics, activities, crafts and skills. Some *providers*, *interested parties* and especially the State, may see such courses as offering a means of keeping the unemployed and the idle off the streets and harmlessly occupied. Such *providers* are instrumental in their approach, but are concerned with political rather than vocational ends. They may be called *political instrumentalists*. They may be instrumental also in hoping that courses for *tasters* and *hedonists* will encourage the students to greater interest in learning and study, thereby increasing the the numbers of skilled individuals. They are enablers if they intend or do increase the desire of individuals to learn and who find learning a worthwhile, enjoyable and lifelong activity. Society as well as individuals benefit from these opportunities. Unfortunately present government policy towards adult education seems to be designed to prevent such a happy progression.

Applying the Categories

The examples I have given so far explain and illustrate the categories I have proposed. The reader will, of course, have realised that they are not mutually exclusive. In this section, I propose to apply the categories to a range of more complicated situations in order to throw a better light on what is really happening.

A particular course may, from a student's point of view, be both *instrumental* – improving job prospects – and *enabling*, giving a greater understanding of society, of theory and of general principles, wider information and knowledge, and increased self-confidence. It could also be enjoyable (we hope it would be), so that the student could pursue it for *sybaritic* reasons. And if the student subsequently obtained a better job as a result, then the outcome would be *climbing* as well. The same course might not be instrumental for another student. A course designed to fob off women (*repressive-deceiving*) might yet convey skills and knowledge which enabled women to challenge the ideological bias of what they had been taught. Clearly this example applies to feminists who have criticised traditional education as 'men's studies'. Such feminists are able to use the skills they have learnt to expose the fallacies of what they have been taught.

Drop-outs may be victims of *repressers* of any variety, or *self-repressers*, but some may simply be dissatisfied with the particular education they have experienced or course they have been following; or their *instrumental* needs or *enabling* or *sybaritic* desires may not have been met. Some pupils and students drop out for reasons unconnected with the course, for example as a result of family illness, financial disaster or change of job. Nonetheless it does not follow that drop-outs have gained nothing from their studies.

The education of upper- and middle-class women or aristocratic men in the eighteenth and part of the nineteenth century was intended to produce a 'cultivated uselessness' (Delamont, 1978a). This could be interpreted as a *hedonistic* education or, more imaginatively, as *instrumental* to the class or social life of the individuals concerned. It can also be interpreted as a *denial* of the value of education. When we scrutinise the nature of the education received, whether at home, in schools for young ladies, in public schools or universities, we find from the writing of the period that the outcome was too often genteel or boorish ignorance, 'accomplishments' or riots by schoolboys – in 1818 a riot by boys at Winchester College was put down by two companies of soldiers with fixed bayonets (Barnard, 1961: 18)[15].

Some of those writing about the education of girls and women from Wollstonecraft onwards have stressed the necessity for an education that would be both *instrumental* and *enabling*. Education needed to be *instrumental* so that women would be able to earn a decent livelihood for themselves when they needed to, as they often did during the nineteenth century (as in other periods). The reasons were various: many women did not marry owing to the imbalance between the sexes; the failure of the family fortune; or late marriage (Banks and Banks, 1965). And some women could no longer endure 'faddling, twaddling and the endless tweedling of nosegays in jugs' as Florence Nightingale's friend, Mary Clarke, put it (Woodham Smith, 1955: 34). An *instrumental* and *enabling* education was what the early feminists who pioneered girls' education sought to provide. For some women, such education provided also the *sybaritic* pleasures of learning, of knowing and, as one of the Girton pioneers put it, the pleasure of having a room of her own, the *right* to get on with her own work and not to be at the beck and call of others[16]; in other words, a right to autonomy.

Not all parents were enthusiastic about an *instrumental* and *enabling* education for their daughters. One father withdrew his daughters from Cheltenham Ladies College when he found they were being taught arithmetic! Sciences had to be disguised as domestic science or geography, a subject not taught at boys' schools (Delamont, 1978a: 144). The education such parents wanted their daughters to receive had, in Delamont's words, to be useless. This was at best *deceiving*, but in effect a *denial* of the value of education. But such parents would have seen the education described by Delamont as being *socially instrumental* in helping their daughters to make a good marriage; they also feared that men would not want to marry clever or learned women. There was a mismatch between the purposes of the founders of these schools and the parents who financed them with the fees they paid, with the result that the schools faced continuing financial problems.

Middle-class parents were clearer about what they wanted for the education of their sons: primarily an *instrumental* education that would open careers and professions and which was at the same time sufficiently broad to enable their sons to *climb* or at least to retain their existing social position. The new public schools, such as Cheltenham, Wellington, Marlborough, Rossall, Haileybury, answered these needs and specifically prepared boys for the army, civil service, colonial service, business and the Church (Simon, 1960: 302). Because of the harmony between the intentions of the founders of the schools and the parents, these schools were not faced with the same financial problems as the girls' schools.

The emphasis in the nineteenth century on creating an exact segregation of social classes within the educational system has created both structures and habits of mind that have survived in adapted forms to the present day, in the 'public' boarding schools, independent day schools, grammar, secondary modern and grant-maintained schools. It can be seen also in the former tripartite system in which the distrust of technical subjects was perhaps reflected in the small number of technical schools that were ever created. We can see it in early specialisation, a peculiarity of English education, and narrow curricula (and in the past excessive concentration on the classics), and in the related system of competition for State Scholarships in the years before and immediately after the Second World War.

In 1920 a few State Scholarships, to be awarded on the results of the second school examinations (equivalent to Higher School Certificate or 'A' level) were created to enable clever poor children to go to university. This was an apparently *meritocratic* proposal, but a very narrow one, as there were only 200 Scholarships each year for all of England and Wales (Barnard, 1961: 267). They were therefore very competitive; they were almost immediately abolished, but re-introduced in 1924. However, in 1943 the Norwood Committee recommended that the purpose of the school-leaving examination for 18-year-olds would not be to provide evidence of a good general education, and this recommendation seems to have been a rationalisation of existing practice (David, 1980: 156-9). The effect was to put strong pressure on clever pupils to achieve in their chosen subjects to the neglect of their more general education. This effect can be interpreted as a *de facto denial* of the right to a general education. The *denial* also acts in an arbitrary way, since it forces pupils to choose between subjects at too early a stage, before the nature of subjects and disciplines is known to pupils and before pupils have a clear idea of their own interests, skills and aptitudes. The narrowness of the examination-curriculum has been justified on the grounds of relieving pupils from the strain of examinations and enabling them to choose subjects which interest them. It is unfortunate, but characteristic, that recent attempts to widen 'A' level courses and examinations have so far been unsuccessful, despite several attempts.

Conclusion

The *denyers* clearly deny there is a right to education. The *excluders* and *deceivers* clearly deny a *universal* right to education, even though they find grounds to justify their own access to education.

The *instrumentalists* have a narrow view of what education is and hence restrict the right to education to instrumental ends and in particular to vocational ends. As a consequence, access to education will be closely linked to the numbers and kinds of jobs that are available or are expected to be available. Therefore selection must be an important part of this approach. Training provided by Training and Education Councils (TECs), apparently *instrumental* in intention, may be even more restrictive in the type of training provided. It seems unlikely that a broad professional and technical training appropriate to related trades will be provided or even specialist training. Rather, some courses seem to be little better than *deceiving repression* aimed at reducing the numbers of the unemployed. The result is that *instrumentalists* do not subscribe to the notion of a *universal* right to education.

Meritocrats are a rather different case, although they resemble *instrumentalists* in some ways. *Climbers* are seeking occupational and/or social advancement. Occupational advancement leads first of all in the same direction as that followed by *instrumentalists*. But some occupational advancement and certainly social advancement require a wider general and cultural education than *instrumentalists* would think necessary. *Meritocrats* might also differentiate between the sexes, and offer a more general and cultural education to girls and more *instrumental* and vocational education to boys. Such discrimination would, of course, be contrary to the provisions of the Sex Discrimination Act 1975. As with *instrumentalists*, the education offered is likely to be selective and also competitive, thereby contravening the principle of universality, but, on the other hand, likely to be less narrow, and therefore a right to a less restricted education for those admitted to it.

The *enablers* and the *sybarites* are quite different. They accept the universality of the right to education and that it should be a broad education. Indeed, they are concerned to encourage as many as possible to make as much use as possible of rights to education, both in the interests of society as a whole, and in the interests of the *recipients* of education themselves.

Conflict is inherent in the notion of rights and certainly in the ways in which rights have been won, as was shown in chapter 1. More specifically in relation to education, conflict is involved in the opposition between on the one hand *denyers* of a right to education and *repressers* of both kinds, and on the other those demanding better access to a broader education. Conflict of a different kind, namely competition, is involved in *ladder-making, climbing* and in *instrumentalism*.

A broad *enabling* education with relevant *instrumental* value would assist both women and the disadvantaged the better to operate the machinery of the State for their own advancement. Indeed such an education is needed for everyone if democracy is to endure in a State. Feminists have emphasised the value of education in raising consciousness and building self-confidence in order to achieve political goals, again a combination of *instrumental* and *enabling* purposes. Liberal concepts of education, of educating the whole person, are reflected in the attitudes of *enablers* and *sybarites*. These are the concepts that offer the widest right to a broad education.

Notes

1. This is the popular version of 'I believe it will be absolutely necessary that you should prevail on our future masters to learn their letters', speech in the House of Commons by Robert Lowe, Viscount Sherbrooke on the passing of the Reform Bill, 15 July 1867. Brian Simon (1993) Education and Citizenship in England, *Paedagagica Historica* XXIX (3), discusses Robert Lowe's views, pp. 689-692.

2. I use the terms 'professional' and 'trades' to include all levels of expertise from the most highly trained to all levels of manual work.

3. See also: 'The decay of Cambridge as a place of learning threatened to overwhelm the university. I believe that for the first half of the century the scholarship and science of Cambridge were a laughing stock on the Continent. . . ' Sir Walter Besant, *Autobiography*, 1902, quoted by L. and H. Fowler (1984) *Cambridge Commemorated*, Cambridge, CUP, p. 208

4. 'It is a very common practice, however, to send young men to the university, who have no claims but those of poverty to urge, and who are thus forced by the mistaken benevolence of their patrons out of their proper sphere of life, into professions for which they are neither qualified by their habits nor attainments, though the provisions of the ancient statutes would appear in many case to point out such persons as the proper objects of the bounty of our foundations. ..' Peacock, *Observations on Statutes*, quoted by L. and H. Fowler, p. 209. A case of rights lost? See also previous note.

5. The Taunton Commission recommended the establishment of three types of school to correspond to three levels of the middle class, with three different school-leaving ages (Barnard, H. C., (1961) , p. 130)

6. Advice which should be recommended to Conservative MPs in relation to the Scott Report on arms to Iraq, the questions of the misleading of the House of Commons and of the prosecution of innocent men leading to the collapse of their business and the consequent unemployment of the workforce.

7. Report of the Poor Law Commissioners on the Employment of Women and Children in Agriculture, 1843, quoted by Ray Strachey, (1928) *The Cause*, reprinted London: Virago, (1978), p. 57. Similar comments were made about the women who worked at the mines, Angela V. John (1980) *By the Sweat of their Brow,* London: Croom Helm.

8. Reports of the Committee on Education of the Privy Council, 1852-53, Appendix by the Rev. F. C. Cook on Normal School Examination Papers, Christmas 1852, PRO, ED 17/17, pp 298, 332, 339.

9. In *The Uses of Literacy*, Hoggart argues: Most mass entertainments are in the end what D. H. Lawrence described as 'anti-life'. 'They are full of a corrupt brightness, of improper appeals and moral evasions. To recall instances: they tend towards a view of the world in which progress is conceived as a seeking of material possessions, equality as a moral levelling and freedom as the ground for endless irresponsible pleasure. These productions belong to a vicarious spectators' world; they offer nothing which can really grip the brain or heart. They assist a gradual drying up of the more positive, the fuller, the more co-operative kinds of enjoyment, in which one gains much by giving much. They have intolerable pretensions; and pander to the wish to have things both ways, to do as we want and accept no consequences'.

10. For example Lobban, Foster-Carter and others in Weiner and Arnot (1987) *Gender under Scrutiny*, London: Hutchinson.

11. Rosenthal and Jacobsen also found that the more the children assumed to be least able gained in IQ, the more the teachers viewed them 'negatively' (p. 113).

12. I use the term 'trades' specifically to include manual work.

13. Ruskin College was founded to provide higher education for trade unionists and the Labour Movement and at the same time to provide a route to university courses. There has been tension on more than one occasion between those who wanted 'impartial' education and students and staff who gave priority to solidarity with the Labour Movement. Simon (1974: 311-323) gives an account of the struggle in 1907. In 1988 David Selbourne, a tutor, published articles in *The Times* when it was being picketed because Rupert Murdoch had sacked 5,000 printers, contrary to the solidarity which the students expected.

14. I prefer 'seekers' to 'researchers' since research is simply a job for some employed in research.

15. Barnard gives other examples of riots by schoolboys and of severe bullying, pp. 18-19.

16. Emily Davies, founder of Girton College, put it like this: 'In a College, as is well known, a student has the inestimable advantage of being free from distraction. This great boon – the power of being alone – is perhaps the most precious distinctive feature of college life', *Questions Relating to Women*, p. 149, written in 1878, quoted by M. C. Bradbrook, 1984, *That Infidel Place,* Cambridge: Girton College, p. 40. Virginia Woolf in *A Room of One's Own*, makes a similar point.

Chapter 4

Education in human rights instruments: what benefits for women?

In this chapter, I examine the ways in which education appears in human rights instruments. How do these provisions meet women's needs? What rights to education do they accord? When were they accorded? to whom? In the next chapter I consider how these rights are implemented and enforced. We shall see that education is included in a wide range of instruments – a testimony perhaps to the importance of education to human rights.

Some of the instruments I shall discuss (listed in Appendix 1) are Declarations which have, of course, no binding force, although some authorities, Sieghart (1983)[1], hold that the Universal Declaration of Human Rights (the Universal Declaration) has the force of customary international law, that is, States are bound by it whether or not they have signed (or ratified) it. About half of these instruments were agreed in the eleven years between 1958 and 1969, justifying the reputation of the 1960s as a decade of liberation and reform internationally, as it was in Britain also, with reforms in the laws, for example on abortion and homosexuality.

The UN uses a variety of means to promote aspects of human rights. One has been the declaration of special years, such as Human Rights Year 1968, International Education Year 1970, Year for the Elimination of Racial Discrimination 1971, Women's Year 1975, Year of the Child 1979, of Disabled Persons 1981, and so on[2]; the UN declares Decades also: the Decades of Development from 1961, for Women from 1980-1990, of Disabled Persons 1983-1992, of Cultural Development 1988-1997 and others. These techniques do produce some results; for example in this country Human Rights Year 1968 produced a mass of publications on discrimination against women. As a result of the Mexico City Conference which initiated the Decade for Women, projects to assist women's equality were initiated in many countries, governments removed restrictions on women, for example in Brazil (Tabak, 1981: 66-80) and set up institutions to work for the improvement of the condition of women, for example in Australia. The International Year of Disabled Persons led to much more attention being given to improving facilities for persons with disabilities, such as British Rail's publicity about arrangements to help passengers with disabilities.

Intergovernmental Conferences leading to programmes of proposed action are aimed at improving the administrative practices and policies of Governments so as to achieve improvements in human rights. Examples are the Human Rights Conferences in Tehran in 1968 and Vienna 1993, the Rio Conference on the Environment in 1991 and the Women's Conferences in Mexico City in 1980, Copenhagen in 1985, Nairobi in 1990 and Beijing in 1995. Such Conferences have a parallel Forum open to NGOs and individuals.

The representatives of NGOs are playing an increasingly important part in these Conferences. In 1985, only a handful of government delegations held meetings with representatives of NGOs, but in Vienna in 1993 and Beijing in 1995, such meetings were the norm, at least among Western governments; some Western Governments have included representatives of NGOs in their official delegations. Preparatory meetings between government officials and representatives of NGOs were held before the Vienna Conference in the African, Latin/American and Asia-Pacific regions and among the Arab NGOs (Azzan, 1993: 89-100). It is clear that representatives of NGOs are now occasionally able to contribute to the negotiations and to influence the content of the final document. On the other hand at the Vienna Conference, some Asian Governments attempted to prevent NGOs from being heard (*ibid.* p. 98). Azzan discusses the preparations and difficulties of the NGOs, and the relationships between the well-established and recognised International NGOs and the regional and national NGOs. She points out the problem of distinguishing between human rights organisations and organisations that are primarily political such as Government-Appointed NGOs (GANGOs) and Peru's 'Shining

Path' representatives. She found that the NGOs representing women, children and indigenous peoples were the best organised at Vienna and that the main necessities for NGOs were to obtain a right to be heard at the Governmental Conference and to ensure that past gains were not lost.

Although the Declaration of the Vienna Conference has been criticised for vague language that makes few definite demands on governments[3], it nonetheless clearly recognised women's human rights as human rights, the importance of education and of education for human rights.

It will be seen from Appendix 1 that there are no regional instruments relating to Asia or the Arab countries. Proportionately fewer Asian governments than those in other regions have ratified UN Conventions on Human Rights (Yamane, 1982). There has, however, been a movement of lawyers and others, LAWASIA, towards developing instruments on human rights and, in 1982 and subsequently, Conferences have been held to discuss a Model Convention for Human Rights in Asia. The emphasis in 1982 was to be on research, teaching, advice to governments, elaborating standards and providing information, rather than on direct enforcement. The standards recommended as a starting point were those of the UN in general and those set out in some of the major instruments such as the Social Covenant, the Civil Covenant and its Optional Protocol. The Conventions on Race, Apartheid and Refugees and those of the Specialised Agencies were specifically mentioned (*HRI Reporter* Sept.-Nov. 1982), although not the Women's Convention. Six years later, the UN Human Rights Centre in conjunction with the Government of the Philippines was able to organise the first Asia-Pacific Human Rights Seminar attended by 23 Asian Governments in May 1990 (*Human Rights Newsletter*, 3(3) July 1990). A further step was taken on 2 July 1993, when the Foreign Ministers at the ASEAN (Asian and South East Asian Nations) Conference agreed to consider establishing a regional human rights mechanism (Council of Europe *Information Sheet No. 35*, 1994: 142).

The Arab League set up a Regional Arab Commission on Human Rights in 1968 following the Six-Day War, a Chairman was appointed, but no meetings were held. In 1970, the League set up a Committee to draft an Arab Charter of Human Rights, but no progress has been made since 1971. The Commission on the Status of Arab Women has an observer at the UN Commission on the Status of Women, which noted in 1978 that the Arab League had adopted a Plan of Action relating to the Status of

Women. Its report also dealt with family law, education and the elimination of illiteracy, the role of women in development and in promoting better nutrition, and the portrayal of women by the mass media. In 1979, the Baghdad Symposium on Human Rights and Fundamental Freedoms in the Arab Homeland noted 'the distressing circumstances in which women in most Arab states find themselves'. Most Arab states have ratified a few of the UN Human Rights Conventions (Vasak, 1982: 580); by 1995 only twelve out of 21 Arab States had ratified the two Covenants. Again, as in Asia, it is the NGOs which are leading the struggle for human rights (Youssoufi, 1987: 33-35, and report of the Workshop in Amman, January 1994, *The Review*, 1994: 92-95).

Provisions concerning Education

I turn now to the content of the instruments themselves to show the emphasis given to different aspects of a right to education and illuminate the meaning given both to education and to the right to education in international human rights law. The sources for a right to education in some form or other lie in at least 29 important human rights instruments from 1944 onwards. They are listed in Appendix 1 together with a brief explanation of technical terms in Appendix 2. A few of the instruments are Declarations, representing intent and are commonly precursors to Conventions providing for implementation and/or enforcement. Most of the instruments however include measures for implementation at least. These measures are discussed in the next chapter. We shall see that the provisions of Conventions are often stronger than the preceding Declarations. The recommendations of the Vienna and Beijing Conferences build on the provisions of the instruments discussed in this chapter; it is convenient to use them as a summing up for the developments set out in this book.

The instruments can be divided into five groups:

(i) universal instruments of the UN, such as the Universal Declaration of Human Rights 1948 (the Universal Declaration) and the Charter of the UN which includes educational and cultural co-operation and the advancement of education among its purposes;

(ii) UN instruments concerned with issues, such as the International Convention on the Suppression and Punishment of the Crime of Apartheid 1973 (the Apartheid Convention);

(iii) UN instruments concerned with particular groups of individuals such as the Convention relating to the Status of Refugees 1951 (the Refugees Convention) and the Convention on the Elimination of All Forms of Discrimination Against Women 1979 (the Women's Convention);

(iv) instruments of Specialised Agencies of the UN organisations, such as the Unesco Convention against Discrimination in Education 1960 (the UNESCO Education Convention), and ILO instruments; and

(v) instruments with regional application, agreed by some or all of the Governments of the region, such as the European Convention on Human Rights and Fundamental Freedoms 1950 and its Protocols (the European Convention), and the African Charter of Human and Peoples' Rights 1981 (the African Charter). The Helsinki Final Act 1975 also comes into this category, although it includes the USA and Canada as well as the Soviet Union and other Central and East European States. Legally it is a statement of intent on European security which had the aim of building confidence, reducing tension and increasing co-operation between East and West and is a very wide-ranging instrument. The collapse of the Soviet Union has not destroyed these aims, which were followed up in the Charter of Paris 1990. Successor States normally take on the obligations and rights of their predecessors.

Non-Discrimination

All instruments have a provision concerned with non-discrimination, either directly prohibiting discrimination or expressing the right of each person to enjoy the rights provided in the instrument. In the Universal Declaration Art. 2 reads:

Everyone is entitled to all the rights and freedoms set forth in this Declaration, without distinction of any kind, such as race, colour, sex, language, religion, political or other opinion, national or social origin, property, birth or other status.

This list appears in some ten instruments with only minor variations[4]. The Children's Declaration 1959 adds 'whether of himself or of his family', the African Charter 1981 'ethnic group', the European Convention 1950 'association with a national minority', and the Social Charter 1961 (not to be confused with the European Social Chapter of the European Union) 'national extraction', the Race Convention 1966 'descent' and the Children's Convention 1989 includes disability and applies the rule to the child's parents or legal guardians. Other instruments have shorter lists: for example, 'race, language, creed or any other factor' in the American Declaration 1948, one of the few instruments not to mention sex specifically; 'race, colour, sex, belief, tribal association or trade union affiliation' in the ILO Convention on Social Policy (Basic Aims and Standards) 1962. The Charter of Paris for a New Europe 1990, a follow-up to the Helsinki Final Act 1975, has a very different list; it expresses the determination of the signatories 'to combat all forms of racial and ethnic hatred, anti-Semitism, xenophobia and discrimination against anyone as well as persecution on religious and ideological grounds'. These are two of some nine instruments with no catch-all phrase. Age, marital status and sexual preference do not appear in any list, but would presumably be covered by the catch-all phrase and perhaps by such phrases as 'all human beings' or 'the population' in those instruments which have no catch-all phrase.

There are few specific references to women or to the 'girl-child'; they are however protected by the non-discrimination Articles. The Declaration on the Elimination of Discrimination Against Women 1967 is naturally more specific. It refers in several Articles to 'women, married or unmarried' and the Convention on the Elimination of All Forms of Discrimination Against Women 1979 (CEDAW or the Women's Convention) in Art. 2 condemns 'discrimination against women in all its forms' and in numerous Articles demands equality with men. The Women's Convention goes further and defines discrimination against women as:

> any distinction, exclusion or restriction made on the basis of sex which has the effect or purpose of impairing or nullifying the recognition, enjoyment or exercise by women, irrespective of their marital status, on a basis of equality of men and women, of human rights and fundamental freedoms in the political, economic, social, cultural, civil or any other field (Art. 1).

The Right to Education

Five instruments provide specifically a 'right to education' (the Universal Declaration 1948, the American Declaration 1948, the Social Covenant 1966/76⁵, the African Charter 1981, the Children's Convention 1989/90). The European Convention in its First Protocol (P1) states the right in the negative: 'No person shall be denied the right to education', but the European Court of Human Rights (ECtHR) has interpreted that as a positive right in the *Belgian Linguistic* cases (1968). The Apartheid Convention 1973 includes the denial of the right to education within the crime of apartheid (Art. IIc). Both the Children's Declaration 1959 in Principle 9, the Children's Convention 1989/90 in Art. 28 (1) and the ILO Convention on Social Policy (Basic Aims and Standards) 1962 in Art. 15(3) provide that employment shall not be allowed to impede a child's access to education. The UNESCO Convention provides that resident foreign nationals should have the same access to education as local nationals (Art. 3(e)).

Disadvantaged Groups

Some groups of individuals are particularly disadvantaged in their access to education, or in the content of the education they receive or both. Several instruments deal with these difficulties. The International Convention on the Elimination of All Forms of Racial Discrimination 1966 (the Race Convention) does so briefly.

The Women's Declaration 1967 (Art. 9) claims equal rights for girls and women in education: (a) equal conditions in access to and study in all types of educational, professional and vocational establishments, (b) the same choice of curricula, the same examinations, the same standards of teaching staff, premises and equipment, (c) equal opportunities to benefit from scholarship and grants, and (d) to have access to continuing education and adult literacy programmes, and (e) access to 'educational information to help in ensuring the health and well-being of families', a coded reference to family planning. The Women's Convention 1979 includes these provisions with slightly more detail and adds three more rights in education in Art. 10:

(c) The elimination of any stereotyped concept of the roles of men and women at all levels and in all forms of education by encouraging co-education and other types of education which will help to achieve this aim and, in particular, by the revision of textbooks and school programmes and the adaptation of teaching methods;

(f) The reduction of female student drop-out rates and the organisation of programmes for girls and women who have left school prematurely;

(g) The same opportunities to participate actively in sports and physical education;

Furthermore the Article refers specifically to the needs of women in rural as well as urban areas and in Art. 14, on the rights of women in rural areas, specifies their right:

(d) To obtain all types of training and education, formal and non-formal, including that relating to functional literacy, as well as, inter alia, the benefit of all community and extension services, in order to increase their technical proficiency.

In relation to education therefore, the Convention sets higher standards than the Declaration. The Convention also deals with the roles of men and women in the family. The Preamble states that 'a change in the traditional role of men as well as the role of women in society and in the family is needed to achieve full equality between men and women' and 'recalls' that discrimination against women is an obstacle to the prosperity of society and of the family. Art. 5(a) requires States to take steps

(a) To modify the social and cultural patterns of conduct of men and women, with a view to achieving the elimination of prejudices and customary and all other practices which are based on the idea of the inferiority or the superiority of either of the sexes or on stereotyped roles for men and women.

The reference to customary practices could be used to cover practices such as genital mutilation and honour crimes. The requirement to modify the traditional roles of women and men is developed in the Children's Convention which provides that 'Both parents have common responsibilities'.

In the next chapter we shall see in what ways these admirable principles are being advanced.

The rights of children with disabilities, recognised in the Children's Declaration 1959, were added to in the Children's Convention to cover special treatment, education and care for children who are physically, mentally or socially handicapped to include training, and services such as rehabilitation and health care services, which should be provided free of charge when possible; States should promote international co-operation in order to improve the treatment provided for disabled children. Primary education should be compulsory and free to all, a variety of forms of secondary education available and accessible to every child, higher education accessible on the basis of ability, educational and vocational information provided, and measures to encourage regular attendance and reduce drop-out adopted. Discipline should be provided in a manner consistent with human dignity; and international co-operation should be encouraged. The Convention further provides that States 'shall take all effective and appropriate measures with a view to abolishing traditional practices prejudicial to the health of children. ' (Art. 24(3))

The Social Charter (of the Council of Europe) makes provision for the right of those with physical or mental disabilities to vocational training, rehabilitation and resettlement (Principle 15 and Art. 15).

The rights of migrant workers and their children to education are most fully dealt with in the Helsinki Final Act 1975, re-affirmed in the most general terms in the Charter of Paris 1990. The Final Act provides that States should 'regard with favour' the provision of vocational training and free instruction in the language of the host country and that they should 'ensure' that the children of migrant workers have access to the education usually provided under the same conditions as local children and in addition that they should permit the migrant workers' children 'to receive supplementary education in their own language, national culture, history and geography'. The ILO has done much work for migrant workers, especially concerned with their rights at work and their rights to social security. Migrant workers are also protected in EU legislation, especially those who are nationals of EU States, and no discrimination is allowed against the latter, as will be seen in the next chapter.

Refugees and stateless persons are to have the same access to elementary education as nationals and treatment not less favourable than that accorded to aliens as regards other levels of education and in the recognition of qualifications, remission of fees and award of scholarships

(Conventions relating to the Status of Refugees 1951, Art. 22, and to the Status of Stateless Persons, Art. 22).

Aims and Purposes related to Education

Four themes can be identified in the aims and purposes related to education set out in the instruments, but not all are in Articles specifically concerned with education. Much of what appears in the documents will look like high-minded ideals and nothing much more. It would, I think, be wrong to put these phrases down simply as 'being against sin'. The phrases are fought over in the Conferences when they are being drafted; they provide leverage for politicians, administrators, NGOs and citizens to make demands on governments, public authorities and private organisations.

The first theme is that of developing the human person. Many instruments contain phrases such as 'the full development of the human personality', 'the sense of the dignity of the human personality' for example in the Universal Declaration, the Social Covenant, the Race and Children's Conventions, and in the Women's Convention also 'the social significance of maternity'.

The second theme is concerned with the promotion of democracy, peace and international understanding, included in nearly all instruments[6] and is expressed in many instruments in phrases such as 'the strengthening of respect for human rights and fundamental freedoms', the promotion of 'understanding, tolerance and freedom among all nations, racial and religious groups', the furthering of 'the activities of the United Nations for the maintenance of peace', 'effective participation in a free society'[7]. The Charter of the Organisation of American States (OAS), amended by the Protocol of Buenos Aires 1967, specifically provides that education should be 'oriented toward the overall improvement of the individual, and as a foundation of democracy, social justice and progress' (Art. 45). The Helsinki Final Act 1975 seeks the promotion of better mutual understanding to the advantage of all peoples and of future generations and sees the study of foreign languages and civilisations as a means of strengthening international co-operation. This idea is developed in the Charter of Paris with particular reference to the environment by emphasis on 'the significant role of a well-informed society' and the promotion of 'public awareness and education on the environment'.

The third theme is the encouragement of education, science and culture, for example in the amended Charter of the OAS: 'the eradication of illiteracy', extension of primary, secondary and higher education, strengthening adult education and ensuring that 'the benefits of culture will be available to the entire population' (Art. 48), in the Helsinki Final Act the encouragement of education, science and culture and in the Charter of Paris the desire for the establishment of cultural centres in the cities of other participating States.

The fourth theme is concerned with vocational education and education as a means of improving the standard of living and included in instruments such as the ILO Convention on Social Policy and the European Social Charter.

The first three themes are *enabling* and *sybaritic* and the second is politically *instrumental* for those concerned with obtaining, maintaining or improving democracy, human rights and freedoms. The fourth theme is both *instrumental* and *enabling*.

The education of children in the American Declaration of the Rights and Duties of Man 1948 includes all these themes. The Convention on the Rights of the Child in Art.29 goes further than that Declaration by providing also for:

(c) the development of respect for the child's parents, his or her own cultural identity, language and values, for the national values of the country in which the child is living, the country from which he or she may originate, and for civilisations different from his or her own;

(d) the preparation of the child for responsible life in a free society, in the spirit of understanding, peace, tolerance, equality of sexes, and friendship among all peoples, ethnic, national and religious groups and persons of indigenous origin;

(e) the development of respect for the natural environment.

The reader will notice that this is the first document in which 'he' referring to both sexes has been replaced by 'he or she' – evidence of progress.

Levels of Education

Most instruments refer to particular levels or forms of education – basic, primary, secondary, further, vocational, higher or continuing education – single-sex schools and so on. Further and vocational education have attracted more provisions and more detailed provisions than any other level. Most of these provisions refer to individuals, rather than to groups, although some instruments are concerned with the access to education of particular groups of people.

Access to Education

Provisions on fundamental (or basic) education provide that it should be free (the Universal Declaration), and strengthened for those with no or incomplete primary education (the Social Covenant and the Women's Convention). Nearly all instruments provide that primary education should be free and compulsory[8]. The American Declaration is unusual in imposing on every person a duty 'to acquire at least an elementary education'. A few instruments refer to secondary education (the Social Covenant, the OAS Charter, and the Women's and Children's Conventions) and these urge the provision of more secondary education, the Children's Convention adding varied forms of secondary education and financial assistance in case of need; and the Social Covenant and the Children's Convention urge that free secondary education should be progressively introduced.

Vocational Education

Provisions on vocational education are the most specific. This difference may reflect the fact that the majority of these provisions form part of instruments that have a fairly clear enforcement procedure, but many instruments contain general statements in favour of vocational and technical education, for example the Universal Declaration, the Philadelphia Declaration of the ILO 1944, the amended OAS Charter and the Children's Convention. The Social Policy (Basic Aims and Standards) Convention of the ILO 1962 prescribes broad systems of education, vocational training and apprenticeship as a preparation for a useful occupation and for high productivity through skilled labour and training in new techniques (Art. 16(1)). The Women's Convention is concerned with women obtaining the same treatment as men in career and vocational guidance and in all forms of technical and professional education and vocational training. The European Social Charter is exceptional in the detail in which it spells out how the obligation of States may be fulfilled. States undertake to provide or promote in consultation with employers' and workers' organisations, vocational guidance services, technical training, access to higher technical and university education on the basis solely of ability, to supervise apprenticeships, provide training and retraining for adult workers and encourage utilisation of facilities by providing them free or with financial assistance and by treating supplementary training that is undertaken by workers at the employer's request as part of normal working hours.

Higher Education

Higher education is to be available to all on merit (Universal Declaration, Social Covenant, Children's Convention), and in order to maintain a high level 'the corresponding regulatory or academic standards are [to be] met' (the amended OAS Charter, Art. 47c).

Continuing and Adult Education

The Women's Declaration and Convention and the amended OAS Charter specifically mention continuing and adult education.

Rights of Parents

The Universal Declaration accords parents 'a primary right to choose the kind of education that shall be given to their children'. The Social Covenant allows parents to ensure the education of their children according to their religious and moral convictions, as do the Civil Covenant and the American Convention, but as part of the right to freedom of conscience rather than as a right to education. The Protocol of the European Convention limits this right to a duty on the State to respect parents' religious and philosophical convictions. In contrast, the Children's Convention does not mention parents' rights as such in connection with education, but instead requires the State to respect the rights and responsibilities of the extended family and community and provide appropriate guidance to the child in the exercise of her or his rights; furthermore the child's views must be given due weight.

Single-sex and Private Schools

Some parents and children may prefer a single-sex school. Some may be unable to obtain the sort of education they desire in a State school. Both single-sex and private schools are expressly permitted in the Social Covenant, and the UNESCO Convention recognises that separate religious and linguistic schools are not discriminatory when allowed by the State.

Rights of Teachers

The instruments give little attention to the rights of teachers. Only the Social Covenant and the UNESCO Convention deal with teaching staff whose material conditions, the Covenant declares, should be continuously improved. Apart from these provisions, teachers must rely on the right to freedom of conscience to teach their religion, and on rights to freedom of expression and on employment rights in other instruments.

The Curriculum

References to the curriculum are relatively sparse. The most important and potentially far-reaching is that in the Women's Convention on the elimination of stereotyping, quoted on pp.83-84. The provision goes further and is more explicit than the more general provision in the Race Convention 1966:

> States Parties undertake to adopt immediate and effective measures, particularly in the fields of teaching, education, culture and information, with a view to combating prejudices which lead to racial discrimination and to promoting understanding, tolerance and friendship among nations and racial and ethnical [sic] groups, as well as propagating the principles and purposes of the Charter of the United Nations, the Universal Declaration of Human Rights, the United Nations Declaration on the Elimination of All Forms of Racial Discrimination and this Convention (Art. 7).

Far vaguer, although later, is the provision in the African Charter 1981:

> The promotion and protection of morals and traditional values recognised by the community shall be the duty of the State (Art. 17(3)).

The Children's Convention provides for access to scientific and technical knowledge and for modern teaching methods, and the development of respect for human rights and freedoms and for the environment. It also provides for a child's right to play and recreation, and protection against exploitation either by employment interfering with education or in other ways. Furthermore, the Convention recognises the important contribution of the mass media to information relevant to children's social, spiritual and moral well-being, physical and mental health and States' role in encouraging the mass media in publishing material of social and cultural benefit to children and children's books. This is a remarkable recommendation to States in relation to the mass media.

The Helsinki Final Act gives cautious support to 'the contribution that national minorities or regional cultures can make... in various fields of education', and recommends that States undertake to facilitate this contribution 'taking into account the legitimate interests of their members'. It also advocates wider provision for the study of foreign languages and civilisations, and the exchange of lecturers and teaching through the media in both higher and continuing education for this purpose. The Final Act deals with these matters in some detail suggesting such measures as meetings, exchanges of staff, students and materials. It also draws attention to the importance of the mutual recognition of qualifications and access to scholarships and fellowships. The Charter of Paris adds concern for the environment:

> We emphasise the significant role of a well-informed society in enabling the public and individuals to take initiatives to improve the environment. To this end, we commit ourselves to promoting public awareness and education on the environment as well as the public reporting of the environmental impact of policies, projects and programmes (Council of Europe, *Human rights*, 1992:460).

The same principle applies also to education and participation by the public in the promotion and protection of human rights. We see here the further emergence of a right to a good environment, already hinted at in the Children's Convention.

A different aspect of education appears in the UN Convention Against Torture, which imposes on States the duty to ensure that all those concerned with law enforcement, civil and military, police, medical staff, public officials and others, are educated and informed about the prohibition against torture, and the infliction of physical or mental pain and suffering (Art. 10).

Conclusions

We can now take stock of the substantive provisions concerning the right to education and assess their nature. I have not traced the processes of drafting the provisions, because once agreed, signed and ratified, instruments have an independent existence, although Courts and committees for implementation do take into account the prior negotiations when interpreting the provisions.

The UN has always attached importance to education, included in the Charter itself, as well as in the numerous instruments discussed in this chapter; it should be available without discrimination as to persons. Education is seen as an unchallenged good, both for the individual and for society. No comfort in this approach for the *denyers* of the value of education. Education has become a fundamental freedom at least at the level of primary and basic education, necessarily so in a literate, global economy.

What levels of education do the instruments provide for? While States are required to provide universal, free and compulsory primary and basic education – which many do not at present – secondary education is to be expanded as resources become available. This is understandable in view of the difficulties facing many countries of the South. Here is an opportunity for exclusion in practice, although not in principle. Higher education according to ability seems to be a reasonable *meritocratic* proposal, especially as it has traditionally referred to intellectually demanding education which is not what everyone wants. Should we think instead of higher education together with continuing and adult education, so that those who do not want conventional higher education have good access to an education which meets both their needs and their desires? The major instruments which I have examined show little concern for continuing and adult education. Since the majority of people in the world have received or receive relatively little education, surely non-discrimination requires more attention to be given to adult education.

What sort of education is envisaged in the instruments? As we have seen, one recurring theme is high-minded idealism, such as 'the full development of the human personality', phrases lacking practical applications, but pointing to *enabling* and *sybaritic* education. Later instruments are more specific: the Women's Convention on ending stereotyping, the Helsinki Final Act on the teaching of foreign languages, the Children's Convention on scientific and technical knowledge, and the Women's and Children's Conventions on the types and availability of books. These specific provisions can have *instrumental* aspects as well.

The provisions on the teaching of human rights and on the environment are general enough in the instruments. However the General Conference of UNESCO in November 1974, the Council of Europe from 1978 and the European Community in 1982 each agreed Recommendations on the teaching of human rights[9] (which there is not space to discuss in this chapter). These are documents which can be used with teachers and others concerned with teaching human rights and with teaching generally. These provisions are *enabling* and should assist women and men to safeguard their own human rights and those of others. For those who value human rights and democracy, they are *instrumental* as well.

The requirement to teach human rights to those concerned with law enforcement is protective of citizens' rights, but also protective, *instrumental* and *enabling* for law enforcers; it will help to keep them out of trouble.

Provisions concerned with ensuring that ethnic groups should be able to retain and develop their own culture should enable them to maintain their own identity and could be *sybaritic* both to them and to others outside their culture. Culture is used both in the anthropological sense and in the sense of ethnic and 'high' cultures. We are all enriched by access to other cultures. We need not become insecure in our own because we have understanding of another culture and can take pleasure in its manifestations. These provisions are *enabling* and *sybaritic* for ethnic minorities and for outsiders as well as a contribution to international understanding. Were members of minority groups to be confined within their own culture and excluded from the mainstream, they would indeed be suffering from *repression* – and discrimination.

The rights to vocational guidance and vocational education are clearly *enabling* in assisting young people, and indeed older people, to find their most appropriate occupation or profession, or to change it. The references to science (which may be used in its Continental sense of scholarly work and research) provides support for *seekers*.

The right of parents to have a major or deciding role in the education of their children, which could lead to the restriction of girls' education to domesticity and marriage and of boys' to their father's occupation and consequent conflicts between parents and children, is absent from the Children's Convention. It recognises a child's right for her or his views to be given due weight for the first time in an international instrument – another *enabling* provision.

We can see that the educational provisions have developed and become more specific over time, that they recognise some of the *instrumental* needs of women and men, and provide a departure point for a more *enabling* and *sybaritic* education for all.

Notes

1. Sieghart discusses the legal status of The Universal Declaration and of Art. 55 of the Charter (which deals with human rights) on pp. 51-55, 6.1 and 6.2.1.

2. Other UN Years include Book Year 1972, for the Eradication of Poverty 1996 and of Older Persons 1999.

3. Examples of criticism of the Vienna Declaration can be found in *The Review* of the International Commission of Jurists, 1993, No. 50, Special Issue on the Vienna Conference.

4. Other instruments with such a list include the two Covenants, the UNESCO Convention, the Children's Declaration and Covenant, the American Convention, the African Charter, the European Convention and the European Social Charter.

5. Where two dates are given, the first refers to the date when the Convention was adopted and the second to the date of entering into effect. See also Appendix 2 for a brief explanation of technical terms.

6. The instruments with such phrases include the Universal Declaration, the two Covenants, the Race, Women's and Children's Conventions, the amended OAS Charter, the UNESCO Convention.

7. Instruments with such phrases include the Universal Declaration, the two Covenants, the UNESCO Convention, the amended OAS Charter, the Women's and the Children's Conventions.

8. The following instruments provide that primary education should be free and compulsory: the Universal Declaration, the Social Covenant, the Children's Declaration and Convention and the Charter of the OAS. As the Women's Convention requires *equal* access to all levels of education, women are provided for in this way; and in Europe, free primary education already exists.

9. The UNESCO Recommendation concerning Education for International Understanding, Co-operation and Peace and Education relating to Human Rights and Fundamental Freedoms is quoted in full in Thomas Buergenthal and Torney, 1976, *International Human Rights and International Education*, pp. 152-162. The Committee of Ministers of the Council of Europe has adopted several resolutions on the subject, the latest of which is Recommendation No. R(85)7 of 14 May 1985 on Teaching and Learning about Human Rights in Schools, and refers to earlier Resolutions. The European Parliament adopted a Resolution on 29 October 1982 on the Teaching of Human Rights in the European Community, OJ No. C 304/255 of 22 November 1982.

Chapter 5

Implementation and enforcement

Part I – Global instruments

The means for implementing human rights provisions are complicated. They are based on bodies and procedures that have grown over time in response to varying pressures. Education may be dealt with through a variety of bodies and procedures. It is therefore necessary to review briefly some of their main characteristics.

There are two types of legal foundation for international human rights bodies and procedures. One is the Charter of the UN and Resolutions of the General Assembly, or of subordinate bodies and the bodies they in turn create, and the equivalent constitutions and decisions of the Specialised Agencies of the UN. These are known as non-treaty provisions or procedures.

The other legal foundation lies in bodies and procedures created by treaties, Conventions, which may be those of the UN itself, of Specialised Agencies or of geo-political regional bodies, such as the Council of Europe, the Organisation of American States (OAS) or the Organisation of African Unity (OAU) (Tardu 1988, Opsahl 1989, Byrnes 1994). The European Convention on Human Rights and Fundamental Freedoms 1950 and the European Social Charter 1961 were created by the Council of Europe, the OAS is the parent of the American Declaration of the Rights and Duties of Man 1948, the Charter of the OAS as amended by the Protocol of Buenos Aires 1967 and the American Convention on Human Rights 1969, and the OAU of the Charter of Human and Peoples' Rights. Governments become parties to a Convention by first signing and then ratifying it. The Convention comes into effect for all States that have ratified it when the number of ratifications specified by the Convention have been received by the relevant Secretariat.

The European Union, a supra-national organisation, is rather different in kind from the international bodies. Its Directives are binding, either directly or indirectly through national legislation, and have been especially important for women in relation to employment and social security. The European Social *Chapter*, part of the Treaty of Maastricht and important for social and economic rights, is also binding on member States, except on the United Kingdom which has opted out.

There are three types of procedure: information-procedures whereby bodies receive information about compliance with human rights or about breaches of human rights; complaints-procedures whereby bodies are able to investigate individual or group complaints; and procedures in Courts (Tardu 1988, Opsahl 1989, Byrnes 1994). Bodies may use all three types, two or only one of them. Related to these distinctions are the differences between monitoring, promotion, protection, implementation and enforcement, but these differences are not always clear-cut.

The bodies, Committees, Councils or Commissions, set up by non-treaty Resolutions and by Conventions have power to consider human rights problems and in some case individual complaints. Their composition, powers, functions and resources have a number of similarities, but their individual histories differ markedly. Over time, most have tended to secure increases in their power and a wider remit. At the same time, governments have tended to become less suspicious of their activities and more willing to co-operate.

What follows is a summary of common patterns. The members of some bodies are government representatives, but in most cases they are independent experts, persons of 'high moral character', of 'recognised competence' and 'acknowledged impartiality'. Governments, States parties to a Convention, may nominate three such persons, who are not always required to be their own nationals (thus an expert whose own government would not nominate her or him can be nominated). States Parties then elect members with due regard to geographical distribution and representation of civilisations and legal systems. Members are commonly elected for four years with staggered elections and are re-eligible. Thus continuity is provided for, enabling expertise to be built up. These bodies vary in size from 10[1] to 45[2] or 53[3]. They elect their own officers and control their own procedure. However, the length and frequency of meetings is sometimes restricted by superior bodies. They are serviced usually by the UN Human Rights Centre in Geneva. All human rights bodies are short of resources. The Centre for Human Rights receives only 0.7% of the UN budget. The US is among those governments which fail to pay their contributions to the UN (Bossuyt, 1993: 51).

The Conventions require States Parties to submit regular reports on compliance with the Conventions including difficulties or obstacles in doing so. The monitoring body examines the government representatives on the report in the light of other information received, usually from nongovernmental organisations (NGOs), that is pressure-groups, interest-groups, voluntary bodies. The monitoring body then produces its own report. The emphasis is normally on assisting States to comply. In dealing with individual complaints (technically, and euphemistically, communications), monitoring bodies seek 'friendly solutions'.

Committees which examine individual complaints, and Courts begin by considering whether the complaint is admissible: does the complaint come within the Convention being administered, is the State complained of a party to the Convention, is the complaint submitted within the prescribed time-limits, does the author of the complaint have the standing to make it, is there evidence other than reports in the media to substantiate it, is it being examined by any other international body, have domestic remedies within the State been exhausted? In effect, has the Committee or Court jurisdiction to consider the complaint, whether or not it proves in the end to be well- or ill-founded? The conditions of admissibility vary slightly among different bodies. After the complaint has been declared admissible, the merits are considered.

Until 1967, the UN human rights bodies and that of UNESCO had received many complaints of violations, but held that they were able to 'take no action'. Meanwhile the European Convention had been adopted in 1950, come into effect in 1953 and by the mid-sixties a jurisprudence, or case-law, had begun to be built up on the basis of a small number of cases. In 1966 after years of negotiation, the UN Covenants on Economic, Social and Cultural Rights, and on Civil and Political Rights and the Optional Protocol to the latter Covenant (which permitted individual complaints) were adopted. The attitude to human rights was changing. Bodies and the government representatives on them, which had declared they could take no action now began to find ways of acting. It seems clear that diplomats who again and again received reliable reports of violations must have influenced the governments to which they reported to change their stance, but the most effective pressure came from NGOs and media reports of violations. How some of them did this, the obstacles they found and overcame is the subject of the next sections of this chapter.

The UN Commission on Human Rights

The UN Commission on Human Rights was created by the Economic and Social Council (ECOSOC)[4] in 1946 and was originally composed of 18 representatives of governments; by 1992 the membership had increased to 53 representatives elected for three-year terms. The Commission meets annually for about six weeks. For the first 20 years, the Commission was primarily concerned with drafting human rights instruments: the Universal Declaration of Human Rights, the two Covenants on Civil and Political Rights and on Economic, Social and Cultural Rights, also the Conventions on the Political Rights of Women 1952 and on the Nationality of Married Women 1957 (Schwelb and Alston, 1982: 233). These are important measures, setting standards, legitimating protests and demands, and establishing procedures for the enforcement of the standards.

From 1953, the Commission's work was affected by the preference of the US for persuasion and its opposition to binding international conventions on human rights. However from 1971-76, the Commission was able to act as a drafting chamber for such conventions, but was unable to resolve the political issues connected with them. Since 1977, it has worked productively on new conventions and better standards, but its work overlaps that of other UN bodies and in 1991 it called for an inventory of all current standard-setting work (Alston, 1992: 137, n. 41).

For its first 20 years, the Commission refused to consider individual petitions despite their number; in 1951-52, there were 25,000 (Alston, 1992: 140). There was opposition from the US because of the treatment of the Blacks in the US, from Western countries because of their colonialism and from the USSR because of Stalinism. After the adoption of the two Covenants and under pressure for action against colonialism and racism from new Asian and African members, ECOSOC adopted Resolution 1235 (XLII) of 1967 in response to a request from the Committee of Twenty Four on Decolonisation to take action on violations of human rights and on South Africa and apartheid. This Resolution authorised the Commission to examine information about 'gross violations' and the practice of racial discrimination 'notably' in Southern Rhodesia. Resolution 1503 (XLVIII) of 1979 lays down the procedure for carrying out this examination. It permits the Commission to receive from its Sub-Commission on the Prevention of Discrimination and Protection of Minorities, created in 1947 and composed of individual experts, complaints of violations of human rights in any country from all available sources, and to make thorough studies and report to ECOSOC. The Sub-Commission was empowered to set up a working group of five of its members to meet annually for not more than ten days to consider communications and the replies of governments and to report to the Commission. The Commission considers what action to take, whether to investigate, appoint an *ad hoc* committee or strive for a friendly solution. All these proceedings in the Sub-Commission and the Commission are confidential and the complainant excluded. This procedure, originally intended for racism and colonialism, has since 1979 been increasingly used in creative ways to expose a wider range of violations in more countries. The 1503 procedure is a petition-information procedure in practice.

However, the Commission may decide in the light of the Sub-Commission's report to transfer the examination to the procedure under Resolution 1235 which is not bound by the confidentiality required under Resolution 1503. Under these combined procedures, the Commission has developed tools for investigating and publicising major violations of human rights. These tools include the appointment of Special Rapporteurs (under a variety of titles) with no clear means of selection, but often diplomats, and with usually vague terms of reference. Up to 1992 no woman had ever been appointed (Alston, 1992: 165-9). Under these circumstances, the reports have reflected differing approaches: fact-finding, accusatorial, condemnatory or conciliatory, and have been of varying quality. Alston (1992: 169-71) considers they have been poor in comparison with those of the Inter-American Commission on Human Rights and of the ILO, and there have been significant problems of reprisals against witnesses.

There are two types of investigation, one concerned with a specific country (country reports) and the other, thematic reports about a problem of human rights involving several countries, for example on The Disappeared 1980, Torture 1986, Religious Intolerance 1986, Mercenaries 1987, Arbitrary Detention 1991, among other issues. At its 1993 session, the Commission condemned the rape of women in Yugoslavia as a war crime and requested the Special Rapporteur to make an investigation and report back within three months (Council of Europe, *Information Sheet No. 32*, 1993: 106). The following year the Commission adopted a similar resolution, but without a reference to the Special Rapporteur (*Information Sheet No. 34*, 1994: 121). In 1995 the Commission strongly condemned the Federal Republic of Yugoslavia and the 'self-proclaimed Bosnian Serb authorities' for continuing to refuse to permit the Special Rapporteur to investigate, and recognised the primary responsibility of the political and military leaders for the violations occurring in the territory they controlled (*Information Sheet No. 36*, 1995: 135). In the same year, the Commission called upon governments to prevent the traffic in women and children and their exploitation, the development of sex-tourism and the export of labour (*ibid*, p. 136). Furthermore, the Commission encouraged the Special Rapporteur to recommend where advisory services or technical assistance would help governments to eliminate and punish gender-based violence in the family, in the community and where perpetrated or condoned by the State (*ibid*, p. 138). In several years the Commission has urged action on poverty as being incompatible with human rights and called upon governments and NGOs to contribute to the Decade for Human Rights Education.

The procedure is intended to be more co-operative than adversarial, but there has been a tendency for States to support those investigations likely to injure or reflect badly on their enemies. The ending of the Cold War has led to co-operation from Central and East European governments and has made it difficult for member States which are developing countries simply to stand aside as observers (Strohal 1993). The forms of pressure that can be proposed by a Special Rapporteur or Working Group are routine requests for information, requests for urgent action, visits to a country, prompt intervention and reporting to the Commission. In relation to individuals, the intention is to try to protect them by showing international official interest in their fate. The Group working on Disappearances has produced frank, incisive, balanced and well-structured reports which have made much information public and have been used effectively by NGOs and in US State Department reports, but the Commission has been less than assiduous in itself making use of the material. Debates in the Commission on these reports have been undisciplined and rhetorical, so that Special Rapporteurs and Working Groups complain that their reports have been ignored (Alston, 1992: 179-80).

The Commission has also organised seminars, conferences and training programmes on human rights and has provided advisory services, some of them severely criticised. The Commission has made attempts to examine the conceptual content of rights, but so far with little success.

The procedures of the Commission have been substantially criticised in particular for the secrecy of the procedure under Resolution 1503. For example Theo van Boven, the Director of the UN Division of Human Rights from 1977-82, has written:

> Is it satisfactory to place so much emphasis on the consideration of situations in confidential procedures, thereby shutting out the international community and oppressed peoples? Are certain procedures in danger of becoming, in effect, screens of confidentiality to prevent cases thereunder from being aired in public? (Statement of 4 February 1980 reprinted in van Boven, *People Matter: Views on International Human Rights Policy*, 1982: 65, quoted by Lutz, 1989: 222 and Alston, 1992: 153)

and Iain Guest wrote:

> confidentiality has not persuaded governments to cooperate with the United Nations... 1503 has become truly dangerous to human rights – and... it offers a useful refuge to repressive regimes (*Behind the Disappearances*, 1990: 441, quoted by Alston, *ibid*).

Since the mobilisation of shame is the only significant weapon available to most human rights bodies, publicity is essential.

Other criticisms concern the slowness of the procedure, the lack of any emergency procedure, the politicisation of decisions in the Commission, the lack of preventive measures, and the lack of immediate and effective sanctions.

The Commission is clearly viewed as important, because there is intense competition among States to become members, more States are involved in it than in any other UN body, NGOs spend much time and effort on it and it is subject at times to intense lobbying by governments (Alston, 1992: 209).

For all its weaknesses, the Commission on Human Rights is an important body which has, after a very slow start, developed valuable and sometimes effective procedures and has given useful consideration to issues that lie on the progressive rather than the conservative agenda. The repeated presentation of well-documented evidence of violations of human rights both by NGOs and their own Rapporteurs has contributed to a 'radicalisation' of the diplomats making up the Commission. Resolutions and reports do not, of themselves, change circumstances, but they do mark a change in what is considered legitimate.

The Human Rights Committee

The Human Rights Committee under the Civil Convention is an expert Committee of 18 members elected for four years and re-eligible. The members must be nominated by their own State; they have varied professional backgrounds as law professors, judges, Cabinet Ministers or with experience on other international human rights bodies. Despite the differing professional, cultural and political backgrounds of its members, but aided by considerable continuity of membership, the Committee has built up a community of purpose. There have, however, been only two women members, a Canadian from 1983-84 and Professor Rosalyn Higgins from 1984-94 (now the first woman appointed to the International Court of Justice). Both the Chairman and the Working Groups of three to five members have been influential. The practice of the Committee has been to make decisions by consensus rather than by voting. Opsahl, a former member of the Committee, considers that consensus has led to slower, but more effective, progress by carrying all the members and enabling the Committee to present unanimous and therefore more compelling decisions (1992: 383-4). The Committee normally meets three times each year for three weeks.

The Committee has two mandates: to consider the reports of those States that have ratified the International Covenant on Civil and Political Rights 1966 (the Civil Covenant); and to hear complaints against those States which have ratified the Optional Protocol 1966, which permits individual petitions. Fewer States have ratified the Protocol than the Covenant, and most of those European States which have ratified it have excluded from its jurisdiction matters which might go to the European Commission and Court of Human Rights.

States Parties to the Covenant are required to submit their first report within a year of ratification, subsequent reports every five years and also when requested by the Committee. In the first report States must report on each Article of the Covenant, explaining not only their Constitution and legislation, but also what happens in practice. For subsequent reports, States are sent a list of questions, but Committee members may raise other matters as well. Persistence by the Committee has resulted in most State reports being submitted eventually (McGoldrick 1991). The meetings are held in public so NGOs, the press and public may attend. NGOs are able to assist the Committee, at least informally, by their comments on Governments' reports and to publicise the result of hearings. Tyagi (1983) discusses the importance of co-operation between the Committee and NGOs.

In 1985, the UK presented its second report[5]. Questioned about the UK's piecemeal approach to human rights and legislation such as the Police and Criminal Evidence Act 1984, the Mental Health Act 1983, the British Nationality Act 1981 and the Data Protection Act 1984, the Government representative told the Committee that the Government were considering 'partial incorporation of relevant provisions of the Covenant or European Convention on Human Rights', but did not know whether government lawyers had ever quoted provisions of the Covenant or the European Convention in any litigation (para. 527). Questions were asked on non-discrimination and equality between the sexes, including on immigration and recourse to *habeas corpus*, bail and other judicial safeguards, naturalisation (paras 541-544, 546), the practice of religion (para. 547), and the actual enjoyment of equality by women. The UK representative claimed that there was no distinction between men and women in relation to participating in public affairs and that the small proportion of MPs who were women small was not the result of discrimination, but because women had difficulty in reconciling family life and a professional career and gave preference to the former (pp. 104-106, paras 541-547 at 545). Other questions were about, for example the treatment of prisoners, freedom of religion in Northern Ireland, ownership of the media, censorship, rights of trade unionists, the right to a fair trial and so on. In its general comments on the report, the Committee concluded:

additional written laws and a statutory Bill of Rights could improve the system of protection of human rights and better define adequate guarantees and remedies. (para. 579, p. 580)

In 1995, the UK was severely criticised *inter alia* for its refusal to incorporate the Covenant into domestic law and to accede to the Optional Protocol, for its failure, despite previous criticisms, to amend the law on immigration and nationality. When the Committee learned that only 77 copies of the Government's report had been distributed, it made a specific request that wide publicity should be given to its comments and the report of the hearings (Justice, 1995: 1-2). There have been some Press reports of the hearings.

Reports from some other States are clearly inadequate, for example the Committee complained that the Afghan report referred only to the Constitution and legislation, and not practice, and had rejected the adverse report of the Special Rapporteur.

The Committee is considerably handicapped because there is not sufficient secretarial, research or other support staff for members or for the Committee as a whole. As a result, during sessions, members have to rely on the services of their missions and work in their hotel rooms. It also means that the members, who hold other posts, are dependent on their spare time for the research needed to do their work on the Committee effectively. For these reasons, they find the information and help that NGOs can provide of crucial importance (See chapter 2). Furthermore, as a consequence of the understaffing, the Committee is ill-provided for when it wishes to follow up previous reports, and the Summary Record of proceedings is not available until weeks or months later (Opsahl 1992: 381-2).

Despite these difficulties, the Committee has developed its methods of work and its guidelines to States. Since 1981, it has presented General Comments, addressed to all States, on complying with reporting, implementing rights, the application and content of individual Articles and suggestions for co-operation between States. These Comments are a means of building up a jurisprudence of standards to which States can be expected to conform. The drafts of these Comments are debated in public session, amounting to an almost quasi-legislative activity. In 1981, General Comment 3/13 contained the following passage:

[The Committee] recognises, in particular, that the implementation does not depend solely on constitutional or legislative enactments, which in themselves are often not *per se* sufficient. The Committee considers it necessary to draw the attention of States parties to the fact that the obligation under the Covenant is not confined to the respect of human rights, but that States parties have also undertaken to ensure the enjoyment of these rights to all individuals under their jurisdiction. This aspect calls for specific activities by the States parties to enable individuals to enjoy their rights.

and General Comment 4/13 on sex equality stated:

(2) First, article 3, as articles 2(1) and 26 in so far as these articles primarily deal with the prevention of discrimination on a number of grounds, among which sex is one, require not only measures of protection but also affirmative action designed to ensure the positive enjoyment of rights. This cannot be done simply by enacting laws. Hence information has generally been required regarding the role of women in practice with a view to ascertaining what measures, in addition to purely legislative measures of protection, have been or are being taken to give effect to the precise and positive obligations under article 3 and to ascertain what progress is being made or what factors or difficulties are being met in this regard.

(3) Secondly, the positive obligation undertaken by States parties under that article may itself have an inevitable impact on legislation or administrative measures specifically designed to regulate matters other than those dealt with in the Covenant but which may adversely affect rights recognised in the Covenant. One example, among others, is the degree to which immigration laws which distinguish between a male and a female citizen may or may not adversely affect the scope of the right of women to marriage to non-citizens or to hold public office.

The General Comment goes on to recommend States to use specially appointed bodies to review legislation that might adversely affect the rights specified in the Covenant[6]. The Committee stresses that it is for States to *ensure* protection of rights, not merely themselves refrain from violating them.

The Committee's other mandate deals with individual complaints[7]. By 1991, 55 of the 96 States which had ratified the Covenant had also ratified the Optional Protocol. Cases under this procedure are heard in closed session, but the Committee's views on them have always been published. When a State refuses to answer a complaint or answers with a mere denial, the Committee concludes that the complaint, provided it is supported by credible evidence, is well-founded.

The dictatorship in Uruguay led to many complaints between 1977 and 1984. Cases concerning women revealed arrest without warrant, torture, rape, kidnapping from Brazil and from the Venezuelan Embassy in Montevideo, and other crimes; and also the psychological suffering of a mother not knowing what had become of her daughter, who had in fact been arrested and kidnapped by the military[8]. After the fall of the dictatorship, the views expressed by the Committee assisted the release of political prisoners (Opsahl, 1992: 423). Unfortunately cases usually take three years from the submission of a complaint to a decision by the Committee. Payment of compensation is often recommended.

Since 1989, the number of cases has grown exponentially (Opsahl 1992: 423) and cases have been prepared by a Special Rapporteur, now assisted by the Secretariat. If the Working Group is unanimous, it can declare a complaint admissible, but trivial cases are rejected and the Committee may refuse to consider complaints against national legislation. Unusually there is no time-limit within which complaints must be submitted.

In two of its most important decisions, the Committee held that there is a separate and general right to equality in relation to any legislation – a ruling which arose out of a married woman's claim to equality in social security (*Broeks* v. *Netherlands, Zwaan de Vries* v. *Netherlands* 1987; Opsahl 1992: 430; *Vos* v. *Netherlands*, 1989: 232; Cook, 1990: 787). This ruling contrasts with the view of the European Court of Human Rights, as we shall see, that a claim for equality must be linked to a specific right in the Convention.

Women's rights as family members have been upheld. In *Lovelace* v. *Canada* (1981), Sandra Lovelace, a Malakeet Indian, had lost her Indian status on marrying a non-Indian, unlike an Indian man marrying a non-Indian woman. She had left the Reserve but returned with her two children after a divorce, although under Canadian law she was no longer entitled to do so. The Committee asked for information about the number of mixed marriages, the legal rules applying to place of abode, where Lovelace had lived before marriage and so on, information which the Canadian Government supplied. Lovelace listed nine disadvantages of her loss of status and stated she had nowhere to live except in the Reserve. The Committee decided *inter alia* that her right to have access to her language and culture in community with other members of her group had been interfered with[9]. A case raising rather similar issues about the right to private life concerned Mauritian women who complained that immigration laws restricted the right of their foreign husbands to acquire Mauritian nationality. Their claim also was upheld by the Committee (*Aumeeruddy-Cziffra v. Mauritius*, 1981; Cook, 1990: 785; 2 *Human Rights Law Journal*, 1981: 139-143). In all these cases, States have amended their legislation to conform to the Committee's invitation to take account of its views. A Special Rapporteur is appointed to monitor follow-up.

Cases concerning education are rare. In Finland, children had to attend classes in religious education, but the Hartikainen parents, who were atheists, objected. The Finnish Religious Freedom Act provides for alternative religious instruction on 'history of religions and ethics'. The Government, asked by the Committee to specify domestic remedies, admitted that there was no binding way of resolving the conflict between domestic legislation and the Covenant. Hartikainen was asked to supply the signatures of others if he wished to pursue the claim as General Secretary of the Union of Freethinkers in Finland, which he did. The Committee thought that history of religions and ethics was not incompatible with Art. 18(4) of the Covenant:

> if such alternative course of instruction is given in a neutral and objective way and respects the convictions of parents and guardians who do not believe in any religion.

Two years later the Finnish Government reported that the legislation had been amended, that a senior official was to be employed 40 days a year to inspect the instruction in ethics and history of religions and that a working group on the topic was to draw up a teachers' guide and further develop the subject[10].

Opsahl observes that the Commission's work on communications is better prepared and more time spent on them than on reports, and that the case-law developed contributes to the interpretation of the Articles of the Covenant. Reporting raises more issues and more important issues and, because the discussion occurs in public, NGOs and public opinion, and sometimes governments, support the Committee's work. McGoldrick (1991) notes that no State or region has avoided criticism, that the process requires States to consider seriously their human rights record, and that many have responded positively. Opsahl found however little co-ordination with the Specialised Agencies. He observed continuing controversy over the proper role of the Committee. While some Western members wanted the Committee to act as a supervisory body, some Socialist and Third World members wanted the Committee to be a forum for the exchange of information and for co-operation intended to achieve consensus between different approaches (*ibid*, p. 433). This controversy could be a problem for Committee members also: if they antagonised States or other members of the Committee, they might not be re-elected (*ibid*. p. 435). For reasons such as these, as well as the limitations of its resources, the Committee had been very cautious (*ibid*, p. 435). Nonetheless Opsahl considered that although the Committee had had only a marginal impact on one third of the 96 States Parties, there had been satisfactory results in two thirds of States, both better reporting and better implementation. Cohn (1991) finds that reports of the Committee have led to changes in legislation in a number of countries, but is unable to include an analysis of the effect in practice. McGoldrick (p. 504) in appraising the work of the Committee considers it to have been 'substantial, positive and constructive' and quotes other similar assessments.

The Commission on the Status of Women

'The Commission was created as an instrument of negotiation among governments, not as an agent of change' (Reanda, 1992: 300). This statement sums up the difficulties confronting this Commission and its members. It is clear from the tortuous history of the Commission from its inception in 1947 by ECOSOC that it was not intended to do much for women and in this it has reflected the attitude of governments. The Commission chose as its guiding principles Equality, Development and Peace. Despite the difficulties, the Commission has achieved something.

The members of the Commission, almost invariably women, have been government representatives and therefore bound by the instructions of their governments. Some have disagreed with their governments, the Commission has protested, but rarely pushed its protests to resolutions. The Commission was for the greater part of its existence confined to short biennial meetings, only once as long as three weeks. However in 1994, it held an intersessional meeting and in 1995 the session lasted five weeks to consider the implementation of the Nairobi Forward-Looking Strategies, the Draft Platform for Action for the Beijing Conference prepared by the Division for the Advancement of Women[11] and the Regional Platform of Action of the Economic Commission for Europe (ECE)[12]. The Platform prepared by the Division covered such topics as creating a gender-sensitive educational system (para. 63(c)), the development of curricula, textbooks and teaching aids free of sex-stereotypes (para. 66(a)), the promotion of gender studies (para. 66(d)), the impact of the mass media, including commercial advertisements, on violence against women and the need to promote a violence-free society (para. 98(c)) and the need to enact laws that granted parental leave to both men and women (para. 126(b)). The ECE document also included the attack on gender stereotypes (para. 124) and the need for legislation to support parental leave for men as well as women (para. 137). The Commission has been deprived of resources, was not permitted to take evidence from NGOs and has been subjected to far greater supervision and limitations on its activities than other comparable bodies (Reanda, 1992).

For its first 25 years, the Commission concentrated on trying to ensure formal legal equality for women and gave special attention to education (Reanda 1992). It worked mainly by sending out questionnaires to governments. Its report on the answers in 1986 was only three pages long and showed that only 17 governments had replied (Coliver, 1989[13]). In the earlier stages these enquiries were a useful contribution to documenting, publishing and organising seminars drawing attention to the extent of formal legal discrimination against women in virtually all countries. The Commission reviewed the reports of States and stimulated technical assistance to women especially in developing countries.

The Commission also received communications, but was able to do nothing about them under the 'no action' principle (above p. 97). By 1982, the Commission was receiving many complaints of discrimination against women including from bodies such as the Food and Agriculture Organisation (FAO) for example about the confiscation of land and of discrimination in agricultural employment and credit in rural programmes. As a result, the Commission referred these complaints to a working group which has produced short (and weak) reports (Jackson, 1992: 449). In 1995, the Commission considered ten non-confidential communications concerning mass rape and 'ethnic cleansing', genital mutilation, the climate of terror in Bangladesh, access to reproductive information, women's health, the economic blockade of Iraq, the portrayal of women in the media and the impact of extremism on women. These communications came both from NGOs and individuals in the US, France, the UK, Iraq and Bangladesh[14.]

From the mid-60s to the mid-80s, the Commission put its main emphasis on integrating women into development. In this work it achieved some success in ensuring that women were included in programmes for the UN Decades of Development from 1961-1990. It also proposed a Convention to implement the 1967 Declaration on the Elimination of Discrimination Against Women and was instrumental in preparing the draft Convention (Jackson, 1992: 445). This is also the period of the development of the Second Women's Movement. It was pressure from the NGOs that led to the nomination by the General Assembly of the first International Women's Year and the Conference held in Mexico City in 1975. This Conference and its two successors in Copenhagen in 1980 and Nairobi in 1985 completing the Decade for Women were crucial in bringing to the international agenda new issues concerning women, such as violence, health, nutrition, women's role in agricultural production and so on. The Conferences also prompted several governments to create machinery to consider the condition of women and to improve it.

The Commission was excluded from the preparation for the first two Conferences and an attempt was made to abolish it in 1980. However counter-proposals ensured the Commission's survival and a strengthened role in preparing for the Nairobi Conference, the supervision of the Plans and Programmes arising from the Conferences and expanding the Commission's role.

These developments have led to the third stage in the Commission's history, that of 'mainstreaming': ensuring that women are included as an integral part of all programmes and projects within the UN system. The membership of the Commission has been increased to 45, its monitoring role has been strengthened and arrangements made for co-ordination throughout the UN system. In 1991, it decided to focus on a number of key issues and to seek to establish quantitative goals.

The members of the Commission may have been unduly timid and lacking in persistence in their attitude to governments, as Coliver believes (1989: 32), but their position was very weak, and the Commission seems sometimes to have been marginalised by the ECOSOC. Pressure from the Women's Movement on governments has changed official attitudes, and improved opportunities for the Commission. We have yet to see how far the greatly increased membership and the existence of conservative governments and legislatures in some Western countries will affect the Commission's work.

The Committee on the Elimination of Discrimination Against Women (CEDAW)

The Committee on the Elimination of Discrimination Against Women (CEDAW) was created by the Convention on the Elimination of All Forms of Discrimination Against Women 1979. It has both similarities and dissimilarities with the Commission on the Status of Women (the Women's Commission) and with the Human Rights Committee. CEDAW's 23 members are experts, not representatives of governments. It has been more active than the Women's Commission. As a result of its work in examining the reports of member States of the Convention, it has begun to draw up regulations and guidelines on implementing the Convention. Like the Women's Commission, it is hampered by lack of resources with the result that no adequate records can be kept of meetings with the consequent loss of institutional memory. At the 1994 session, Mr Mathiasan, the Deputy Director of the Division for the Advancement of Women, warned the Committee that they might have to choose between the report on the effect of structural adjustment programmes on women, or the report on Article 2 of the Convention or two reports which might be of lower quality[15]. The Committee is also handicapped by short sessions, in this case limited to two weeks a year by the Convention itself – a unique provision. ECOSOC supported requests for longer meetings to last for three weeks once a year[16].

Unlike the Women's Commission, the Committee has no power to investigate communications, but it does enjoy at least informal access to NGOs. By 1994, 131 States had ratified the Convention, and many State reports had been submitted. By 1995, 13 initial reports, seven second, three third and two fourth reports had yet to be considered, but only six could be considered in the three-week session of January 1995[17] and 35 initial reports were outstanding, some of which should have been submitted in 1982. This evidence of activity and support ensured the survival of the Committee at a time of rigorous cost-cutting (Jackson, 1992: 455). However, many States have ratified with declarations or reservations limiting the effect of the Convention as applied to their country. There is no adequate means of ensuring that these reservations do not undermine, contrary to normal international law, the substance of the Convention. To overcome this difficulty, the Committee considered in 1995 whether to require States to report on reservations, explaining why they were necessary and the effect on women's human rights and law, and to provide a timetable for their withdrawal[18].

In 1983, the Committee drew up Guidelines for the form of States' reports. The report must be in two parts, the first dealing with legislation and measures taken to implement the Convention, the second with specific information related to each Article and including obstacles to implementation. Further, the reports must include relevant statistical data. States' reports vary greatly, from Australia's 200 pages with statistical appendices in 1986 to Mali's two pages in 1987. Portugal in 1984/85 included material from both governmental and non-governmental sources (Jackson 1992:457). Libya's eight-page further report, considered in 1993, showed that prostitution was illegal and punished severely and that therefore there were no arrangements for rehabilitating prostitutes[19]. In contrast, Tunisia's initial and second report of 216 pages seems a thorough document[20]. CEDAW has pursued States whose reports have not complied with the Guidelines and has sought additional information where necessary. It has made General Comments on States' reports and it has addressed suggestions and general recommendations to individual States (Coliver, 1989: 35-36).

The report is presented often by a male diplomat who may be ill-informed on the subject, sometimes facing a fellow national on the Committee who is expert. There are two sources of tension in this situation: inexpert versus expert, and male versus female. Questioning is made more difficult for the Committee by the lack of a reference file with a record of previous oral submissions to the Committee and previous questions put by the Committee (Jackson, 1992: 461).

The Committee's relations with other bodies need further development. Although CEDAW's reports are sent automatically to the Women's Commission, the latter seems to have made little use of them (Jackson 1992), but the report of the Director of the Division for the Advancement of Women, adopted by the General Assembly in December 1993[21] noted that the Commission had regularly taken up concerns raised by the Committee. CEDAW is rather isolated from other human rights bodies, since it is serviced from New York (formerly from Vienna) like the Women's Commission, not from Geneva as are the other human rights bodies, but since 1988 the Chairperson has been included in the biennial meeting of Chairpersons of Human Rights Treaty Bodies (Jackson, 1992: 463). Close relations need to be established with INSTRAW (the International Research and Training Institute for the Advancement of Women) and UNIFEM (the United Nations Development Fund for Women). The Committee has suggested that INSTRAW could provide technical assistance to States to develop their statistical data especially in relation to women. UNIFEM supports many grass-roots projects which are not referred to in States' reports, and has reported to CEDAW.

Representatives of Specialised Agencies are able to attend meetings of CEDAW and to submit information. Such reports are circulated as background papers. In 1991, a representative of the ILO was actively involved.

NGOs are able to attend CEDAW's open meetings as observers and some are able to send information to individual members of CEDAW, but there are mixed views on the Committee as to how far NGOs should have direct access. Furthermore, many NGOs may not know how to reach Committee members.

Jackson considers that the question and answer sessions when government representatives are presenting reports, need restructuring to avoid repetition and to make better use of the limited time available. CEDAW is now beginning to develop a 'jurisprudence' interpreting in more detail the requirements of the Convention. These matters could be dealt with more easily if the Committee had more time and resources and were able to discuss them at pre-sessional meetings.

UNESCO

I turn now to the procedures specific to Unesco. They raise several important questions about how monitoring bodies work:

- should government representatives be members of such bodies?

- how important is stability and continuity of membership?

- what rights should the authors of communications and victims of breaches of rights have in such procedures?

- what powers should monitoring bodies have to carry out investigative or fact-finding missions?

- does confidentiality or publicity produce better results?

- should monitoring bodies verify governments' claims to have taken action on complaints?

UNESCO's procedure contrasts markedly in many of these respects with those of other human rights bodies.

Alston (1980: 667) notes that human rights resolutions have been passed by virtually every General Conference, the 'Parliament' of UNESCO which meets every two years. Despite their obligations under the Convention Against Discrimination in Education 1960 (the Education Convention), governments have failed to reply to UNESCO's questionnaires on their compliance[22]. Since UNESCO lays greater emphasis on its programmes to promote human rights, its monitoring and complaints-procedures are a lesser part of its work (Alston, 1980: 668-9).

Until 1967, UNESCO held to the doctrine that it had no power to take action on communications, a doctrine challenged by the Secretariat and by experts on international law. In 1967, the Executive Board, the governing body of UNESCO, decided communications could be referred to the Special Committee on Discrimination in Education and in 1978 laid down a more developed procedure in Decision 3. 3 (Alston, 1980: 671).

The outstanding characteristic of this procedure is its strict confidentiality and emphasis on finding a friendly solution. It was believed that States would comply with requests if secrecy were maintained. It is difficult to demonstrate that this belief is well-founded, since the Resolutions, Reports and *Comptes-Rendus* of the General Conference throw no light on any action. Two types of communication are identified: 'cases' deal with complaints concerning one or more individuals; and 'questions' concern 'massive, systematic or flagrant violations of human rights and fundamental freedoms' including for example 'policies of aggression' or those resulting from foreign occupation, 'colonialism, genocide, apartheid, racialism or national or social oppression' within UNESCO's competence (para. 18 of Decision 3. 3).

In principle, Decision 3. 3 enables any person or group to make a complaint against any government concerning a very broad range of human rights. In practice, UNESCO's remit is limited to persons and groups working in education, science and culture, and rights associated with such activities. For this reason a precise description of the victim is required: 'pensioner' and 'worker' are too vague. A medical practitioner must be a researcher or a teacher. As in the procedure under Resolution 1503 (see above, p. 99), the communication must be based on reliable information and not on reports in the mass media, must be presented within a reasonable time, must not be anonymous, or contain abusive material, although the Secretariat can remove this. The requirement of exhausting domestic remedies is generously interpreted; an attempt is sufficient. Unusually, there is no provision excluding complaints that have been or are being dealt with in another human rights organ (Partsch, 1990: 494-6).

The procedure goes through three levels, the Secretariat, the Committee on Conventions and Recommendations, and the Executive Board. Both the Committee and the Board are composed of representatives of governments, elected by the General Conference. The Committee of 24, half of the Executive Board, has a shifting membership usually of civil servants or diplomats (Partsch, 1990: 490-1).

Communications are examined first by the Secretariat, in practice the Office of International Standards and Legal Affairs (not the Division of Human Rights and Peace) which considers whether the complaint comes within the remit of UNESCO. If it does not, normally the author of the complaint is informed and the papers filed without further action. If it does, the Office informs the author of the conditions of admissibility and asks for agreement to send the communication to the Government concerned and to the Committee under his/her/their name(s). A detailed questionnaire is enclosed requesting all the information needed for a decision on admissibility and sometimes leading to a lengthy correspondence. All this is sent to the Government concerned when satisfactorily completed. That Government usually has one month in which to respond before the matter is put on the agenda of the Committee, and its representative is expected to attend.

The Committee, which meets twice a year, considers admissibility often on several occasions, in the light of all the material supplied by the author, the relevant Government and by the Office or Director-General. The Committee may have power to investigate the claims of the parties to the complaint 'in exceptional circumstances' subject to special prior permission of the Executive Board, a procedure which seems never to have been used (Partsch, 1990: 498). Having determined admissibility, the Committee considers the merits. If the Committee finds none, it dismisses the complaint and informs the author and the Government accordingly. The author is not informed of the Government's case and has no opportunity to challenge it. There appears to be no appeal against the Committee's decision. If the Committee finds a violation, it tries to reach a 'friendly solution', and sends a report summarising its findings and recommendations to the Executive Board. It may also ask the Director-General to intervene. The Board, meeting in private, would be expected to adopt the Committee's report (Weissbrodt and Farley, 1994: 395).

Weissbrodt and Farley were able to examine 64 cases which went to the Committee between 1980 and 1991 and which were already closed. Information about them was obtained with the help of the International Human Rights Law Group and from other sources. The cases cannot be identified individually, but they came from all geo-political regions and involved 190 individuals; 27 cases, the largest single group, concerned students and teachers, 15 concerned journalists, poets, authors, and publishers, three concerned doctors and the remaining 19 concerned religious leaders, former government officials, and participants in public demonstrations. The treatment victims complained of included imprisonment, refusal of passports, exile, withdrawal of citizenship, withdrawal of licence to publish, dismissal, and denial of promotion. The rights violated were chiefly concerned with freedom of expression, of religion and of association. The individuals affected had, for example criticised their government or government policy, tried to organise public meetings or attempted to publish and circulate religious tracts.

How did the Committee deal with these cases? Weissbrodt and Farley divide the cases into three groups. Five cases were declared admissible; 18 inadmissible; and 42 were kept pending, but repeatedly considered without a decision on admissibility for from one to five years. Weissbrodt and Farley consider that the 17 inadmissible cases should have been held admissible because they met all the criteria and were concisely and clearly drafted.

The Committee sent one member to a Latin-American country, the location of three cases declared admissible, and which were under consideration at 19, 17 and 9 meetings, for $9^1/2$, $8^1/2$ and $4^1/2$ years respectively. The results of this mission were discussed by the Committee and the Executive Board in private, but never sent to the authors of the communications. Diplomatic confidentiality, it seems, was unsuccessful in obtaining an improvement.

In two cases, the Committee asked the Commission on Human Rights, which was sending a representative to the countries concerned, to intervene on behalf of the victims. The representative visited one victim in prison, found that he was suffering ill-health as a result of torture and had been denied access to a nursing home for treatment. The Committee accepted the Government's denial of torture and assertion that the victim had been released and was residing in a nursing home. The author of the complaint on behalf of the victim was informed from another source that the victim was being held in a nursing home subject to restrictions on freedom of movement. The Committee refused to investigate this possibility.

The UNESCO procedure is, in practice, based on nagging governments and making appeals for clemency. It produced improvements for 93, just under half, of the victims in the survey. At least 43 individuals were released from prison but in five of these cases the individuals remained subject to restrictions, in three cases sentences were reduced, one individual was able to return from exile, in another case citizenship was restored (but not as a result of UNESCO's efforts), three victims were granted passports, and in one case 21 individuals got their jobs back and a licence to publish. These gains are not negligible; some of these successes may have been assisted by changes of regime.

This leaves 97 individuals where UNESCO was unsuccessful. Ten persons remained in prison and one died in detention. Nothing is known of the fate of the remaining 86.

Several of the weaknesses of the UNESCO procedure are now apparent. The procedure is slow and there is no emergency procedure. Weissbrodt and Farley found that there is no clear distinction between considerations of admissibility and of merits (see above, p. 97). The requirement that the complaint should not be ill-founded leads inevitably to a consideration of merits and to confusion between the two stages, as Partsch (1990: 497) and Weissbrodt and Farley have noted.

The failure to engage in fact-finding may reflect the fear of intervening in the internal affairs of States and also a belief that UNESCO should not play the role of an international judicial body. This idea is expressed in para. 7 of Decision 3.3: UNESCO 'basing its efforts on moral considerations and its specific competence, should act in a spirit of international co-operation, conciliation and mutual understanding; and recalling that UNESCO should not play the role of an international judicial body.'[23]. Perhaps for this reason the author of a complaint is excluded from any part in the procedure. As a consequence, there is no means of verifying the accuracy and reliability of a Government's response to enquiries or its statements on any action taken, a problem compounded by the secrecy by which the procedure is surrounded. Weissbrodt and Farley note that the Committee has been too willing to strike cases off the agenda when Governments fail to respond after repeated nagging. Furthermore the Committee even in 'successful' cases, has contented itself with the immediate result and has not taken up the issues of principle raised.

These failures may result from the composition of the Committee. Partsch notes (1990: 490-1) that the government representatives elected to the Executive Board have a double function: to represent their government, and to exercise the powers delegated to them by the General Conference in the name of that body. Government representatives may well prefer diplomatic representations to more active methods of dealing with violations of human rights. It is also a large Committee for its purpose and the shifting membership militates against building up expertise. There is no evidence that strict confidentiality assists satisfactory settlements.

There does not seem to be evidence of action on 'questions' (massive violations). When the Committee has concluded its examination and finds that there is a question, it must refer the question to the Executive Board and the General Conference for discussion in public. Partsch quotes

(1990: 505) the former President of the Committee, G. H. Dumont, as saying in 1989 that nine *situations ou cas de portée générale* ('situations') had been settled by the Committee. 'Situation' seems to be a term for an accumulation of individual cases which are not admitted to amount to a 'question'.

UNESCO has concentrated on developing programmes concerned with education, human rights and programmes for the advancement of women, rather than on dealing with communications. These programmes are of two kinds. First the advancement of women is one of the 'transverse' themes running across the main programmes. Programmes under this heading have been concerned with, for example literacy and civic education, especially in Africa, women in democratising countries in Central and Eastern Europe, gender studies in Moscow, journalism for women in Asia, Africa and the Arab States, a documentation centre for women in the Cameroons, building a regional network of women scientists and technologists in Asia, improvements in the environment for women in marginal urban areas in Chile, workshops on women's participation in cultural activities in Burkina Faso and Brazil (Report of the Director-General for 1990-91, p. 88). The Director-General also noted that work specifically for women was often cut, and that women held only 5% of research and study grants (*ibid*, p. 89). Secondly, projects for women are included in the major programmes on education, for example on basic education, primary and secondary education, the role of women teachers (*ibid*, pp. 4-5), on girls' and women's access to technical and science education (*ibid*, p. 11) and on the development of Women's Studies in European Universities (p.12). Projects for women and girls appear thinly in other major programmes.

It seems clear that UNESCO's Committee dealing with communications has achieved a few helpful results, but is limited by the ideology behind Decision 3. 3 and by the nature of its membership. The secrecy and the way in which cases have been handled suggest that they have not been used to develop codes of good practice, although secrecy by itself need not necessarily lead to this omission. The real value of UNESCO's work for women lies in its programmes. These are both *instrumental* and *enabling*.

The International Labour Organisation

The International Labour Organisation (ILO) is the oldest of the Specialised Agencies. Nearly a century before it was founded the British philanthropic industrialist, Robert Owen, and the Frenchman, Daniel Legrand, advocated the creation of such a body. The ILO's origins lie in the International Association for Labour, founded by individuals who set up an International Labour Office in Basle in 1900. Conferences in the first two decades of this century adopted Conventions on health and safety, and the American Samuel Gompers, the Frenchman Léon Jouhaux and the British G. N. Barnes were the leaders in seeking means for international regulation of labour standards. As a result, the ILO was set up and included in the Treaty of Versailles in 1919. The Covenant of the League of Nations specifically refers to securing fair and humane conditions of labour for men, women and children (Art. 23(a)). This provision was expanded in the Declaration of Philadelphia 1944 (see chapter 2).

ILO Conventions and Recommendations are negotiated and adopted by Governments, and their implementation is subject to supervision and the hearing of complaints by the ILO. The ILO's tripartite structure (of governments, employers' associations and organisations of workpeople) has been particularly helpful in making these processes rather more effective than they have been in some other bodies. There is however little or no access for other NGOs. The ILO also works through direct contacts, technical assistance, research and publication either on its own or with universities, and through promotional activities.

Conventions and Recommendations are adopted after they have been agreed at two consecutive Annual Conferences by a two-thirds majority (Leary, 1992: 587). The Annual Conference consists of 2,000 to 3,000 delegates; each member State sends two representatives of government, and one each of employers' and of workers' organisations. The others are advisers. The two-thirds majority means that governments cannot be overruled by or overrule united employers and workers. Since 1919 some 176 Conventions have been adopted, some of which are revised versions of earlier Conventions.

Conventions, when ratified, are binding on member States, which have to report annually on implementing them for the first two years after ratification, and then every two years. In addition the Governing Body, tripartite in the ratio 2: 1: 1, chooses some Conventions and Recommendations which all States are required to report on whether they have ratified them or not. These reports are examined by the Committee of Experts on the Application of Conventions and Recommendations. Governments have to submit the reports of the social partners (employers' and workers' organisations) on their report at the same time. The social partners may send additional observations. The Committee of Experts, composed of 19 experts appointed by the Governing Body on the proposal of the Director-General for a term of three years, has the support of the expert and experienced staff of the ILO in examining the numerous reports received. Its findings, published together with its recommendations to the government and always couched in the politest diplomatic language, are transmitted to governments and the Conference. On unratified Conventions and on Recommendations, the Committee suggests ways of overcoming difficulties. Wolf (1984: 283 n. 39) reports that in about three-fifths of cases, governments take the action necessary to correct weaknesses. The Committee also reports to ECOSOC on the implementation of the Covenant on Economic, Social and Cultural Rights.

From the 1995 Report of the Committee of Experts we learn for example that a number of complaints have been raised against the UK in previous years, because it fails to allow free prescriptions to victims of industrial accidents, it has not updated sufficiently regularly the lists of industrial diseases and toxic substances, and the conditions for claiming unemployment benefit are unduly harsh. The Committee found that the UK Government's determination to recognise only a Staff Federation at the General Communications Headquarters (GCHQ) was an interference with the workers' right to choose their own Union, that the Government should restrict itself to establishing a general framework for the internal organisation of trade unions and not interfere in detail, that a general prohibition of sympathy strikes even when the original strike was lawful could lead to abuse, and that workers should not be penalised as a result of industrial action:

> In the Committee's view, legislation should provide for genuine protection in this respect, otherwise the right to strike may be devoid of content. (p. 200)

The German Report on Convention 100 on Equal Pay led the Committee to question the way in which light work (*leichtlohngruppe*), an almost exclusively female category, was distinguished from heavy work. The Committee asked the Government to show how 'physically light' jobs had been reclassified upwards to take account of mental or nervous strain including posture, time-controlled or repetitive work, noise and other environmental and social stress (pp. 256-7).

The Report on India raised again the question of enforcement of the equal pay legislation and that on Sweden asked what the Government was doing about the underpayment of women managers in County Councils.

Convention 111 on Discrimination (Employment and Occupation) 1958 deals with all types of discrimination. The Comments on the Brazilian report regretted that the Bill prohibiting employers from seeking a medical certificate of sterilisation from female employees had not as yet become law (p. 295). The Comments on New Zealand's report noted that the Government relied on market forces to enable women, Maoris and Pacific Islanders to obtain equality and that the New Zealand Combined Trade Unions was dissatisfied with this policy which, it believed, would not achieve equality in this way. The Committee requested more information from the Government (pp. 309-312). Minor requests for information are not specifically referred to in the Committee's Report. When Governments have failed to send in Reports in due time, the Committee repeats its previous Comments, for example on Jamaica which for the third consecutive year had sent in no report (p. 259).

The Annual Conference holds a general discussion based on the Report of the Committee of Experts, discusses a survey of unratified Conventions and a few selected cases (Meron, 1982: 284). The Conference Committee on Standards (some 200 members made up of equal numbers of governments, employers' and workers' representatives) questions government representatives on the basis of the Report of the Committee of Experts. The trade unionists and employers are most active in this process. The Conference Committee has a good reputation for objectivity. Their Report has 'special paragraphs', the term of art replacing the blacklist of governments failing to comply with their obligations (Leary, 1992: 599-601).

All members of the ILO are bound by the special procedures on Freedom of Association, established in 1951, whether or not they have ratified the relevant Conventions. Complaints, which may be made by governments, employers' or employees' organisations, are considered by the Committee on Freedom of Association (FAS) which is composed of nine members, three each from governments, employers' and workers' organisations, appointed by the Director-General. The Committee examines all complaints of infringements of freedom of association, reports to the Governing Body on the probability of the complaint being substantiated, decides whether to make recommendations to the government or to send the complaint to the Fact-Finding and Conciliation Commission. This procedure is widely and increasingly used. Complaints are sent to governments, which are likely to be asked to send a representative for an oral hearing, and the government's response may be sent to the complainant. While the procedure has primarily moral or persuasive value, some governments have released imprisoned trade unionists or permitted the return of some of those exiled.

Since 1951, 1,700 cases concerning both employers' and workers' organisations have been heard. The only case against the UK has concerned the lack of independence from management of the Staff Federation at GCHQ[24]. Mr Malcolm Rifkind, the Foreign Secretary, in 1995 announced the ending of the management's power of veto over the activities of the Staff Federation, after the ILO threatened to name the UK in a 'special paragraph', the procedure normally reserved for military dictatorships (*The Guardian*, 1 April 1996). Other recent cases include complaints against New Zealand that new legislation there on employment contracts violates the right to organise and bargain collectively, and against Cameroon on the right for teachers in higher education to secure recognition for their Union and allegations of intimidation of their Union members (*ILO at Work*: 1. 5).

Under the contentious (litigation), as opposed to the fact-finding, procedures, a workers' or employers' body may complain against any State that is not complying with a Convention. The Governing Body may send a complaint to the government concerned or refer it to a Commission of Enquiry consisting of three independent and highly qualified experts appointed by the Governing Body on the recommendation of the Director-General. The Committee receives documents and hears witnesses and may also invite evidence from those who, it thinks, may be able to help in the investigation. Strict time-limits are applied and the Commission reports with recommendations. In the 1960s and 1970s up to 1982, 13 such complaints were dealt with; four concerned forced labour, seven freedom of association and one discrimination in employment. The normal supervisory body usually follows up the recommendations.

In 1984 the World Federation of Trade Unions (WFTU) brought a case against the Federal Republic of Germany in connection with the *Berufsverbot*, forbidding those with Communist or fascist affiliations to be civil servants. The WFTU cited a number of individual cases concerning teachers who were civil servants. The Commission of Enquiry consisted of a Finn who had held, among other offices, several very senior UN posts concerned with human rights, a Swiss and a Venezuelan, both senior labour lawyers. The Commission declared it was not reviewing the decision of the Governing Body but examining the case *de novo*, and that this was a fact-finding and not an adversarial judicial proceeding. It invited evidence from neighbouring States and from trade union organisations. It obtained guarantees from the German Government that no prejudice or disadvantage would be suffered by anyone giving evidence. The Commission considered a wide range of international documents on human rights concerned with discrimination on grounds of political opinion and decisions of the European Court of Human Rights on these individual cases (*Ms Glasenapp* and *Mr Kosiek*, 1982). The European Court of Human Rights decided in favour of the Federal Republic of Germany in both cases by a majority of 16-1. The ILO Commission also used the General Survey of the Committee of Experts. The Commission made a site visit in 1986. It considered each of the individual cases and reached its decision in 1987 by a majority of 2-1 against the German Government[25] in contrast to the European Court.

In addition to these procedures, staff of the ILO may be authorised to enter into 'direct contact' with governments, a procedure which provides scope for discussion and negotiation. The ILO provides help to developing countries by linking standards, technical assistance and human rights, for example in drafting legislation. For example, it has advised on how co-operatives can mitigate the effect of structural adjustment programmes and privatisation (*ILO at Work*: 2. 13 and 5: 39). It has worked on equal opportunities (2. 16 and 2. 19), sexual harassment (4. 36), ways in which workers, both men and women, can combine work with family responsibilities through shorter hours, child-care services, flexible schedules and so on, provisions that are set out in Conventions 156 and 165 (*ILO at Work*, 5. 38) – neither of which has been ratified by the UK. The ILO is giving particular attention to the situation of women in social security (*ILO at Work*, 5. 42) and is promoting policies and programmes to counter the adverse effects of stress (*ILO at Work*, 4. 32). The ILO has also provided training for women, for example in textiles and clothing, management and accounting for a women's co-operative in Bolivia (*World of Work*, (12) May/June 95: 8), and support for women homeworkers in India and South-East Asia (p. 13).

In 1960 the ILO created the International Institute for Labour Studies as a centre for advanced work on how labour markets can contribute both to economic development and social progress and social coherence in the face of change and globalisation (*ILO at Work*: 1. 10). From the mid-60s, the ILO has questioned the belief that growth would necessarily bring jobs, a doubt recognised in the Employment Policy Convention 1964[26] and endorsed in 1976 by the Tripartite World Conference on Employment, Income Distribution and Social Progress and the International Division of Labour. The Conference Declaration noted that wide-ranging policies were needed to promote strategies of full employment and to meet basic needs in developing countries for food, shelter, clothing, safe water, sanitation, transport, health, education and active participation of the people. These policies would have to include redistribution of income, land reform, more labour-intensive technologies, mobilisation of the unemployed for production, improved productivity of the poor, increased investment in traditional agriculture and informal urban sectors, and institutions to secure popular participation (Trubeck, 1984: 238-9). In the last years of the twentieth century, such policies are needed in developed countries as well and, especially, in the UK. It can be seen from the range and methods of its work that the ILO does not separate civil and political rights from social and economic rights.

The ILO's methods of setting standards, supervising and monitoring their enforcement, investigating alleged infringements and providing technical assistance make a coherent, integrated and systematic set of procedures. The example of GCHQ and the UK Government show that they can be effective as well and that publicity can be more effective than confidentiality. The presence of workers' representatives is *enabling* in giving them access to a means of control over workers' lives by participating officially in the setting and implementation of standards at work.

The ILO seems to be better staffed and less meanly resourced than the UN organs concerned with human rights. The participation of representatives of employers' and workers' organisations is a crucial factor in its success, both adding to its authority and to the realism and practicality of the measures it proposes. Their presence and the unusually strong position of the Director-General result in the ILO being less politicised than other organs of the UN.

Notes

1. Convention Against Torture 1984, Convention on the Rights of the Child 1989.

2. Commission on the Status of Women, originally 15 increased by stages to 45 in 1990.

3. Commission on Human Rights, 18 at first meeting in 1947 and increased by stages to 53 in 1992.

4. The Economic and Social Council (ECOSOC) was created by the UN Charter and reports to the General Assembly which elects the members of the Council.

5. A/40/40, 1985, pp. 97-114, paras 518-580.

6. Report of the Human Rights Committee to the General Assembly, Official Records, Thirty Sixth Session, Supplement No. 40 (A/36/40), Annex VII (1981).

7. There is also an inter-State procedure, but it has never been used and is not likely to be. States do not like making such complaints against each other; they are all vulnerable.

8. A/36/40 (1981) pp. 143-146, 185-189; A/38/40 (1983) pp. 173-179, 186-191, 216-229; A/39/40 (1984) pp. 164-168.

9. A/36/40, pp.166-175; A/38/40, pp.249-253.

10. A/36/40, pp.147-152; A/38/40, pp.255-256.

11. E/CN. 6/1995/2 of 27 February 1995

12. E. CB. 6/1995/5/Add. 4 of 6 January 1995

13. She quotes UN Doc. E/CN. 6/1986/11.

14. E/CN.6/1995/CR. 31 of 4 January 1995.

15. CEDAW/C/SR/257 of 4 February 1994.

16. E/1994/INF/6, para. 1994/7.

17. CEDAW/C/1995/2 of 31 October 1994.

18. CEDAW/C/7/Rev. 1 of 3 February 1995.

19. CEDAW/C/LIB/1/Add. 1 of 4 October 1994.

20. CEDAW/C/TUN/1-2.

21. Res. 48/104, para. 554.

22. The failure of governments to reply to UNESCO's questionnaires is confirmed by a scrutiny of the General Conference *Comptes-Rendus*.

23. Quoted by Weissbrodt and Farley, pp. 395-396, n. 10.

24. Personal communication.

25. CD-ROM at the ILO Office in London. I am grateful to Lee Swepston of the ILO Geneva for additional information.

26. This Convention was ratified by the UK in 1966 and the Equal Remuneration Convention in 1971 after the passing of the Equal Pay Act 1970. The UK has not ratified the Discrimination (Employment and Occupation) Convention 1958 and has denounced (i. e. withdrawn from) six Conventions related to wages, conditions of employment and holiday pay, and also from the Conventions on night-work for women and young persons and underground work for women.

Part 2 – Regional instruments

The European Convention on Human Rights and Fundamental Freedoms

The European Convention on Human Rights was drawn up in 1951 by the member States of the Council of Europe, in order to give legal effect to some of the intentions of the Universal Declaration of Human Rights. The Convention came into force on 3 September 1953, and deals chiefly with civil and political rights and education. There are now 11 Protocols (additions) to the Convention, not all in force, some conferring additional rights and others making changes in structure and procedures.

The Convention established the European Commission of Human Rights and the European Court of Human Rights. Both have one member for each member State and no two members should be nationals of the same State. The members of the Commission are elected for six years by the Committee of Ministers, and the members of the Court for nine years by the Parliamentary (Consultative) Assembly of the Council of Europe. They serve as individuals in an independent capacity. The function of both Commission and Court, sitting in Strasbourg, is to hear complaints from individuals and organisations which consider their rights under the Convention have been injured, and inter-State complaints. Both the Commission and the Court can provide legal aid. Jurisdiction under the Convention extends to the activities for which a government may be considered responsible outside its own territory. Thus Turkey is responsible for the conduct of Turkish soldiers in the north of Cyprus. The Convention was innovatory in establishing the right of individual petition, that is in allowing individuals to sue a government, provided the government had agreed to the relevant Article, before an international tribunal, thus endowing individuals with legal personality in international law for the first time. States wishing to join the Council of Europe now must be prepared to ratify the Convention, and accept the compulsory jurisdiction of the Court and the right of individual petition. As this is also a requirement for membership of the European Union, it is no longer, in practice, possible for any member State to withdraw from these obligations.

The role of the Commission is to examine whether applications are admissible (see above, chapter 5, part 1). No formality is required for making an application; a simple letter is sufficient. At present, all applications go to the Commission first. If an application is admissible, the Commission sends it to the government concerned and the forwards the government's reply to the individual, carries out any further enquiries, makes a finding on the merits and seeks to arrange a friendly settlement, which may result in the government paying compensation to the complainant. This result is achieved in about 15% of cases (Mowbray, 1994: 546). These proceedings are confidential. If it is impossible to arrange a friendly settlement, the Commission sends a full report either to the Committee of Ministers of the Council of Europe or to the Court to decide the case. In fact the Committee has always agreed with the Commission[1]. Although the details of the work of the Commission are confidential, the Committee of Ministers may authorise publication of the Commission's report. In any case, brief information about cases is published by the Committee.

The Court may also receive cases direct from States: there have been only a few. Since 1 October 1994, individuals, groups and organisations may refer cases against those States which have ratified the Ninth Protocol directly to the Court. (The UK has not yet even signed it.) The Court hears cases in public and issues judgements on the merits and on 'just satisfaction' (compensation) and costs, if any, to be paid by the government.

It is the Committee of Ministers which supervises the execution of these judgements. Governments are required to report on whether and when they have paid any compensation or costs ordered and whether they have taken any other measures to amend legislation or procedures to comply with the requirements of the Convention as determined by the Court. The Committee of Ministers is persistent in this task. Some governments have delayed or failed to make payments. In 1991, the Committee changed its Rules in order to make its Resolutions binding on governments. This change seems to have been effective; for example, the Government of Italy had failed to pay compensation recommended by three successive Resolutions of the Committee from January 1989, but did order such payment on 30 April 1992 after the Committee's fourth Resolution and the change in the Rules; the payment was made on 18 May, and the Committee satisfied itself this had been done (Council of Europe, *Information Sheet No. 31*, 1992, *Sallustio*, and *Minniti*).

Over the years the Court's procedures have been eased, so that for some years, it has been possible for individual applicants to appear before it and to present their case, even when they are also represented by lawyers. The Commission has always presented its report at the Court's hearings which are public. It is possible for members of the public to follow the proceedings, as copies of papers are provided. Simultaneous translation is in the two official languages of French and English.

The workload of the Commission and the Court has increased very substantially over the years. In 1977, the first year for which this figure is available, the Commission opened 2,181 provisional files; in 1995, it opened 10,201. Many of these applications are clearly outside the scope of the Convention or the Protocols, are out of time, do not relate to a member State of the Convention or are otherwise clearly inadmissible. The number of applications registered, that is which appeared on the face of them to be within the jurisdiction of the Convention, was 138 in 1955, 373 in 1977 but 3,481 in 1995. In 1977, 32 registered applications (8.6%) were found admissible but 807 (23.2%) in 1995. The increase in the proportion of admissible cases may well reflect the increasing proportion of cases presented by lawyers and which are therefore better prepared: between 4% and 23% until the early 1970s, but thereafter between 28% and 51% (Council of Europe, Commission 1995, *Survey*). The work of the Court has also increased dramatically; in the first 17 years, 1959-1975, the Court gave 20 judgements, 102 in the next eleven years, 113 in the following four and from 1991-1993, 213 judgements (European Court, *Aperçus*, 1994).

The increased workload reflects three principal factors. First, more States have recognised the right of individual petition (the UK did so in 1964) and the compulsory jurisdiction of the Court (recognised by the UK much earlier). Secondly, the work of the Commission and the Court and the provisions of the Convention have become much more widely known. Thirdly, there are now 32 States Parties to the Convention, and another eight States have signed it including Albania, Russia and Ukraine[2], compared with the ten which ratified the Convention in 1953. The range of members is wide, from Iceland to Turkey, from San Marino to Germany and including Baltic, Central and East European States.

The governments against which the largest number of registered applications (those considered admissible) was made in 1994 were Italy at

507 (up from 142 in 1993), France at 439, the UK at 216, Germany at 188, Turkey at 187, and Poland and Sweden at 161. The reason for the high figures for Italy lies in what appears to be a campaign by Italian lawyers to reduce the inordinate delays in the Italian courts – a campaign which may be having some success. Many French cases concern North Africans, or applications for compensation from haemophiliacs and others suffering from HIV as a result of infected blood transfusions. British cases reflect the lack of a modern Bill of Rights and the dualist system by which international treaties bind the Crown, but cannot normally be used in the Courts, although this is changing. In addition to the very numerous cases concerning fair trial, especially excessive delays in civil and criminal cases from a few countries, there are a considerable number of cases concerning custody of children, most of them brought by divorced or unmarried fathers, as well as some cases from transsexuals.

The increase in the volume of work and the complex procedure has led to long delays in completing cases so that some have taken as much as five to eight years before they are finally settled. To hasten the flow of work, the Commission and the Court have been divided into Chambers, and the length and frequency of sittings have been increased, but there are limits to such measures as long as Commissioners and Judges are part-timers with other jobs. A more far-reaching solution was agreed in Protocol 11 which provides for the creation of a single full-time Court combining the functions of the present Commission and Court. The new Court will begin work one year after all member States have ratified the Protocol. At present [July 1996], 19 States including the UK have done so, and all member States have signed. The new Court will operate in Chambers of seven judges and a Grand Chamber of 17 judges. Cases will normally be heard by a Chamber, which may refer those involving a serious question of interpretation or application of the Convention to the Grand Chamber, as may any party to a case within three months of a judgement. This was the price that governments demanded for allowing individuals direct access to the Court (Mowbray, 1994)[3].

There is a substantial literature on the development of the case-law of the Commission and Court. All that is practicable here is to describe briefly a few recent cases on education and a few of particular relevance to women.

Two of the education cases concerned corporal punishment in private schools, both against the UK. *Costello-Roberts* (1993), is the more interesting, not for its facts – a seven-year-old was hit three times with a rubber-soled gym shoe and his parents were unsuccessful in claiming a violation of Art. 3 which prohibits torture or inhuman or degrading treatment – but for the Court's statement of the State's responsibility in relation to education. First, the State has an obligation to secure to children their right to education under the Convention (and under the Convention on the Rights of the Child, 1989, Art. 28), and this includes a school's disciplinary system. Secondly, this right is guaranteed to children in both State and independent schools. Thirdly, the State cannot divest itself of this responsibility by delegating it to private bodies or individuals.

The second case (*Y* v. *UK*, 1992) ended in a friendly settlement by which the British Government paid £8000 compensation in addition to costs. Y, aged 15, had been caned, leaving long weals, heavy bruising and swelling. The parents obtained no remedy, although the police considered there was evidence of actual bodily harm, and the County Court, in a civil action, decided the parents had entered into a binding contract with the school by which they accepted corporal punishment of their child. The Commission held that the punishment was a violation of Art. 3.

The next case is very different. Mrs Hoffmann, after her marriage and the birth of two children, became a Jehovah's Witness unlike the rest of the family (*Hoffmann* v. *Austria*, 1993). The marriage broke down and a divorce followed. The Austrian Supreme Court granted the father's application for custody on the grounds that the lower Courts had ignored the Religious Education Act, the risks of the social marginalisation of the children and of their being denied a blood transfusion if they were brought up as Jehovah's Witnesses. The European Commission, in considering Mrs Hoffmann's application, considered that her right to family life had been violated since she had been discriminated against on account of her religion, contrary to Art. 9. By a 5-4 majority, the European Court concluded that the Austrian Supreme Court had in effect reached its decision essentially on the issue of religion and this was not acceptable. Mrs Hoffmann received 75,000 Austrian schillings for costs and expenses actually incurred.

Two cases concern Art. 10 on freedom to give and to receive information. In Germany, Ms Vogt, a secondary school teacher and civil servant, was dismissed on account of her activities as a member of the Communist Party. The Commission concluded that her rights to freedom of expression and of association had been violated (1994). The Court came to the same conclusion. This decision is in line with the ILO cases on the *Berufsverbot* discussed part 1 of this chapter.

The case of *Open Door Counselling Ltd* and *Dublin Well Woman Centre Ltd* v. *Ireland* (1992) is the nearest the European Court has come to having to decide on the compatibility of abortion with the Convention. In fact it was possible to avoid the issue because the case was about the validity of the injunction granted by the Irish Supreme Court prohibiting the applicants in perpetuity from providing information about abortion facilities available abroad contrary to Art. 10 on freedom to receive and impart information. Two Irish women of child-bearing age joined the applicants in the case. The Court held that, although the restriction had a legitimate aim, the protection of the unborn in accordance with the Irish Constitution and Irish moral values, its terms were disproportionate, excessive and outside the margin of appreciation (scope of discretion) open to States. The Court recalled that freedom of expression includes information on ideas that offend, shock or disturb the State or any sector of the population and that the 'perpetual' character of the restraint was also disproportionate. Furthermore, the Court pointed out that the information was in fact available from other sources without the benefit of impartial counselling. Open Door Counselling Ltd received IR£68,985.75p. for domestic costs and costs in Strasbourg less legal aid, and Dublin Well Woman Centre Ltd IR£25,000 for loss of income and IR£100,000 similarly for costs.

The Commission has decided several cases concerning abortion from which it is possible to deduce five principles including that the foetus does not have an absolute right to life, that the life of a person already born has priority and that an individual has a right to pursue the development and fulfilment of her or his personality (Rendel, 1991).

Art. 7 of the Convention provides that:

No one shall be held guilty of any criminal offence on account of any act or omission which did not constitute a criminal offence under national or international law at the time when it was committed.

SW was found guilty of raping his wife and CR of attempting to rape his, the Courts in England holding that the common law principle that a husband could not be guilty of raping his wife no longer applied (1992). The Commission considered that there had been no violation of Art. 7, as has the Court (1995).

In 1985, Ms Patricia Lavisse attempted to create in Strasbourg an association for the protection of surrogate mothers and for the moral enhancement of surrogate motherhood. Under the law in Alsace-Lorraine (though not elsewhere in France), associations have to be registered with the local Court. The Prefect, the local representative of the central government, objected to the registration on the grounds that the association's purposes were contrary to the law criminalising incitement to the desertion of children. Appeals through the French Courts were unsuccessful. The Cour de Cassation had declared surrogate motherhood contrary to certain provisions of the Civil Code. The French Government used rather technical arguments to oppose Ms Lavisse's application. The Commission declared the case inadmissible (1991).

Victims of child abuse were unable, because of the rules limiting the period within which claims could be brought, to take legal action because they were out of time (*Leslie Stubbings and others* v. *UK, and DS* v. *UK*, 1993). Both applications have been referred by the Commission to the Court and in the first case the Commission concluded that there had been a violation of the right to a remedy.

The conception of a mother's role was the issue in *Schuler-Zgraggen* v. *Switzerland* (1993). Mrs Schuler-Zgraggen contracted tuberculosis in 1976 and received half-pension, but in 1979 she was dismissed and then received full pension. Fortunately her health improved and family circumstances changed so that she was 60-70% able to look after her child from 1986. The authorities cancelled her pension. She appealed, but the Courts assumed that as a mother of a young child, she would in any case have given up work. The European Commission by a majority vote agreed with this view and referred the case to the Court. The Court, *inter alia*, found that the Swiss Federal Insurance Court had made its decision solely on the assumption that women gave up paid work on the birth of a child and went on to argue:

The advancement of the equality of the sexes was today a major goal
of the member States of the Council of Europe and very weighty
reasons would have to be put forward before such a difference of treatment could be regarded as compatible with the Convention. The Court
discerned no such reason in the case before it. (p. 55)

Mrs Schuler-Zraggen received costs. The Swiss authorities awarded her a
full pension from 1986, but failed to take into account the eight-year lapse
of time. Therefore the Court in a second Judgement of 31 January 1995
awarded her 25,000 Swiss francs in interest for that period.

The Court's view of family relationships is seen in a case which
concerned a married woman, Mrs Kroon, who had been deserted by her
husband, and who had established a stable relationship with another man,
Mr Zerouk, and had a son with him; her first marriage was subsequently
dissolved (1994). Since the boy was born during the first marriage, the
couple were unable to secure the recognition of the biological father as the
legal father. The Court did not accept the Government's suggestion of
'step-parent adoption' which would require Mr Zerouk to marry Mrs
Kroon. The Court held that such a solution was incompatible with the
notion of respect for family life (Art. 8) which required that biology and
social reality should prevail over a legal presumption that in the present
case benefited no one and was contrary to their wishes.

The Court had reached a Judgement in an earlier case clearly expressing a liberal view of family relationships:

> The Court recalled that the notion of the 'family' in this provision is
> not confined solely to marriage-based relationships and may
> encompass other *de facto* 'family' ties where the parties are living
> together outside of marriage. A child born out of such a relationship
> is *ipso iure* part of that 'family' from the moment of his birth and by
> the very fact of it. (*Keegan* v. *Ireland*, 1994[4])

Art. 8 on respect for family life has a much wider ambit than might be
expected. Mrs López Ostra used this Article successfully when her health
suffered as a result of pollution from a plant treating waste a few metres
away from her home. She was not alone as many other townspeople also
suffered (*López Ostra* v. *Spain*, 1994). The Town Council evacuated those
affected promptly and subsequently ordered a partial cessation of the

plant's operations. However, Mrs López Ostra continued to suffer and claimed protection from the unlawful interference with her home and her physical and psychological integrity caused by the nuisance. She lost in the Spanish Courts, but the European Court considered that the Town Council was at fault because, despite the prompt evacuation, it must have been aware of the continuing nuisance after the partial cessation of the plant's operations and had resisted her applications in the Spanish Courts. Accordingly, the European Court awarded her 4,000,000 pesetas in compensation and costs before the Commission and Court. She had received free legal aid in the Spanish Courts.

Art. 8 is also being used by Ms June Buckley, a Gypsy, to contest the refusal of the local authority to allow her to park her caravan on land she owns (1992), a claim upheld by the Commission. The same Article has been used by various individuals whose premises have been searched or telephones tapped in connection with criminal prosecutions.

The European Commission and Court of Human Rights have to combine upholding the provisions of the Convention and establishing a high standard of human rights throughout the area of its remit with allowing a reasonable margin of appreciation (scope of discretion) to States to have regard to the traditions and sensitivities of their citizens. It is deplorable that the British Government should apparently be seeking to extend this doctrine at the very time when States with little experience of either democratic government or human rights are becoming Parties to the Convention. *The Guardian* (2 April 1996) reported that the Government is seeking the support of other member States to change the procedure for appointing judges by informally submitting names to other Governments before nomination because:

> Account should be taken of the fact that democratic institutions and tribunals in member states are best placed to determine moral and social issues *in accordance with regional and national perceptions* (my emphasis).

This proposal, if accepted, could destroy the work of the Commission and Court in improving the standard of human rights not only in Britain and in Europe, but also throughout the northern part of the Eurasian Continent.[5]

The European Social Charter

The European Social Charter was adopted in 1961 by the member States of the Council of Europe to be complementary to the European Convention; it came into effect in February 1965. The Preamble includes the usual non-discrimination clause covering sex, race, religion and so on, but the rest of the Charter is in two parts. Part I of the Charter lists 19 aims of policy including for example:

> all workers have the right to a fair remuneration sufficient for a decent living for themselves and their families (Aim 4),

> Mothers and children, irrespective of marital status and family relations, have the right to appropriate social and economic protection (Aim 17).

Other aims concern the protection of employed women, children and young persons (Aims 8 and 7), trade union rights (Aims 5 and 6), vocational guidance and training including for disabled people (Aims 9, 10 and 15), just, safe and healthy working conditions (Aims 2 and 3), access to health services and social security (Aims 11, 12, 13 and 14) and free choice of employment (Aim 1). The remaining three Aims concern the family (Aim 16) and migrant workers (Aims 18 and 19). No aim specifically refers to equal pay, although such an aim can be implied from the Preamble and Aim 4. The scope of the Charter was extended by the Additional Protocol of 1988 which covers equal opportunities and equal treatment, workers' rights to be informed and consulted and to take part in deciding their working conditions, and the right of elderly people to social protection.

Part II, consisting of Articles corresponding to each Aim, specifies what the State is required to do. For example, Art. 8 paras 1-3 provides that employed women should have paid maternity leave, that employers may not dismiss a woman during her maternity leave and that nursing mothers shall have time-off to feed their infants.

In order to enable States with differing systems of social and economic policy to accede to the Charter, a complicated arrangement is set out in Part III. States must accept that they are bound by at least five of Articles 1, 5, 6, 12, 13, 16 and 19, and at least 10 Articles or 45 (out of 67) numbered paragraphs. Four Articles have only one paragraph. The emphasis is on those Articles concerned with rights of trade unions and with social security.

The reporting provisions resemble in several ways those of the ILO. Every two years States must report on those Articles they have ratified and, when requested by the Committee of Ministers, on unratified Articles. These reports are examined by a Committee of Independent Experts of seven members, appointed for six years by the Committee of Ministers, and a representative of the ILO in a consultative capacity. The conclusions of the Committee of Experts on the reports are then considered by the Governmental Committee, consisting of representatives of all member States, together with two invited representatives each of international employers' and international workers' organisations and observers from NGOs (Harris, 1984: 261-263). There has been continuing friction between the vigorous Committee of Experts and the Governmental Committee which tends to see its function as one of protecting the Governments and Ministers it represents.

The Governmental Committee passes its report to the Committee of Ministers, which may by a two-thirds majority of its members and after consultation with the Parliamentary Assembly make recommendations to a member State.

This system has proved to be weak and cumbersome. Since responsibility for the European Social Charter was transferred to the Human Rights Division of the Council of Europe in 1989, attempts have been made to strengthen the supervisory role from one described as 'self-supervision' to something more effective. Amendments in the Protocol of Turin 1991 and not yet in force, provide for greater participation by international organisations of employers and workers, greater independence and powers for the Committee of Independent Experts, more precise and effective functions for the Governmental Committee, the Committee of Ministers and the Parliamentary Assembly, and greater publicity. The Governmental Committee has decided, following a decision of the Council of Ministers, to work on the basis of its new terms of reference from the Twelfth Cycle of reports relating to 1988-1989. The improvements were also prompted by the applications for membership from States in Central and Eastern Europe and from developments in the European Community. The Social Charter is more specific in the obligations of States than the Community Charter of Fundamental Social

Rights for Workers of the European Union, to which little other than a non-binding Action Programme was added by the Treaty of Maastricht 1992.

Despite the difficulties, the Social Charter has achieved some useful results. Some Governments have changed legislation to comply with recommendations. Harris (1984: 308-311, Appendix III) gives some examples. The French Government declared its intention to end discrimination against foreign women in access to maternity allowance. Ireland legislated for the first time for periods of notice of dismissal and ended its marriage ban on women in the civil service. Italy improved substantially its maternity benefit for certain categories of employed women. The UK extended substantially periods of notice of dismissal, and took measures to ensure that seriously ill or disabled children of migrant workers were no longer prevented from joining their family (and see below, p. 139-140).

Art. 7(3), providing that those still subject to compulsory education should be prohibited from working in circumstances or on work which would deprive them of the full benefit of education, has prompted debate in the Committee of Experts and the Governmental Committee. Problems have arisen in several countries on account of the nature of the work, the number of hours worked and the employment of young relatives in family businesses. The Governmental Committee, while adhering to the intention of the Charter, took a more permissive approach than the Committee of Experts (Council of Europe, *Case-law,* 1993: 72-75).

Women's right to maternity pay and maternity leave led to separate and dissenting opinions from members of the Committee of Experts as well as to varied opinions among the Governmental Committee (*ibid.,* pp. 92-100). The Charter provides that employed women should be able to take a total of twelve weeks leave divided before and after childbirth and receive pay, adequate social security benefits or allowances from public funds (Art. 8(1)). The case-law of the Committee of Experts has recommended that the pay or benefit should amount to 100% of normal pay, but accepted 90% as adequate, and that no distinction should be drawn between permanent, temporary or part-time workers or their occupations. Ireland had reduced the amount from 80% to 70% of average earnings, which the Committee did not think was sufficient. The UK's provisions did not satisfy its obligations under the Charter, because only some women received 90% and for only six weeks. After that they, like women who had not worked continuously for the same employer for two years or more, received only the lower rate of statutory maternity pay, and some received only maternity allowance which is even lower. The Committee concluded that although the allowances were paid over 18 weeks, the amounts were not adequate. The Committee insisted:

> it is essential that the mother should not suffer prejudice in the form of a substantial reduction in her income, implying a kind of sanction on maternity, for this would constitute a socially harmful instance of discrimination. (*ibid*, p. 93)

The separate opinion considered the history of the Committee's case-law and paid particular attention to the provisions of relevant ILO Conventions.

The Netherlands was criticised for reducing the period of maternity leave in cases of premature births, and Germany for allowing only one month in cases of stillbirth (*ibid*, pp. 92-93).

The Committee has for some years been concerned that women should take a reasonable period of leave after the birth, which it considered should be obligatory for six weeks, although the rest of the period of leave should be optional (*ibid.*, p. 94). A dissenting opinion argued that proper protection of women could be secured in other ways and did not require an obligatory post-delivery period of leave. The Governmental Committee expressed much concern about whether women would be subjected to undue pressure to return to work too soon, but concluded by a majority that a compulsory period was not needed (*ibid.*, pp. 98-99). These discussions arose from the report of the UK, where no compulsory period exists.

Under the wide-ranging Art. 16, States 'undertake to promote the economic, legal and social protection of family life' by means of benefits, fiscal arrangements, provision of housing and so on. This provision partially overlaps Art. 8 of the European Convention safeguarding the right to respect for private and family life. A Dutch case arose under both instruments. The Dutch authorities proposed to deport a Moroccan, whose residence permit had expired. He was divorced from his Dutch wife and father of a Dutch child. The Committee of Experts took into account the judgement of the European Court of Human Rights which considered both his and his daughter's right to family life had been violated (*Berrehab*, 1988). The European Court had awarded the father and daughter 20,000 guilders for travel expenses and mental suffering caused by the separation. The Committee considered the child's right to receive visits from her father had been infringed and wanted to know what steps the Government was taking to prevent the recurrence of such circumstances. In its next report, the Dutch Government showed that it had abandoned the proposed deportation (*Case-law, ibid.*, pp. 130-131). The Governmental Committee agreed it was right for the Committee to use the case-law of the European Court of Human Rights in interpreting the Charter (*ibid.*, p. 133).

In the General Introduction to their Conclusions, the Committee of Independent Experts also questioned whether the needs of large families and of homeless families were being met, stressed the importance of general preventive measures such as adequate housing, urban policies and help for those looking after children, elderly parents or disabled persons. The Committee considered that 'all measures to reduce and re-arrange working hours to facilitate family life should be encouraged' (*ibid.*, p. 131).

The Committee of Experts noted five examples in British legislation of restrictions on the right to strike: the ban on secondary picketing; the impossibility for trade unions to take action against the actual employer who hires labour through an intermediary firm; the highly complex and restrictive legal and regulatory provisions on strike ballots; the narrow definition of lawful trade disputes; and the right of employers to seek an interlocutory injunction to stop a strike before a Court has decided, on the merits, whether the strike is unlawful or not, thus 'reducing the effective-ness of the right to strike in achieving collective agreement' (*ibid.*, pp. 60-61). The Committee of Experts, the Governmental Committee and the Committee of Ministers agreed in finding this legislation (and the low level of maternity pay discussed above) was not in conformity with the Charter (Recommendation No. R Ch 5(93)3, p. 65). Both the Committee of Experts and the Governmental Committee had reached this conclusion on previous occasions. It will be remembered that the ILO reached a similar conclusion on British legislation concerning the right to strike. So we see that international experts, government representatives and Ministers of friendly States are agreed in finding British legislation on the right to strike unacceptable in a developed industrial and supposedly democratic country.

The European Court of Justice and the European Union

The Treaty of Rome 1957 in Art. 119 gave women a right to equal pay for the same work; this provision has been the legal basis for the four Directives of great importance to women, those on Equal Pay 1975, which includes all forms of pay, pension contributions, payments in kind and so on and work of equal value, Equal Treatment 1976, Equal Treatment in Social Security 1978 and the Pregnancy Directive 1992. The Treaty, in Art. 128, also gave the European Commission[6] limited responsibilities to establish general principles for a Community policy on vocational training, a provision which the Commission and the European Court of Justice (ECJ) have expanded to include vocational higher education and school education in so far as it gives access to vocational training. By 1988, the Commission had developed a limited policy on education in schools to include information technology, equal opportunities, the inclusion of children with special educational needs in mainstream schools, consumer education in primary schools, illiteracy, school failure, languages and the European dimension. Art. 126(1) of the Treaty of Maastricht provides a firm legal basis for this work, but does not seem to give the Community enhanced powers (Barnard, 1992: 126). Art. 126(3) recommends co-operation with the Council of Europe which has already done much work on education.

The Treaty of Rome provides that Community law shall be supreme in those matters ceded by member States to the Community. There are three means of enforcing this supremacy. The Commission may take enforcement proceedings against States which are not complying with Community law and has taken such action against most, if not all, States including the UK in relation to equal pay and equal treatment. The second method is for a Court or Tribunal to refer a case to the ECJ where one or both parties believe the effect of Community legislation is unclear. Many such cases have gone to the ECJ. The third method is for individuals to sue others in national courts from which appeal lies to the ECJ or its Court of First Instance.

The ECJ adopts a teleological approach, considering the purpose of Community legislation – very different from the English literal tradition of interpretation or a 'formulaic' interpretation. It has established general principles of law, adopting elements from national legal systems (Brown and Jacobs, 1977: 217). These include the protection of fundamental human rights, legal certainty and non-retroactivity, proportionality, equality, and legal professional privilege and confidentiality (*European Community Law*, 1990: 51-52). The protection of fundamental human rights means in practice recognition of the European Convention on Human Rights and other international instruments of human rights as well as national constitutional provisions on human rights. Although the European Union has not acceded to the European Convention, all its member States have done so. When the ECJ upholds a right not previously upheld and which could affect legal relationships already in existence, the Court usually provides that that right shall affect future rather than existing contracts. 'Proportionality' means that measures and penalties should be proportionate to the purpose intended or to the wrong to be punished. The principle of equality has supported women's claims and protected Community nationals from discrimination in another State of the Community.

In many cases, the ECJ has ruled on Directives in ways favourable to women. A few examples illustrate this. Discrimination on grounds of pregnancy is discrimination on grounds of sex because only women become pregnant (*Dekker* v. *Stichting Vormingscentrum Voor Jonge Volwassen*, 1990). Job evaluation schemes are discriminatory if they use values which represent the average capabilities of employees of only one sex (*Rummler* v. *Dato-Druck*, 1987; Palmer and Poulton, 1987: 104). Part-time workers are entitled to the same rate of pay per hour as full-time workers where it can be shown that one sex would be more disadvantaged by a lower rate for part-time workers (*Jenkins* v. *Kingsgate (Clothing Productions) Ltd*, 1981; *Bilka-Kaufhaus* v. *Weber von Hartz*, 1986). Compulsory earlier retirement for women is unlawful when the employer is part of the public sector (*Marshall* v. *Southampton and South West Hampshire Area Health Authority (No. 1)* 1986. The necessity to identify a requirement or condition, as in British equal value claims, has been removed (*Enderby* v. *Frenchay Health Authority and Secretary of State for Health*, 1993). In this case speech therapists, overwhelmingly women, were claiming equal value with pharmacists and clinical psychologists, predominantly men. Married women who gave up their jobs to look after an invalid were refused the Invalid Care Allowance paid to married men and single people who did so. The ECJ found this discrimination to be unlawful, because contrary to the Social Security Directive (*Drake* v. *The Chief Adjudication Officer* 1986). There were signs that the Government would abolish the Allowance; this was prevented by a strong campaign by pressure-groups (Luckhaus, 1986).

In a very interesting decision, the ECJ held that Family Credit in the UK fell within the ambit of the Equal Treatment Directive because the benefit is intended to keep low-paid workers in employment and assist their access to employment. The prospect of that benefit encouraged them to accept such work (*Meyers* v. *Adjudication Officer*, 1995). Ms Meyers had been refused Family Credit on the ground that her income was too high; she claimed that the cost of child-care should be deducted, which then brought her income within the prescribed limit. The UK Government claimed the benefit was a measure of social security. The ECJ preferred to treat it as equal treatment.

These are strong moves towards formal legal equality. However the ECJ has now drawn back. In relation to maternity leave, it held in *Gillespie* v. *Northern Health and Social Security Board* (1996) that it is direct discrimination to treat a woman less favourably than a comparable man while both are at work, but not so when she is on maternity leave. She may however compare her treatment with that of a man who is temporarily disabled from working. This comes close to treating maternity leave as sick leave. The Court added that the level of maternity pay must not be so low as to undermine the purposes of maternity leave and that a woman was entitled to receive pay rises including back-dated pay awards.

In another pregnancy case, the ECJ concluded that a pregnant woman recruited on an indefinite contract could not be sacked even if she were not available, because of her pregnancy, at the critical period for which she had been recruited (*Webb* v. *EMO Air Cargo (UK) Ltd,* 1994).

The decisions in two German cases concerning social security are disturbing (*Nolte,* 1995 and *Megner* 1995). The ECJ decided that national legislation could exclude certain part-time workers from social security benefits in order to achieve the aim of providing opportunities for 'minor' employment. The part-timers affected were those working fewer than 15 hours per week and earning less than one seventh of average earnings. The overwhelming majority of such part-timers are women. Instead of proving that such measures were necessary to achieve this objective, it was sufficient for the legislature reasonably to consider them necessary. The Court rejected the contention of the German Government that such workers were not part of the working population.

144 · WHOSE HUMAN RIGHTS?

A further setback for women seeking promotion came in *Kalanke* v. *Freie Hansestadt Bremen* (1995). The City of Bremen required women to be given preference over equally qualified men candidates in promotion to grades in which women were under-represented. Under-representation was defined as women constituting less than at least half of the staff in the relevant pay-grade and department. The ECJ ruled that this provision was contrary to the Equal Treatment Directive.

Fenwick and Hervey (1995: 443-470) argue that formal legal equality is not enough to secure substantive equality for women. Formal legal equality 'perfects' the labour market by removing arbitrary decisions by prospective employers. It does not address adequately women's actual weakness in the market. Three recent decisions illustrate this problem. Ms Habermann-Beltermann was dismissed when she became pregnant because regulations forbad the employment of pregnant women on night-work, but she had been able to work only nights because of her family responsibilities. Nonetheless the ECJ upheld the regulation (*Habermann-Beltermann* v. *Arbeiterwohlfahrt, Bezirksverband Ndb. /Opf. eV,* 1994). Lower pensions for women because of women's greater longevity were outlawed in *Barber* v. *Guardian Royal Exchange* (1989) but in *Neath* v. *Hugh Steeper Ltd,* (1993) the ECJ accepted that separate actuarial calculations for men and for women were permissible – a clear retreat from *Barber*. And despite the helpful aspects of *Enderby* on the burden of proof and refusing separate collective bargaining as a justification for indirect discrimination, the Court nonetheless held that the state of the labour market could be a possible justification for indirect discrimination on the grounds that a shortage of individuals with particular skills would lead to higher pay. However there was a shortage of speech therapists and it had not led to higher pay.

We can speculate on why the ECJ should have withdrawn from positions it had previously taken. It is not unusual for Courts to follow an 'activist' period in which they develop the law by a more conservative and cautious period. The ECJ (and the European Court of Human Rights) have been severely (and unjustly) criticised by the UK Government for their jurisprudence. Furthermore, governments appoint the judges and are therefore able to select conservative rather than activist judges.

The Court will give direct effect to a Directive in the event of a government failing to implement it within a reasonable period, so that individuals may then use the Directive in the national Courts without waiting for national legislation, and indeed the Court has ruled that national Courts should take account of Recommendations (which are not legally binding) in their decisions (*Grimaldi* v. *Fonds de Maladies Professionnelles,* 1991).

In relation to vocational and higher education, the ECJ has, in a series of cases, ensured that nationals from other member States cannot be charged higher fees for courses in vocational training and this can include university courses with a vocational bias (*Forcheri* v. *Belgian State,* 1983; *Gravier* v. *City of Liège,* 1985; *Blaizot* v. *University of Liège,* 1988). It has also held that for vocational courses, such students are entitled to maintenance grants on the same terms as nationals of the State where they are studying (*MacMahon* v. *DES,* 1982). The children of migrant workers living with their parents in another member State are entitled to the same benefits as children of nationals of that State, even after the death of the parent (*Casagrande* v. *Landeshauptstadt München,* 1974) and to services for persons with disabilities (*Michel S.* v. *Fonds National de Reclassement Social des Handicapés,* 1973).

Much of the Commission's work in relation to education has been concerned with schemes for making it easier for students to study in other member States for example ERASMUS, and for particular subjects: LINGUA for the teaching and study of languages, PETRA for the development of sciences and technology; and for the mutual recognition of qualifications and so on. It has also made a considerable number of grants for training programmes for women which permit positive discrimination; but they have to be matched by local funds which the UK Government has too often been unwilling to provide.

The Inter-American System

The Inter-American system is complicated, but is particularly interesting for the range of human rights and human rights instruments that come within its purview.

The Inter-American Commission on Human Rights (the Commission) was created in 1959 by resolution of the Organization of American States (OAS) and its position was strengthened by the Protocol of Buenos Aires 1967 which declared it part of the Constitution of the OAS. It derives its powers and functions from two sources, the Charter of the OAS and the

American Convention on Human Rights 1969. Under the Charter its remit covers all States that are members of the OAS and it has the function of promoting the observance and defence of human rights. In this capacity, it has sought to uphold and implement the American Declaration of the Rights and Duties of Man 1948 and all other instruments of human rights. Under the American Convention, which came into force in 1978, it has the principal functions of developing awareness of human rights, advising and making recommendations to governments, preparing reports, obtaining information from governments, taking action on petitions and communications and making an annual report.

The Convention provided for the Inter-American Court of Human Rights (the Court) which has a twofold jurisdiction: it can give advisory opinions and it can decide litigation. Only States, the Commission and other organs of the OAS may refer issues to the Court. Both the Court and the Commission have seven members who should be independent and appointed in their personal capacity, but this is not always the case.

The Inter-American system operates against a very troubled background: military dictatorships, drug cartels, lack of education and of other services, extremes of wealth and poverty that are the greatest in the world, and, what is perhaps worse, governments that are unable to control their military forces and administration and are therefore unable to secure the maintenance of law and its implementation. Furthermore the OAS has been used by the United States as an instrument of foreign policy to uphold Christianity and capitalism and to oppose socialism and communism. For women, society is dominated by male *machismo* and 'Marianism' requiring women to be self-sacrificing, submissive and subservient to others. That the Inter-American system can achieve anything in these circumstances is remarkable.

The Commission conducts on-site investigations into the status of human rights in many countries with oppressive regimes. Its members visit many parts of such countries and have been available for individuals to come to them to report breaches of human rights. In Guatemala very few such complaints were brought. But in Argentina before the fall of the *Junta*, it was very different; in Buenos Aires, there were queues of those reporting disappearances and other abuses stretching around five or six blocks. The Commission's subsequent report made it impossible for the educated middle class any longer to believe that disappearances were anything other than a systematic policy for the extermination of all opposition[7]. This realisation contributed to undermining the regime and its eventual replacement by a more democratic government.

The Commission also investigates individual cases which may be brought by the victim or by another on her or his behalf. Many of these cases concern murder, torture, rape, kidnapping by the military who go unpunished. The Commission receives petitions, seeks further specific information if necessary, and sends it to the government concerned. It seeks to arrange a friendly settlement – a forlorn hope in dictatorships. The Regulations of the Commission provide that facts are presumed to be true if a government does not reply. The Commission seeks to evaluate the evidence by the criteria of consistency, credibility and specificity. This happened when COMADRES, a women's group in El Salvador, made 13 complaints concerning harassment of the organisation and its members from 1980-1989[8]. The Government failed to reply. The Commission rejected five of the complaints because they lacked detail, for example no date, and one because the supporting evidence was inconsistent.

Mrs Raquel Martín de Mejía was repeatedly raped and intimidated in Peru in 1989 and was accused of being a terrorist when her husband, a lawyer, was kidnapped, tortured and murdered. His case was dealt with separately. Her case raised the issue of the tolerance by the authorities of the rape of women by the military. The Commission quoted (p. 175) from Amnesty International:

> government spokesmen commented that rapes are to be expected when troops are operating in rural areas, so criminal proceedings should not be instituted to punish this type of abuse. (*Peru: Human Rights in a Climate of Terror*, 1991, p. 7)

In response to questions about this tolerance, President Fujimori is reported in *The New York Times* of 29 April 1993 as hoping that investigations were being carried out and regretting the tradition of impunity (quoted by the Commission, p. 180). Mrs Mejía received political asylum in Sweden in 1989.

The Commission's Recommendations usually call on governments found at fault to carry out thorough investigations, to amend legislation, to ensure proper trials and to provide remedies. Copies of the final reports are sent to the governments and petitioners concerned and are published in the Annual Report. Further action may depend in part on the petitioners and it is far from clear from the Annual Reports whether the Commission is successful in securing compliance with its Recommendations, but the Commission refers cases to the Court.

The Court came into existence in 1978. Some of its Opinions and Decisions have been wide-ranging and of great importance. Two examples will suffice. First, Costa Rica sought an advisory opinion on the compatibility with the Convention of its draft legislation on naturalisation which, *inter alia*, made naturalisation easier for spouses of Costa Rican men than for spouses of Costa Rican women. The Court unanimously decided that this provision would be discriminatory and contrary to the Convention[9].

Secondly, the Commission and Court have been less successful in dealing with Honduras. In 1981, the disappearance of Angel Velásquez Rodríguez was reported to the Commission. In 1986, the Commission, having received no satisfactory response from the Government of Honduras despite repeated requests, referred the case to the Court (*Annual Report*, 1986: 29-35). In its Decision of 29 June 1987, a judgement of great importance, the Court found that the disappearance of Velásquez was part of a pattern of disappearances (para. 188) and that the Government had completely failed to investigate the disappearance, contrary to its obligations under Art. 1(1) of the Convention to respect the rights and freedoms in the Convention so that any infringement by act or omission of any public authority entailed the responsibility of the State (*The Review*, 1988, 41: 60, quoting para. 182). By 1992, the Government of Honduras had still not paid the compensation ordered by the Court (*The Review*, 1992, 48: 71), but agreed to pay before 31 March 1995[10]. The importance of the decision of the Court lies in its assertion of the wide-ranging responsibility of the State for ensuring that rights are respected. Advisory Opinions 13 and 14 have been valuable in permitting NGOs to appear before the Court independently of the Commission.

Medina (1994: 272-3) suggests that this jurisprudence could be used to take effective action against domestic violence and rape. She quotes para. 172 of the Decision:

> An illegal act which violates human rights and which is initially not directly imputable to a State (for example, because it is the act of a private person or because the person responsible has not been identi-

fied) can lead to international responsibility of the State, not because of the act itself, but because of the lack of due diligence to prevent the violation or to respond to it as required by the Convention. (Medina, p. 272)

Medina argues further (p. 270) that the Commission has failed to use its powers effectively to secure the repeal and amendment of legislation that discriminates against women. In June 1991 the Commission resolved to pay special attention to and report on the observance of the rights of women, along with minors, the handicapped and minorities[11]. This Resolution resulted in a report reviewing the *Situation of Women*[12] which recognised the discrepancy between legal provisions and actual practice, the existence of substantial discrimination and included brief reviews for seven countries (Antigua and Barbuda, Barbados, Bolivia, Brazil, Canada, Costa Rica, Mexico). The *Annual Report* 1994 refers briefly to the working group set up in consultation with the Inter-American Commission of Women with priority to be given to examining the compatibility of domestic legislation with the Convention, and the crimes of rape and inhuman treatment of imprisoned women. In its report on Haiti (1995), the Commission devoted a section to the use of violence against women and sexual abuse as a political weapon (pp. 39-46).

The Inter-American Commission of Women (CIM), also part of the structure of the OAS, was established as early as 1928 and made permanent in 1938. It helped to ensure that equality for women was effectively included in the UN Charter. At the end of the 1980s, it was composed of government representatives, a small organisation with four professional and four support staff, starved of resources. It now appears to be far weaker than it was in the inter-war and immediate post-war periods. It has produced a number of brief studies on the condition of women and passed resolutions on domestic legislation on women in the mid-1980s.

Africa

The African Charter, which was adopted in 1981 and came into effect in 1986, creates, in terms similar to those in the European and Inter-American Conventions, an African Commission on Human and Peoples' Rights of eleven members, serving in their personal capacity for a six-year term. In practice, the persons appointed by governments have usually been government Ministers, and governments have tended to treat the Commission as an extension of themselves (Butegwa, 1994: 504). The Secretary-General of the Organisation of African Unity in Banjul is required by the Charter to provide staff, funding and resources to enable the Commission to carry out its duties. In practice the Commission has no adequate support and only one professional member of staff (Butegwa: 506). It lacks the means to undertake the functions laid upon it in Art. 45 of education and of building up a data-base.

States are required to submit reports on their progress in implementing the Charter by legislation and practice every two years and the Commission may receive communications (complaints) from States, individuals, and also from NGOs if the victim is unable to submit the complaint him or herself (Butegwa: 505). There have been no inter-State complaints. The Commission may consider the complaint provided a simple majority of its members so decide and the complaint must be considered, provided the usual type of conditions have been satisfied. Unfortunately the outcome remains confidential. It is also clear that the Commission lacks the means of conducting any adequate investigation although it is entitled to do so (Art. 46). By 1991, the Commission had received 20 communications, and 35 NGOs were accredited with observer status. The Charter permits a potentially valuable role to NGOs.

In 1990, four periodic reports were received, and each was sent to one Commissioner only, thereby hindering effective consideration by the Commission. In the following year, only five of the eleven Commissioners attended the meeting of the Commission, so that the meeting did not reach the quorum of seven (Norman, 1991: 96).

In addition to these practical problems, there are major problems of substance. The Charter faces both ways: to modern concepts of human rights and non-discrimination, and to traditional African culture. This potential conflict can be illustrated in Art. 17:

1. Every individual shall have the right to education.

2. Every individual may freely take part in the cultural life of his community.

3. The promotion and protection of morals and traditional values recognised by the community shall be the duty of the State.

Elsewhere, the Charter forbids discrimination on grounds of sex (Preamble, para. 8, Art. 2, Art. 18(3)) and it affirms 'adherence to the principles of human and peoples' rights and freedoms contained in the Declarations, Conventions and other instruments' of the OAU and the UN (Preamble, para. 9). It also takes into consideration the 'virtues' of the 'historical tradition and the values of African civilisation' (Preamble, para. 4) and asserts the duty of individuals to 'preserve and strengthen positive African cultural values' (Art. 29(7)).

Numerous authors draw attention to the low status and limited opportunities of African women. Butegwa (1994: 495-499) shows how women in Tanzania and Uganda are excluded from ownership of land. Ilumoka sets out out the discrimination against women in Islamic and customary law in relation to marriage, divorce, abortion, inheritance, rights to land and custody of children (1994, pp. 314-317). Beyani points out that domestic legal standards are heavily weighted against women (1994: 304).

The conflict may be more apparent than real, since the Charter, in adopting principles of human rights, requires the Commission 'to draw inspiration' from the Charter of the UN, 'the Universal Declaration of Human Rights and other instruments adopted by the UN and by the African countries in the field of human and peoples' rights' (Art. 60) adopting principles of human rights and refers to the virtues of African traditions. However these phrases enable men in positions of power – and there has been only one woman Commissioner, Vera Duarte of Cape Verde elected in 1993 (*Information Sheet No. 36*, p. 120) – to justify existing inequality, and account in part for the failure to implement the equality required by the Charter. Even where governments have passed legislation to comply with the Charter, and many have not, little or nothing is done to enforce it. Legislation is published in English (or other colonial language) in capital cities in the Official Gazette and has very limited circulation. Furthermore little or no attempt has been made to publicise such legislation and to educate the public or officials (Butegwa, 1994: 502), despite the duty laid on States in Art. 25 to undertake such education.

The right to education and women's right to education has been further undermined by the effect of structural adjustment programmes (SAPs) which have impoverished the urban and rural poor and subsistence farmers – and that means especially women. The reduction in funds and the introduction of charges for education, health and other services, and the limited access of women to agricultural extension, credit and relevant training have further weakened women's human rights. The programmes also act as a pretext for governments to do nothing about women's right to education or about human rights in general (Kuenyehia, 1994: 429ff). Ilumoka (1994) criticises SAPs more severely, contending that women have been especially harshly affected, their burdens increased and their opportunities reduced, that violence against women and sexual exploitation have increased and that traditional support-groups have been undermined. She argues:

> Questions of social justice and social capacity to bring about change for women are inextricably linked to economic power, and to control of the processes that confer economic power in a society. (p. 318)

From which she concludes that women's rights outlined in international instruments 'are violated *systematically and on a daily basis*' (*ibid.*, emphasis in the original). On this analysis, the economic policies expressed in SAPs are in conflict with the development advocated in Articles 21 and 22 of the Charter and with the rights set out in other instruments of human rights.

A more optimistic view of the Charter is taken by Beyani in discussing the ways in which some domestic Courts have used international Conventions on human rights and women's rights to quash domestic and even constitutional legislation that discriminates against women. In *Ephrahim* v. *Pastory and Kaizingele* (1989), a woman's right to sell clan land on the same conditions as a man was upheld by the Tanzanian High Court on the ground that the Constitution incorporated a Bill of Rights and the Universal Declaration of Human Rights, which both prohibit discrimination on grounds of sex. The nationality of children born to a Botswanan woman married to an American was the issue in *Attorney General* v. *Unity Dow* (1991). The Botswana Court of Appeal held that the woman was able to confer her nationality on her children, overruling the claims of the Attorney-General that the Citizenship Act did not permit this, that Botswana society was patrilineal, and that the Constitution did not expressly forbid discrimination on grounds of sex. The Court held that the Constitution forbad discrimination, although it did not specifically mention sex, Botswana was a party to the African Charter, and the Court stressed the importance of international instruments of human rights.

All the authors cited criticise the confidentiality and note that publicity would both help to inform and educate the public and put pressure on governments which did not comply with their obligations. At the 8th Session of the Commission in 1990, several Commissioners complained that the profile of the Commission was too low, criticised the secrecy and urged seeking the support of NGOs for publicity (Norman, 1991: 95-96).

Conclusion

The instruments and institutions discussed in the last chapter and the two parts of this chapter show a wide range of provisions for securing the promotion, implementation and enforcement of human rights. As we have seen, human rights for women and in relation to education have been advanced. The Europeans, as might be expected, have established effective Courts, and now have a body of case-law built up over 40 years. This jurisprudence is influential throughout the world. The younger Inter-American Court faces the problem of the implementation of its judgements – of little value to victims, if they are not enforced. However judgements which are difficult to enforce are nonetheless valuable in establishing rules and standards that may become enforceable subsequently and are enforceable in other States. The African Commission is made ineffective by the governments of the Continent, predominantly dictatorships, which violate human rights. The most hopeful development in Africa is the growth of NGOs.

In this chapter, it has been possible to discuss only some of the UN organisations concerned with human rights. There has not been space to discuss, for example the Convention and Committee on the Elimination of Racial Discrimination, the Economic and Social Committee or the advisory and technical work of the UN Human Rights Centre. The institutions of the UN and Specialised Agencies that have been considered vary from the not very effective to the much more effective. NGOs have been of crucial importance and, as the example of the ILO shows, their membership can help to prevent institutions from being dominated by unhelpful political conflicts.

Notes

1. In a few cases without the two-thirds majority for the Committee to take action. I am grateful to Mr Mark Neville of the Council of Europe for this information.

2. The others are Andorra, Estonia, Latvia, Moldova and 'the former Yugoslav Republic of Macedonia'.

3. Mowbray gives a helpful account of the proposed changes to the organisation of the Court.

4. While not entirely comparable, this view of the family may be contrasted with that required in the National Curriculum; S.2A of the Local Government Act 1986, replacing the notorious S.28, prohibits local authorities from promoting homosexuality as 'a pretended family relationship'. The Court is saying that those who live together as a family should be treated as a family.

5. Russia is now a member of the Council of Europe, and has signed, but not yet ratified the Convention (October 1996). All members of the Council of Europe are now required to ratify the Convention and recognise the compulsory jurisdiction of the Court and the right of individual petition.

6. The European Commission is the civil service of the European Union (originally Common Market, then European Economic Community). It is bound by the decisions of the European Council (Heads of Governments of member States) and of Councils of Ministers, such as Education, Social Affairs, Agriculture and so on. The Commission does have the power to propose measures to the Councils of Ministers and to take action to try to secure compliance with existing Directives. The Commissioners are nominated by member States, one or two according to the size of the State. They are appointed to their portfolios by the President of the Commission, himself elected by the European Council. The European Council, not to be confused with the Council of Europe, an entirely separate organisation, serves as a kind of Cabinet for the Union. Unfortunately, the European Parliament, although directly elected throughout the Union, has only limited powers, and all attempts to increase them have been strongly opposed by the UK Government.

7. Lecture given by Professor Tom Farer at the Institute of Advanced Legal Studies, 17 November 1995. I have benefited in this section also from the Conference on the Inter-American System for the Protection of Human Rights on that date.

8. Annual Report of the Commission 1995, Case 10,948, pp. 101-112.

9. Advisory Opinion OC-4/84 of January 19, 1984, paras 64-69.

10. Press Communiqué 2/95 of the Inter-American Commission, *Annual Report 1995*, p. 251. In 1996, both the Inter-American Commission and the State of Honduras requested that the case closed. Accordingly the Court decided on 10 September 1996 to end the proceedings. I am grateful to Victor Madrigal-Borloz of the Inter-American Court for this information.

11. Res. AG/RES. 1112, *Annual Report 1991*, 1992: 21.

12. *Annual Report 1992-1993*, 1993: 251-63.

Chapter 6

A right to education in England?

Is there a right to education in England? If so, what is its source? What sort of education does it give a right to? and for whom? It is impossible in the scope of this chapter to cover all the possible circumstances to which these questions give rise. I shall begin by considering a right to education in general terms before turning to more specific aspects. Most of this chapter will be concerned with education at school. This is not to suggest that vocational, further, higher, continuing and adult education are not equally important. They are. Adult education in particular is important for those who were unable, or failed, to profit adequately at school. I shall consider legislation, structures, policy and access to whatever education is available before considering content and remedies.

Children and parents as well as many others, as chapter 3 indicated, need rights in relation to education. Students in further, higher and adult education need rights in relation to access to courses, review of examination marking, financial support, and for adults especially, the availability and accessibility of courses and their cost. Teachers, Heads and other *providers* of education need rights as employees. In addition, they have obligations to those whom they are teaching in relation to maintaining the integrity of what they are teaching and how they are teaching and examining – the approval of *recipients* is not a sufficient test of this – and to society at large. This last issue raises questions of professional independence, which I cannot hope to deal with here. Employers are *parties with an interest* in teachers' retaining this integrity and not merely meeting employers' immediate needs.

Legislation, Structures and Policy

English law does not give a right to education. *Our Children's Education*[1] (1994) claims that a child with special educational needs (SEN) has a right to an education which meets those needs (p. 14), that parents have a right to a good education for their child (p. 15) and that children have a right to advice about the choice of options at 14 and to careers advice (p. 17). Unfortunately, the document is devoid of legal effect. This parents' Charter provides that in case of difficulties, parents may take up the matter with the teacher, the Head of the school, the Governors of the school, the LEA, the Secretary of State – all informal procedures – or through independent appeal Committees or the Local Government Ombudsman.

Education is provided by a multiplicity of bodies, including LEAs, schools, colleges and universities, acting under a variety of statutory and charitable provisions and Charters. The legislation governing the services provided is therefore inevitably complex, but whereas in the past much was left to be worked out between the principal *providers* of education, the then Department of Education for grant and authorisation of capital expenditure and the LEAs for the provision of buildings and staff, legislation now makes detailed prescriptions, which, moreover, the Secretary of State has power to amend by binding regulations (sometimes known as Henry VIII clauses) subject to only minimal Parliamentary checks. This latter practice raises important issues both of the constitutional arrangements in Britain and of human rights.

The Education Act 1944 provides two means of appeal against an LEA. Under S. 68, appeal lies to the Secretary of State who can give directions to the LEA if she or he considers an LEA is behaving 'unreasonably', and under S. 99 the Secretary of State can exercise default powers. Both these methods are used and have led to litigation. Other statutory avenues of complaint are dependent on specific Acts, and are often not well known to parents, resulting in a patchwork rather than a general and consistent means of seeking a remedy.

Duties on others to *provide* education are only as good as the willingness and ability of those others to carry out those duties and the right and ability of individuals and organisations directly affected to enforce those duties. Lawyers Harlow and Rawlings (1984); and Wade (1984) have agreed that the duty to provide education or provide a particular kind of education was not, and probably still may not be, enforceable by individuals, a view prompted by a series of cases. The most striking of these concerned the failure of the former Inner London Education Authority (ILEA) to provide enough teachers for over 300 children who were, as a result, deprived of a school-place (*R*. v. *ILEA* ex p. *Ali and Murshid*, 1990). Woolf, LJ, held that the duty to provide 'sufficient' schools, as required by the Act, was a target duty, which the ILEA had been prevented from carrying out because of lack of resources, a lack, we may add, resulting from the policy of the central government.

Government policy on education in the 1980s and 1990s is attempting to create a 'free market' in education in which schools compete with each other for pupils. All State schools must teach the National Curriculum (independent schools are exempt); they may choose their inspectors from among those who have undergone a rigorous, centrally approved training[2], and are assessed by published league tables of examination results, truancy and various other criteria. Since 1980, successive Education Acts and Regulations have, in principle, given parents rights to receive increasingly detailed information about schools, to choose their child's school, to appeal against refusal to admit a child to the chosen school, to meet the inspectors of the school, to participate through their representatives in the government and management of the school their child attends, and to participate in and to challenge decisions about any special educational needs of their child. The Government claims that this system will enable parents to make an informed choice between schools. It is difficult to see how this policy can overcome the difficulties that were faced, for example by the ILEA, Ali, Murshid and the other parents affected, which was essentially one of underfunding. The basic right to education might, it seems, be enforced in England and Wales only through an application to the European Commission of Human Rights, a method I consider later. However, Gillian Shephard, the Secretary of State for Education and Employment, announced on 28 March 1996 support for more selection of children by schools and an acceptance of grammar schools – a policy which can scarcely be reconciled with the notion of the supremacy of parental choice.

Harris (1993) has described the Government's policy as one of regulation and consumerism. It is also a policy of centralisation and fractionalisation. The effect of Local Management of Schools (LMS), of encouraging the establishment of grant-maintained schools (GM schools) and of funding them centrally is to weaken severely the role of LEAs and to attempt to create increasing numbers of small organisations that will inevitably be weak in the face of central government and of other large, rich or powerful persons or organisations, which are unelected and unaccountable. The Private Finance Initiative (PFI) tends in the same direction. Although the policy, and its intentions, are new, it uses some long-standing institutions and practices: parents have long had the right to be represented on the governing bodies of schools, schools have always been inspected, and education has always received funds from the central government either through LEAs or, in the case of private educational establishments recognised as charities, through remission of or exemption from rates and taxes.

Parents could and can still try to implement a right to choose their child's school through administrative and political methods existing since before 1980: notably by complaints to the schools, to the LEA, to Councillors, to the MP, complaint to the Commissioner for Local Administration (local government ombudsman), or the Parliamentary Commissioner for Administration (the Ombudsman) if the complaint is against the Secretary of State or central government. Furthermore, parents can, if they have exhausted those methods, complain to the Secretary of State for Education under S. 68 and S. 99 of the Education Act 1944 (see above). Other legal action may be available, and publicity in the Press is sometimes helpful. What is new since 1980 is the creation of statutory Education Appeal Committees to deal with appeals against refusal of admission to a school and the exclusion of a pupil from a school, and Special Educational Needs Tribunals for disputes about decisions affecting children with special educational needs.

The right for parents to choose the school their child shall attend would appear to be a valuable right. As we shall see, there are difficulties in practice. David (1995) also sees difficulties in the practice and concludes that 'the albeit limited moves towards equality of opportunity over the period from the 1940s to the 1980s have been curtailed' (p. 276). This is a right of access; the right for the child to remain at a school raises questions about the behaviour of the pupil, the methods of punishment, the powers of the Head and governors of the school to suspend or exclude a child in the case of bad behaviour and what arrangements are made for that child's education in those circumstances. Other questions about schooling concern the choice of subjects to study, including sex education and religious education, and entry for public examinations in secondary schools; for the latter there appears to be no means of enforcement.

The Education Act 1980 set up specific provisions to enable parents to choose schools. LEAs have to provide information about the arrangements for admission and about the schools, including not only their own schools, but also independent schools and those maintained by other LEAs. The information to be provided has increased with successive Education Acts and Regulations and now must include statistics on rates of absence and of truancy, examination results, assessments under the National Curriculum, and the destinations (that is, jobs or further education and training) of school-leavers. They must also provide information on the means of appealing against the refusal of a school to admit a child. The Act requires that Education Appeal Committees should be set up for this purpose (SS. 7-9). Over 15,000 appeals over admissions to schools have been lodged with Education Appeal Committees and several thousands have reached the Secretary of State in each year in the 1990s (Harris, 1993: 18). These Committees also hear appeals against the permanent exclusion of a child from a school (Education (No. 2) Act 1986). Pregnancy is not a ground for exclusion (Circular 10/94, para. 33). Pupils, unless they are 18 or over, may not appeal against exclusion. However children under 18 could appeal to the European Commission of Human Rights, as a 16-year-old boy in the Netherlands did (on quite a different matter) in 1988 (*Erik Nortier* v. *Netherlands*, 1991). The Appeal Committees are subject to the general supervision of the Council on Tribunals as to their composition and procedures.

The principle of 'open enrolment' (SS. 26-32, Education Reform Act 1988 (ERA)) means that schools can admit pupils up to the physical capacity of the buildings, another step in the creation of a 'free market' and one which can make less popular schools unviable, and destroy long-term planning for the education of the community. These provisions have already caused problems. Court decisions have held that LEAs must admit children from other LEAs (*R.* v. *Greenwich London Borough Council* ex p. *Governors of the John Ball Primary School*, 1990) and parents may demand that their children be admitted to schools where there are few pupils from racial or ethnic minorities, so that parental choice has priority over the purposes of the race relations legislation (*R.* v. *Cleveland County Council*, ex p. *Commission for Racial Equality*, 1991).

Parents (and children's) choice of school may also be constrained by the type of schools that are available. In Birmingham in the 1980s, there were five single-sex boys' grammar schools with 540 places and three such schools for girls with 360 places. The EOC, the Court of Appeal and the House of Lords considered that this disparity constituted discrimination against girls. In order to comply with the decision, the LEA considered making all the schools affected single sex or one of the boys' schools co-educational. One of the boys' schools thereupon applied for and became grant-maintained, and left the control of the LEA. As a result, the LEA had 399 places for boys and 397 for girls. But the disparity had not disappeared. When the EOC took this up, both the High Court and the Court of Appeal held that the LEA should take account of all the State provision within its boundary. Grant-maintained schools receive their funds through the Funding Agency for Schools. As a result of these developments, amendments have had to be made to the Race Relations Act 1976 and the Sex Discrimination Act.

In the case of education, for a free market to work effectively, there must be a buyer's market, that is more school places than prospective pupils so as to enable parents (and pupils) to choose the school and type of education they want. But government policy in pursuit of efficiency and economy is devoted to reducing 'excess' school places, so that the number of places more nearly equals the number of prospective pupils. This policy tends towards creating a sellers' market in which schools select pupils (and parents). At the same time, government policy directs that funds, and therefore staff and resources, shall be provided in relation to the number of pupils and on the basis of equal funding per pupil, with only minor exceptions (formula-funding). Furthermore, 'failing' schools are closed and unsuccessful teachers are to be dismissed. Hackney Downs School in London was closed in the middle of the school year in 1995-96 and the pupils redistributed to other schools despite its distinguished record in the past. The consequences of these policies are that it is in the interest of schools to select pupils who will work hard, get good examination results, not make trouble at school and whose parents will support the work of the school.

The underfunding of schools and LEAs has already led to major problems of repair and maintenance in school buildings; it is con-servatively estimated that £3.2 billion needs to be spent in the next five years simply to keep existing buildings open (*Association of County Councils and Association of Municipal Authorities*, 1996); the under-funding of teachers' salaries discourages men and women from entering the profession; and the stress caused by increasingly large classes, and ever more work, especially administrative work, encourages many to seek early retirement or to leave the profession. Schools may therefore be tempted to recruit the children of parents who can contribute generously to school funds – a step towards abolishing free education?

Schools reputed to be 'good' will attract pupils and become more selective. Well-heeled and well-informed parents are likely to be more successful than others in getting their children into such schools, so that schools will become increasingly 'graded' intellectually and socially. These successful schools will grow. Government policy will enable them to expand as money will follow the pupils, and Court decisions and governing bodies' admission policies will enable them to draw children from a wider area. These schools will 'cream' other schools, a result which will be exacerbated by the new policy announced in March 1996 of increasing the schools' right to select. The effect will be most marked on other schools nearby, especially in inner cities.

At the other extreme, the education for the more difficult children, the children of poorer parents unable to contribute to school funds, where there are younger, less experienced teachers and high turnover, or more experienced and therefore more expensive teachers and larger classes, will become less satisfactory. These difficult schools in the run-down areas of cities need more staff, more experienced staff, more facilities and re-sources; and expert support, previously available free of charge from the LEA, must now be bought in as more and more of an LEA's budget has to be devolved to schools. Formula-funding denies the possibility of any redistribution of resources that would assist the most disadvantaged children. It is a *repressive* measure.

The notion of competition between schools is hardly helpful. Schools which find good ways of dealing with particular problems may be unwilling to share them if sharing means reducing their competitive advantage. We may also wonder whether an atmosphere of competition between schools will not be transmitted to staff and pupils within schools, making it more difficult for children to grow into adults who find it easy to work in a team – which means sharing – whom employers say they wish to recruit. But how likely are any individuals to work well in a team when they are insecure in their jobs and at risk of redundancy? Is this policy of competition in fact *instrumental* in preparing an efficient and well-trained work-force?

The Content of Education

The purposes of the education to be carried out in every publicly-maintained school are set out in S. 1(2) of the Education Reform Act 1988 (ERA); the curriculum meets the requirements of the Act provided it:

(a) promotes the spiritual, moral, cultural, mental and physical development of pupils at the school and of society; and

(b) prepares such pupils for the opportunities, responsibilities and experiences of adult life.

These very broad provisions might meet most of the requirements of many human rights instruments when read in conjunction with other educational provisions, depending on how they are interpreted. However the Act specifies the 'core' subjects as Mathematics, English and Science, and in Wales also Welsh; and the 'foundation' subjects as History, Geography, Technology, Music, Art and Physical Education. Other subjects may be taught provided the teachers are willing and time can be found in the teaching programme. The content of education is now largely prescribed by the Department for Education and Employment, set out in the National Curriculum as provided for in accordance with the ERA and must be taught in all State schools. It has been modified several times since it was first introduced in 1988. Neither civic education, human rights and peace, nor social sciences are included as compulsory topics, nor the emotional aspects of personal and sexual relations. In this respect, the National Curriculum fails to meet the requirements of human rights instruments, or, indeed, of the Act's professed aims. These subjects are essential if pupils are to be adequately prepared for the responsibilities of adult life.

Human rights instruments, as we have seen, insist there should be no discrimination on grounds of *inter alia* sex or race. On a number of occasions, the EOC has intervened to persuade LEAs to ensure that their schools do not discriminate by channelling girls and boys into different subjects; in principle at least, such discrimination is less likely to occur under the National Curriculum. However the way in which girls and boys are treated in class is more difficult to deal with. Evidence from the 1980s in relation to science and technology showed girls to be put at a disadvantage and numerous complaints are now made about the exclusion of girls from access to computer clubs and computers: the boys monopolise them. Complaints have been made about the discriminatory way in which some teachers treat Black pupils and research has confirmed these complaints. There is now a large literature on discrimination on grounds of gender and race (Coard, 1971; Rampton, 1981; Stone, 1981; Tomlinson, 1983; Weiner, 1985; Whyte et al., 1985; Eggleston et al., 1986; Arnot and Weiner, 1987; Weiner and Arnot, 1987; Gillborn, 1990; Mirza, 1992). Arnot, David and Weiner give an excellent summary in relation to girls (1996).

Despite, or because of, this evidence of discrimination, there were many initiatives in schools and by LEAs to raise awareness of sexism and racism. There was no national policy or programme and much depended on the activities of individuals.

Has the National Curriculum helped to overcome discrimination and unequal treatment and opportunity? Arnot, David and Weiner (1996) found that teachers and LEA administrators in general welcome the National Curriculum. When asked about the impact on improving equal opportunities between boys and girls, they expressed diverse views. In primary schools, teachers were neutral, but in secondary schools a significant majority thought it had brought advantages. One LEA officer noted that parents now expected their children to have to do everything and so complained less about non-stereotyped activities (Arnot et al., 1996: 113). However teachers also regretted the simplification of the National Curriculum brought in by the Dearing Report in 1993 which has enabled pupils to make choices between subjects at 14. As a result children were making more stereotyped choices. Arnot and her colleagues found that the concept of gender equality or equal opportunities was being replaced by one of entitlement.

Special arrangements are made for religious education and for sex education. Religious education has to be of a broadly Christian character, according to a syllabus agreed by a local standing advisory council on religious education (SACRE) representing the principal religions in the area, and parents may withdraw their children from religious education if they so wish. A few primary schools where the great majority of children are Muslim have now been allowed to teach an Islamic course.

Sex education is under the control of the governors of a school; it is for them to decide whether and what sort of sex education should be taught. The governors must prepare a statement on it and make this statement available to parents. Guidance in Circular 5/94 of 6 May 1994 of the Department for Education advises that 'in addition to the facts about human reproductive processes and behaviour, consideration of the broader emotional and ethical dimensions of sexual attitudes' should be included (para. 10). Parents may withdraw their children from sex education if they wish, provided the topics are not within the National Curriculum. The Science Curriculum at key stage 3 now includes under the rubric of human reproduction: physical and emotional changes in adolescence, the reproductive system including the menstrual cycle and fertilisation, the foetus in the uterus and the role of the placenta. On 12 January 1995, the Secretary of State made an order prohibiting the teaching of any material on AIDS, HIV or other sexually transmitted diseases as part of the National Curriculum (SI 1995/53). It is difficult to see what useful purpose this prohibition serves or how it helps to prepare children for the experiences of adult life.

Citizenship is included as a cross-curricular theme in the National Curriculum, but, despite the plethora of materials produced for core and foundation subjects, nothing has been produced on citizenship education (which includes human rights) since *Curriculum Guidance 8* in 1990. While this document has many useful suggestions about what might be studied, the only human rights instruments referred to are the Universal Declaration, the European Convention and the Children's Convention, thereby omitting the two Covenants which have provisions for implementation, the Women's and the Race Conventions. While gender opportunities in the workplace are mentioned, equality in the family is not. Equal opportunity legislation on gender and race, whether national, supranational or international is only hinted at. The crucial role of NGOs is not made clear and the words 'political parties' appear once only in connection with ascertaining the views of candidates of all parties in a local election (p. 27) despite a section on Democracy in Action which quite properly makes clear that these topics should not be taught in a biassed way. This is Hamlet without the Prince of Denmark.

As social sciences and politics are not included in the National Curriculum, and twentieth century history only at key stage 4, when history is no longer compulsory, a large proportion of young people may leave school with no idea about the working of the political system and the rights and responsibilities of citizenship. In these ways, the National Curriculum fails to meet the standards set in the ERA and those set in instruments of human rights to which the UK Government is a signatory, including not only those discussed in previous chapters, but also the Recommendations of UNESCO and the Council of Europe on this subject. Some teachers are aware of these limitations and are finding ways of inserting human rights and citizenship into the National Curriculum.

We can now see that the aims of the National Curriculum do not adequately meet the requirements of human rights instruments. They do not give priority to the development of the human personality (although the inclusion of Music and Art is wholly appropriate), nor do they deal adequately with human rights and peace. In particular the ways in which the aims have been expressed in National Curriculum documents imply a rather old-fashioned and depoliticising education with technology added in. It does however make provision for the wishes of parents in relation to religious education (which is not new) and sex education. One measure of the success of the National Curriculum is that the pressure-group, the Advisory Centre for Education (ACE), has not received complaints about it[3].

Remedies

We have seen that the admissions procedure with its rhetoric of parental choice has given rise to a very large number of complaints to the Education Appeal Committees. The majority of these complaints is unsuccessful. It has been suggested that the rhetoric about parental choice has led to expectations that cannot be satisfied.

A separate system for appeals exists for parents of children with special educational needs. Some parents may wish their child to be educated in an ordinary State school; others may think their child's needs require special education, whether in a State or independent day or boarding school. There are several issues that may arise: the specialist problem of what education the child requires, the practical problem of where and how that may be provided, and the financial problem for the LEA of how much it will cost. The specialist problem is required by legislation to be set out in the 'statement' of the child's educational needs. The LEA is now required to carry out the process of identifying the difficulty, the needs of the child and the provision to be made in consultation with the parent. The Education Act 1993, amending the 1981 Act, established the present procedure. Since the appeals system set up in 1981 did not work well, the 1993 Act created Regional Special Education Needs Tribunals (SENTs) under legally qualified Chairpersons. The SENTs operate under a President subject to the supervision of the Council on Tribunals. Appeal from a SENT will lie, on a point of law only, to the High Court. LEAs are now required to comply with specified time-limits. Nonetheless it is thought, for example by Harris (1993: 240-243), that LEAs in fact have wide discretion in 'statementing'.

Complaints about discrimination in relation to gender and to race can be brought under the Sex Discrimination Act 1975 and the Race Relations Act 1976[4]. Advice and help in making such complaints can be obtained from the Equal Opportunities Commission (EOC) and the Commission for Racial Equality (CRE). Under these Acts, complaints about education can be taken to the County Courts. There have been few such cases. On the other hand, the EOC has intervened in many useful ways to reduce discrimination or the exclusion of girls (or boys) from subjects they wished to study.

Two other important means of seeking redress remain to be discussed: the Local Government Ombudsman or Commission for Local Administration and the European Commission and Court of Human Rights.

The Local Government Ombudsmen and Ombudswomen

The Local Government Ombudsman has power to examine complaints about LEAs and schools, sent either through Councillors or directly. In relation to LEAs, the Ombudsman can deal with complaints about the working of Appeal Committees, transport to and from school and grants to students. With regard to grant-maintained schools, the Ombudsman can consider only procedural issues relating to Appeal Committees. In both cases, the role of the Ombudsman is to deal with maladministration, the Crossman catalogue[5]: corruption, bias, delay, losing or not replying to correspondence, taking irrevelancies into account, ignoring relevant matters, misleading a person about their rights, failing to notify a person about their rights, unfair discrimination, misuse of powers, general high-handedness. The Ombudsman may conclude that a LEA has behaved unreasonably, but is not entitled to substitute his or her opinion for that of the LEA or Appeal Committee.

There were about three and a half times as many complaints to the Local Government Ombudsman in 1994-95, 1,187 in all, as in 1990-91, when there were 331; the number of complaints concerning education as a proportion of all complaints rose from 3.6% to 7.6% over the same period. Many of these complaints concerned special education, but in the summer of 1994 there was 'a flood' of complaints from parents whose appeals on admission to their choice of school for their child had been rejected by the school Education Appeals Committees (The Commission for Local Administration in England, 1994-95: 6)[6].

Two cases will illustrate how the Ombudsmen and women deal with complaints. Both complaints concern children with special educational needs, whose difficulties were noticed by parents and teachers within a year of the child entering primary school, but neither was 'statemented' until they were in their teens. In a complaint against Leicestershire County Council (Report on Investigation No. 94/B/0524), Claire suffered from severe learning difficulties and at the age of 13 had not progressed beyond what might be expected of a child of seven to seven and a half years. John, in a complaint against the London Borough of Enfield (Report on Investigation No. 94/A/0015) suffered from severe emotional difficulties, such that he was referred to the Educational Psychological Service within two months of beginning at primary school, but he first saw the psychotherapist more than a year later. In both cases, there were delays sometimes caused by shortages of staff, responsibility was passed between different bodies and, in John's case, it took from December 1991 to March 1994 to complete the statementing process.

In Claire's case the Ombudsman found maladministration with injustice to Claire and ordered the setting up of a trust fund equivalent in value to the cost of the special teaching Claire did not receive over two and a half years, and an award of £250 to be paid to Claire's mother for her time and trouble in bringing her complaint to the Ombudsman. In John's case, the Ombudsman found maladministration, but without injustice to John, because the LEA had provided the treatment recommended in the statement before the statement had been completed; £250 was awarded to each of John's parents. The Reports detail the delays throughout the greater number of these children's school years, but they do not seem to have been taken into account in the awards made. The awards are purely token amounts and cannot compensate for the lack of special treatment the children should have received while at their primary as well as at their secondary schools. The Reports do not state when the complaints were received or how long the Ombudsman's investigation took, but it was probably about three months[7].

Some Local Authorities ignore the Ombudsman's Reports and fail to pay compensation when required to do so. All the Ombudsman is able to do is to issue first a 'Further Report' and then, if there is no response within a reasonable time, order the LA to pay for an advertisement in the local Press publishing a statement on the case by the Ombudsman – scarcely a dire penalty. Formal Reports are only a small part of the Ombudsman's work, which makes a contribution to higher standards and better procedures.

Using the European Convention on Human Rights

The nearest approach to a right to education is Art. 2 of Protocol 1 of the European Convention: 'No person shall be denied the right to education', which the European Court of Human Rights has held to enshrine a right to education, but not an obligation for a State to provide any particular type of education or at any particular level (*Belgian Linguistic Case*). The Article continues:

> In relation to any functions which it assumes in relation to education and to teaching, the State shall respect the right of parents to ensure such education and teaching in conformity with their own religious and philosophical convictions.

Where remedies in Britain have failed, a few parents have applied to the European Commission of Human Rights in relation to admission to school, special educational needs, or the organisation of schools, though without success. Applications in relation to corporal punishment in schools have been more numerous and more successful. The Roman Catholic parents of a child apparently of grammar school ability, wanted him to attend a Roman Catholic grammar school, but he failed to win one of the special places for exceptionally gifted children. Despite the efforts of the parents, the LEA was unwilling to arrange transport for him to attend another RC grammar school, and the parents eventually paid fees for him at such a school. The Commission decided that his right to education had not been infringed (*X and Y* v. *UK*, 1977).

Two cases concerned special educational needs. In 1983, Matthew Smith, aged 10, was diagnosed as suffering from dyslexia, and had experienced behavioural and emotional problems until his dyslexia began to be treated. His father put him in an independent school for dyslexic children when the LEA failed to provide adequate educational support or to issue a 'statement' for him until threatened with action in the High Court. As a result, in 1986, a statement was issued under the Education Act 1981 which recommended that Matthew attend the LEA school which had a special department for children with learning difficulties such as Matthew's. The parents appealed successfully to the local Committee, but the LEA held to its original decision. The parents appealed unsuccessfully to the Secretary of State who upheld the LEA's decision on the ground that the proposed education was adequate for Matthew's needs, and that the LEA should not incur the cost of paying for a place in an independent school. The parents were unable to finance a challenge in the High Court. Matthew and his father applied to the European Commission on the ground *inter alia* that his right to education was denied. The Commission held that:

> Article 2 of Protocol No. 1 is not an absolute right which requires Contracting Parties to subsidise private education of a particular type or level. . . . . The Commission recognises that there must be a wide measure of discretion left to the appropriate authorities as to how to make the best use possible of the resources available to them in the interests of disabled children generally. While these authorities must place weight on parents' and pupils' views, it cannot be said that the first sentence of Article 2 of Protocol No. 1 requires the placing of a dyslexic child in a private specialised school, with the fees paid by the State, when a place is available in an ordinary State school which has special teaching facilities for disabled children. (*Matthew Smith* v. *UK* 1989)

The next case is a mirror-image of the previous one. It is a long and complicated case concerning another handicapped child (*Graeme* v. *UK*, 1988). The parents were determined for their son to be educated in an ordinary school, despite his backwardness, small stature and ill-health, and despite consistent medical, educational and legal support for his education in a special school. The Commission held on 5 February 1990 that the parents' religious and philosophical beliefs about the education of their child, their rights as a family and their religious convictions had not been violated. In its decision, the Commission stressed that the best interests of the child and for his education were paramount and superior to the rights of the parents:

> Even assuming that the applicant's philosophical convictions may be at issue in this part of the present case, the Commission refers to the dominant character of the child's right to education in Article 2 of Protocol No. 1 to the Convention.

In Northern Ireland in the 1970s schools were either private Roman Catholic schools or Protestant schools entirely maintained by the State or voluntary schools which could receive 85% of capital and 100% of recurrent costs from the State. Some parents who wanted to establish non-denominational 'integrated' schools (that is schools attracting children from both the Roman Catholic and the Protestant communities) claimed that they were unable to raise 15% of the capital cost. They were unsuccessful in their claim to the European Commission that they had been discriminated against and their right to education violated in being denied support; the Commission decided that there was no obligation on a State to subsidise any type of education and it was reasonable for those who wanted a voluntary school to contribute to the cost (*X and Y* v. *UK*, 1977).

The European Court of Human Rights has also dealt with the content of the curriculum in two important cases. *Kjeldsen, Busk Madsen and Pedersen* v. *Denmark* (1976) concerned the sex education that is a part of the compulsory curriculum in State schools in Denmark. The Court held that parents could not object to the teaching of 'information or knowledge of a directly or indirectly religious or philosophical kind' since 'many subjects taught at school ... have, to a greater or lesser extent, some philosophical complexion or implications'. They went on to say the State must take care 'that information or knowledge included in the curriculum is conveyed in an objective, critical and pluralistic manner. ' (para. 53). The Court followed this view in *Campbell and Cosans* v. *UK* (1982), the first of several cases on corporal punishment in schools. This case was also important for the definition of education that the Court expressed.

They pointed out:

> the education of children is the whole process whereby, in any society, adults endeavour to transmit their beliefs, culture and other values to the young, whereas teaching or instruction refers in particular to the transmission of knowledge and to intellectual development. (para. 33)

The Court included disciplinary processes within education. This is a broad definition of education which can be seen as being within the definitions given by instruments on human rights and discussed in the previous chapter.

The Commission and Court have limited the right to education to the education that already exists; for example in an early case, a prisoner who was denied the possibility of studying technology in prison was un-successful in his application to the Commission which decided:

> The right to education... is concerned primarily with elementary education and not necessarily advanced studies such as technology. Therefore accepting the probability that the prison authorities had no facilities for the study of technology. . . . [there is] no breach of Article 2. (*X* v. *UK*, 1975).

This is a narrower definition of education than that in either *Kjeldsen* or *Campbell and Cosans* and is, in any case a decision of the Commission rather than a judgement of the Court and therefore does not have the same authority.

Apart from the corporal punishment cases and two of the seven *Belgian Linguistic* cases, cases on education have not been successful, apart from a case against Sweden on religious education which was resolved by a friendly settlement (*Karnell and Hardt* v. *Sweden,* and *X* v. *Sweden*, 1971). However, I have argued elsewhere that it might be possible to use Article 2 and Article 14 of the Convention to oppose sexist and racist education and materials[8].

Conclusions

The present system of education in Britain does not *deny* the value of education; on the contrary, the importance of education and training is stressed in the rhetoric. The pressure to improve basic standards is undoubtedly valuable.

The present system is however ostensibly *instrumental* in the importance attached to Technology, but the inclusion of Art and Music as foundation subjects can be considered both *enabling* and helpful to *hedonists* and *tasters*, as well as to those who may wish to pursue a career in musical or artistic occupations. The assisted places scheme can be seen as *meritocratic*, but in view of the role of independent schools, both in education, in their better facilities, their very much smaller classes, and in their high status and the advantages conferred on their pupils in English society more widely, the scheme is socially divisive and therefore *excluding* and *repressive.*

The nursery vouchers scheme, by which parents receive a voucher worth about £1000 to pay for nursery education for 4-year-olds, at present being piloted in three LEAs and to be made universal without further evaluation, is in many ways *deceiving*, as the value of the voucher is less than the cost of providing nursery education. It therefore constitutes a subsidy to those of the better-off whose children are in private fee-paying nursery schools. Since nursery education has been shown to give substantial educational advantages throughout school life, this divisive scheme is also *repressive*, by excluding the children of poorer parents because of the scarcity of nursery places and the lack of resources accorded to most LEAs. It could also be a first step towards re-introducing payment of fees for State education more widely.

The difficulties confronted by unemployed persons who wish to use their time improving their skills and qualifications is open to the same criticism. The Department of Social Security claims that unemployment benefit or job seeker's allowance should not be used to subsidise education or training. This is a perverse argument, because better skills and qualifications are likely to assist an individual in obtaining a job, thereby reducing costs to the DSS.

The attempt to make parental choice, consumerism, a motor for improving standards of education has now been abandoned and is being replaced by selection by schools and the return of selective grammar schools. This is a *repressive* measure likely to reduce the educational opportunities of those who are not selected by the most favoured schools. Will the National Curriculum continue to be implemented in all schools? Since 'failing' schools will be closed and they will not have received additional funds, staff or other support to secure improvement, will there be adequate accommodation elsewhere for the displaced pupils whose education will have been disrupted?

The increasing cost of university courses and the reduction in the grant to students together with the financial difficulties of universities are likely to reduce the number of students, another *repressive* result – or intention? The increasing cost and lack of support for adult education will both deny *enabling* and *sybaritic* education, and also knock rungs out of the *ladder* for those whose school education was unsuccessful.

These difficulties will not apply to those who themselves, or whose parents, are well-off. Thus the education system, while aiming at improved basic educational standards for the many, is offering better chances to fewer individuals by reducing competition for the better jobs in a smaller labour market, and a depoliticising education for all.

Notes

1. The phrasing and grammar of the sub-title of this publication, *The Updated Parent's Charter* (a revision of the 1991 Parents' Charter), is unfortunate; it suggests that the Charter is for one parent who has been updated.

2. Apparently many would-be inspectors fail this training.

3. Personal communication.

4. Complaints concerning employment including pay, pensions, conditions and so on whether in education or other occupations go to the Industrial Tribunals, and on appeal on a point of law to the Employment Appeal Tribunal and thence to the Court of Appeal. Complaints concerning education, goods, facilities and services go to the County Courts and on appeal to the High Court.

5. The Crossman catalogue is so called from the speech made by Richard Crossman, when he was Secretary of State for Housing and Local Government, in the House of Commons on 18 October, 1966.

6. I am grateful to Mr Rob Rundle of the Commission for sending me this and other information.

7. Annual Report, 1994-95: 32, Graph 4.

8. See my Women's Right to Equal Education, in *Women, Equality and Europe*, 1985, Mary Buckley and Malcolm Anderson (eds), Macmillan, pp. 185-203; and European Law and Girls' Education, *Gender and Education*, 1992, Vol. 4(1-2), pp. 163-173.

Chapter 7

Towards a human rights future?

A century ago, there was one human rights organisation – the International Committee of the Red Cross – and two permanent international organisations – the International Telegraphic Union and the Universal Postal Union. Apart from these three organisations, there were sovereign national States and multi-national Empires, which governed their mutual relationships by treaties, customary but unenforceable international law and above all by warfare. They were free to do as they pleased in their own territories in so far as their military, economic and political power permitted.

As we have seen, there is now an elaborate structure of international law, some supra-national law, and a considerable number of international bodies concerned not only with the relations between States, but, what is far more striking, with the relations between governments and their citizens and those within their territories or for whom they have some responsibility. The sovereignty of the nineteenth and earlier centuries has gone and been replaced by a shared sovereignty. It can be seen as a historical, almost Hobbesian Social Contract between States.

This enormous change has come about in the last century and especially in the last half century. It has come about by an accelerating process of gradualism. It has been an uneven process of losses as well as gains, of opportunism, of principles fought for politically, ideologically and with armed force. Change has also been preceded by proposals which have disseminated ideas and prepared minds to consider possibilities not previously contemplated. Unsuccessful attempts at change and at creating new methods and new institutions have prepared the way for more realistic solutions. But why should the growth of international human rights have occurred at all? Will the development of human rights continue? Will the implementation of human rights become more effective? We can identify some immediate causes for change.

The mass slaughter of the First World War was the immediate cause of the creation of the League of Nations by the Treaty of Versailles in 1919. The League was intended to prevent future wars. But the idea of such a body had been talked about for more than a century. The genocide committed by the Nazis was the immediate cause of the Universal Declaration 1948, as we have seen. But there is a very long history of concepts of human rights. Other contributory causes have been the increasing destructiveness of modern weapons resulting from techno-logical development. The media have made ordinary people aware of what is happening. William Howard Russell's despatches to *The Times* told the British public about the suffering of British troops in the Crimean War and contributed to reforms in the Army. Television pictures showed the American public what the war in Viet Nam was costing both their own forces and Viet Namese civilians and led to massive peace demonstrations which contributed to ending the war. But mass slaughter, genocide, atrocities, increased destructiveness resulting from technological develop-ment are nothing new in human history.

Those are some of the events leading to concern for peace. The other aspects of human rights are concerned with freedom, equality and quality of life. A state of war provides an excuse for restricting freedom, and war-fare is a major cause of poverty. Poverty can also be increased by peace-time policies which allow unrestrained economic and social activity both within and between nations. Roosevelt's 'freedom from want' was a response to the inequalities of the American Depression and the spectacle of starvation while food was being destroyed, and contributed to concepts of economic and social rights in the Universal Declaration. The television film *Cathy Come Home* exposed the existence and extent of homelessness in apparently prosperous Britain and led to legislation for housing the homeless. But poverty in the midst of plenty and being homeless are not new, and there have always been more poor women than poor men.

What are relatively new are, first, the immediacy and the amount of information available to people and, secondly, the means by which people can influence governments, although both these factors existed in earlier periods to a much more limited extent. Technological development required education, education required literacy, literacy created a market for mass media, and an increasingly educated population demanded and obtained some measure of participation in government. The views of ordinary people could be heard.

Perhaps the most important change resulted from scientific development, prompting the belief in the late nineteenth century and into this century that 'man' could conquer nature. The concept could be applied to society. There was no inevitability about what is. We could remake the world nearer to our heart's desire.

The mass slaughter in warfare, the genocide and atrocities, the ever-increasing destructiveness of weapons of war, and the impoverishment of our environment continue; inequality increases. The mass media and education can be used to manipulate public opinion, to depoliticise people and distract their attention from what happens elsewhere, or even at home, from the part their own government and, indirectly, they themselves are playing in such outcomes. People's jobs may depend on the sale of weapons, the seats of members of legislatures and governments' tenure of power may depend on people keeping their jobs. Such weapons and, we may add, some goods, methods of production and use of natural resources too often end in destroying the lives, the livelihood and the environment of people much poorer elsewhere. If less-disadvantaged people can be persuaded that such outcomes are for the best in the best of all possible worlds[1], that such suffering is inevitable on the way to an ever-receding better future, if they themselves are not to be plunged into poverty, that in any case the poor deserve their fate, then popular pressure will diminish.

But are such means the only way large numbers of people can earn a decent living? Clearly not. For those who believe in the inevitability of what is – that there is no alternative, that 'you can't buck the market' – then it might seem so. We should observe that those who express these views do not in fact act on such beliefs, since they put plenty of effort into changing conditions of work, asserting that no harm can result, and persuading others to buy their products.

Nonetheless it is true that many people are locked into situations which are profoundly harmful to human rights.

How may human rights contribute to changing matters? Can a human right to education and to education in human rights help? What difference can women's rights make?

Opponents of human rights may be divided into two groups. One group believe human rights are ineffective, a deception and mystification leading the disadvantaged to believe that remedies are available while their oppression continues unabated, and argue that the only realistic means of improving the lot of the worst-off is to transfer power to them, presumably by revolution. The historical evidence shows that revolution is a short route to further tyranny. At the same time such critics of human rights are normally strong supporters of the *enabling* and *sybaritic* functions of education and of its *instrumental* uses. This would imply faith in education as a means of improving the human condition. Can their disregard of human rights possibly be a conscious or unconscious convenient cover for doing nothing while waiting for the revolution? The proper answer to deficiencies in the present methods of implementing human rights is to stick to the long, slow and often tedious process of gaining 'painful inches'[2].

Human rights education about what has been achieved and how the gains have been won can help to refute these opponents. It is not sufficient simply to teach what the rights are; students at all levels will justifiably conclude, in the light of what is going on around us, that that is mere hot air. It is essential that students should also understand what arrangements there are for implementing and enforcing rights, why there are difficulties and how some have been overcome, and that existing rights must be defended to prevent their being whittled away.

The second group of opponents see human rights as a charter for the undeserving (though most of them concede there should be a safety net for the 'deserving poor'), as oppressive regulation, as a barrier to economic efficiency, competition in world markets, maximising profits and doing the best for shareholders, including pension funds. This group, in contrast to the previous opponents, may be *denyers* or *repressers*, or, at best, *instrumentalists* or *meritocrats*.

Cognitive information can challenge the inadequacies of such views. This information can be conveyed through a variety of subjects and disciplines as well as through education specifically about human rights. The danger is that a strict regulation of the school curriculum and restriction of the funds available for further, adult, continuing and higher education could hinder or prevent such a development.

Human rights education has also a moral dimension, as well as a cognitive content. The values of human rights accord with many of the values of most religions, so that many traditional religious beliefs can be linked with at least some modern notions of human rights. Few individuals are wholly amoral or immoral. Most at least profess to support some moral values. Both shame and guilt can be used to try to secure better compliance with the norms of human rights. As we have seen, international institutions of human rights are largely dependent on mobilising shame to persuade compliance. The equality of women and men, the acceptance of a variety of sexual orientations and the ending of discrimination against unbelievers, heretics and apostates are the values of human rights to which traditional beliefs accommodate least easily.

Women are disadvantaged both in the private domain of the family and in the public domain of employment, economic activity and political life. These disadvantages rest on long-existing traditions and profound beliefs about women. As we have seen, the human rights Conventions and documents do offer a challenge to such traditions and beliefs. Whatever the deficiencies of the exact wording of the instruments, they provide legitimation and standing for those seeking future gains. Changing traditions and beliefs, and building human rights are long-term tasks. The same principle applies for other disadvantaged groups. As the Women's Convention makes clear, equality in the home is as much a part of ending discrimination as equality in the workplace and in public life. Equality should mean that boys learn domestic science and parenting and girls learn craft subjects. The corollary is that men should have equal access to paternity leave, and to caring, nurturing and other often creative work in the home and in bringing up children. The European Union has recently agreed the Directive on parental leave – a minimum of three months unpaid leave regardless of gender (1996)[3] – but British people have been denied this step towards equality by the opt-out from the Social Chapter obtained by the present British Government in 1991. Such developments have the potential radically to change the nature and values of society, providing greater choice for individuals and in particular opening to men constructive and creative activities from which they have, hitherto, been largely excluded.

How far do the programmes agreed at the Vienna and Beijing Conferences address these issues and lay the foundations for further progress?

Both the Vienna Declaration and Programme of Action and the Beijing Platform for Action reiterate with renewed vigour what the instruments have already expressed about education. The Vienna Programme gives particular emphasis to education for human rights and especially the human rights needs of women[4], re-affirming the *enabling* and *instrumental* value of such education. The Beijing Platform, a very wide-ranging document with many specific proposals, recommends governments to take action to achieve 'legal literacy' for women. This is a specific, new, *enabling* and valuable recommendation.

The concept of legal literacy is developed in the Beijing Platform[5] as part of human rights education. This section in the Platform urges governments, NGOs, the UN and other international organisations to present and publicise information about international, regional and national instruments on human rights and means of redress in easily accessible form and in indigenous languages. Information on human rights and rights under humanitarian law should be included in school curricula, in adult education and in training programmes, especially for groups such as the military, the police, the judiciary, lawyers and health professionals. Local and regional women's groups, NGOs, educators and the media should be encouraged to participate in educational programmes to make women aware of their human rights. The importance of education in human rights, beginning in primary school, was stressed by Seck (1990) who observed that there was virtually no teaching on human rights in Africa, where there were so many violations. He also gives an account of the activities of the two African Institutes of Human Rights and notes the limited resources available.

The Vienna Declaration and Programme marks a clear advance in recognising the human rights of women as 'an inalienable, integral and indivisible part of universal human rights'[6]. This result was achieved as a consequence of the thorough preparation for the Conference, especially by women from the Third World and the South (Mertus and Goldberg, 1994). They agreed with women from the West and from Central and Eastern Europe who concurred that the way to ensure this result was to concentrate on the issue of violence against women. Arab women wished to include education as an equal priority with violence. Violence is a recognised violation of human rights. MacKinnon (1993) argues convincingly that violence against women is a form of torture although double standards have prevented it from being recognised as such. Whereas violence against men occurs in public places, violence against women occurs in the home, the private domain, as well as in public places, thus demonstrating again most clearly the falsity of the public/private dichotomy. As Devlin observed (1993) private abuses of human rights are legion (p. 999).

The special needs of women and children refugees are acknowledged[7], as well as the problems caused to women, children, elderly persons and those with disabilities during armed conflicts[8]. The appointment of a Special Rapporteur on Violence Against Women was recommended[9]: Ms Radhika Coomaraswamy was appointed for three years in 1994 by the Commission on Human Rights and presented her first report in November 1994. At its session of January-March 1995, the Commission on Human Rights encouraged the Special Rapporteur on Human Rights to deal with problems of violence against women and to make recommendations to governments about situations in relation to which advisory and technical services could be helpful (*Information Sheet No. 36*, p. 138). The Vienna Declaration also condemns and requires action against female infanticide and other forms of abuse of girl-children[10].

Similar recommendations were made for all children, for racial and ethnic minorities and indigenous peoples and for other disadvantaged groups.

Attention is given to poverty in both the Vienna and Beijing documents. More than one billion people in the world live in extreme poverty and the overwhelming majority are women. The Vienna Declaration notes both that poverty limits the exercise of human rights[11] and that extreme poverty is an affront to human dignity[12] and stresses that the alleviation and ultimate elimination of poverty is a priority for the international community and for governments. Sen (1981) showed that poverty and lack of entitlement rather than shortage of food, substantially exacerbate famines, and are one cause of starvation. By 'entitlement', Sen means access to resources by trade, production, an individual's own labour, inheritance or transfer, exchange, social security or employment.

The Conferences themselves have no authority to implement or enforce recommendations. They could and did urge action upon governments and upon UN organisations, recommending legislation, co-operation, the use of advisory and technical services of the UN and the regular monitoring by UN bodies of progress towards full compliance with those recommendations.

The Vienna Conference made a number of recommendations for the practical implementation of human rights including the following. It called for more resources to be made available for strengthening or establishing regional arrangements for the promotion of human rights through the advisory services of the Centre for Human Rights[13], and made a comparable recommendation to governments (para. 74, p. 132). As might be expected, it recommended co-operation between organisations and co-ordination of procedures, supported the work of the Commissioners and rapporteurs, and urged States to ratify Conventions and Protocols which they had not as yet ratified. It also encouraged more work on the establishment of an international criminal Court and the adoption of the draft declaration on 'the right and responsibility of individuals, groups and organs of society to promote and protect universally recognised human rights and fundamental freedoms' (para. 94). Finally, the Conference recommended that the Commission on Human Rights monitor compliance with its recommendations[14]; and the Commission is doing this.

The *Platform for Action* of the Beijing Conference 1995 takes these provisions further. It lists 12 issues as being of critical concern. These include violence against women, stereotyping, increasing female poverty, inequality in economic structures, in decision-making and in the management of natural resources (Chapter 3, para. 44). It notes that 'the rigidity of socially ascribed gender roles' as well as women's limited access to power are among the factors that may lead to insecurity for families.

The Beijing *Platform* also spells out in some detail and in rather specific terms the obligations of States in relation to women's reproductive health, reproductive rights, control over their own fertility and access to information on family planning, contraception, mentioned in terms (para. 106(u)), and information on AIDS/HIV and sexually transmitted diseases.

The *Platform* calls on governments to encourage men to share equally in child-care and household work and to provide financially for their families, even if they are not living with them (para. 107(c)). In connection with both women's education and their participation in the economy, the *Platform* calls on governments, educational institutions, NGOs and the private sector to provide affordable child-care services of high quality and which would take account of the needs of working men and working women (paras 88(b) and 173(g)). For women and men to combine family, social relations, and work and career opportunities requires, as Beck observes (1992), changes in current views on the supremacy of a highly mobile labour market which treats people as if they were mere isolated individuals.

The Beijing *Platform* includes Recommendations for women and the economy (Chapter 4, section F) and urges governments to establish means of reconciling family and professional life. In relation to the mass media (section J), it invites governments to promote information on women's multiple roles. It notes (in section K) the extent of environmental risks in the home and the importance of women's part in managing natural resources for families. Women form the most stable groups in the community because it is predominantly men who are the migrant workers. Section L on the girl-child notes that boys are commonly preferred to girls and treated more favourably; governments are urged to discourage such discrimination in feeding, education, early marriage, genital mutilation and so on.

The *Platform* recommends institutional measures for advancing women (section H), for example obtaining more information on women's un-recognised and unmonetised work in caring for dependants, preparing food and other tasks, and urges the collection of disaggregated and age-specific data on victims and perpetrators of domestic violence, sexual harassment and incest.

Conclusion

The Vienna and Beijing documents carry forward the working out of human rights in more detail, including recommendations on education. They deal specifically with the needs of disadvantaged groups and individuals and especially women. Governments have agreed these documents. Women's needs focus attention on social, economic and cultural rights and on rights of solidarity, rights that men also need. Unfortunately the dominant policies of a few international organisations and of most governments are increasing needs by their economic preferences and priorities, and by arms-sales to oppressive regimes. Women, children and older people are the most numerous groups of victims.

The ending of the Cold War has removed the example of an alternative policy, however much it may have been rejected as a result of political repression. The Declaration to American Peoples at Punta del Este in 1961 linked liberty with economic and social security and was a response to developments in Cuba after Castro won power (Brownlie, 1981:388). It is in accordance with the statement of an East German scholar that the social policies of the former 'Socialist' (more exactly State-capitalist) countries helped to safeguard the rights of workers in the west[15]. The present dominant economic doctrine also is associated with political repression in many countries.

What leverage then have human rights institutions and processes, NGOs and INGOs on the hypocrisy of governments? In chapter 2, we noted that Galtung doubted how far human rights had any leverage on the situations in which individuals, organisations and nations were trapped.

We can interpret the Vienna and Beijing documents as steps to the further development of existing institutions and processes of human rights. They legitimate the challenge to the present dominant and almost exclusive official economic doctrine with its dire social and economic consequences.

We can see the world's society as an intricate, moving web of organisations of many kinds, of procedures and resources and of individual actions. Changing one thread in that web makes little difference, because the web adjusts to take account of the change. For this reason the overlaps between procedures and institutions are an advantage rather than a disadvantage. If or when one method is blocked, recourse may still be had to others. Substantial change requires many small changes over time. Small changes can cumulatively contribute to the building of trust and confidence between different groups, thereby facilitating further trust. Such changes depend on everyone contributing to making these changes and helping us to keep the rights we have. This is an obligation which everyone should (O'Neill, 1986), but not everyone will, recognise. Education for human rights should help women and men to recognise and carry out these obligations in their personal and occupational lives. As Galtung argued, human needs must be addressed, human needs for freedom, for security and for co-operation. These are the needs which human rights seek to meet.

Notes

1. In Voltaire's *Candide*, Dr Pangloss taught that necessity decrees that all must be as it is, and all is for the best in the best of all possible worlds.

2. 'For while the tired waves, vainly breaking, /Seem here no painful inch to gain, /Far back through creeks and inlets making /Comes silent flooding in the main.' Arthur Hugh Clough, *Say Not the Struggle Naught Availeth.*

3. *The Week in Europe*, WE/13/96, 4 April 1996.

4. Part IID, para. 81, *The Review*, pp. 133-134.

5. Strategic Objective I. 3, para. 233, pp. 131-133.

6. Part I, para. 18, *The Review*, p. 118.

7. Part I, para. 24, *The Review*, p. 119.

8. Part I, para. 29, *The Review*, p. 120.

9. Part II, para. 40, *The Review*, p. 128.

10. Part II, para. 48, *The Review*, p. 129.

11. Part I, para. 14, *The Review*, p. 147.

12. Part I, para. 25, *The Review*, p. 120.

13. Part II D, para. 76, *The Review*, p. 133.

14. Part II E and F, *The Review*, pp. 134-136.

15. Personal communication.

APPENDIX I

Instruments containing references to education

This Appendix lists instruments containing references to education, but is not exhaustive. All instruments referred to in chapter 4 are included.

All instruments were agreed in this century. Where one date is given, that is the date when the instrument was agreed; the first of two dates refers to the date when the instrument was agreed, the second to the date when it came into effect.

The abbreviated names of instruments used in the text are shown in square brackets.

United Nations Instruments

The UN Charter, 1945 [*The Charter*]

Universal Declaration of Human Rights, 1948 [*Universal Declaration*]

International Covenant on Economic, Social and Cultural Rights, 1966/76 [*Social Covenant*]

International Covenant on Civil and Political Rights, 1966/76 [*Civil Covenant*]
   [First] Optional Protocol to the Civil Covenant, 1966/76 [*Optional Protocol*]

UN Specialised Agencies

International Labour Organisation

Declaration Concerning the Aims and Purposes of the International Labour Organisation, Philadelphia, 1944 [*Philadelphia Declaration*]

Discrimination (Employment and Occupation) Convention, 1958/60 [*Discrimination Convention*]

Social Policy (Basic Aims and Standards) Convention, 1962/64 [*Social Policy Convention*]

Employment Policy Convention, 1964/66 [*Employment Convention*]

UN Educational, Scientific and Cultural Organisation
Convention Against Discrimination in Education, 1960/62 [*Education Convention*]
Recommendation concerning Education for International Understanding, Co-operation and Peace and Education relating to Human Rights and Fundamental Freedoms

Regional Organisations

Europe

Council of Europe
European Convention on Human Rights and Fundamental Freedoms and its Protocols, 1952/54 [*European Convention*]
European Social Charter, 1961/65
Recommendation No. R (85) 7 of the Committee of Ministers to Member States on Teaching and Learning about Human Rights in Schools

European Union
Directive of 10 February 1975 on Equal Pay (75/117/EEC)
Directive of 9 February 1976 on Equal Treatment (76/207/EEC)
Directive of 19 December 1978 on Equal Treatment in Social Security (79/7/EEC)
Resolution on the teaching of human rights in the European Community, of the European Parliament, No. C 304/255

Organisation on Security and Co-operation in Europe
*(*formerly *Conference)*
Final Act of the Helsinki Conference,1975
Charter of Paris 1990

The Americas
Organization of American States
American Declaration of the Rights and Duties of Man, 1948
Declaration of Punta del Este, Declaration to the Peoples of America, 1961
American Convention on Human Rights, Pact of San José, 1969/78

Africa
African Charter of Human and Peoples' Rights, 1981/86

Issues

International Convention on the Elimination of All Forms of Racial
    Discrimination, 1966/69
International Convention on the Suppression and Punishment of the Crime of
    Apartheid, 1973/76
Convention Against Torture and Other Cruel, Inhuman or Degrading Treatment
    or Punishment, 1984/87

Beneficiaries

Convention Relating to the Status of Refugees, 1951/54
Convention Relating to the Status of Stateless Persons, 1954/60
Declaration on the Rights of the Child, 1959
Declaration on the Elimination of Discrimination Against Women, 1967
Convention on the Elimination of All Forms of Discrimination Against Women,
    1979/81
Convention on the Rights of the Child, 1989/90

APPENDIX 2

A brief explanation of some technical terms*

Accession, adherence: A government agrees to be bound by a Convention or treaty.

Communication: An application or petition to a UN body.

Convention, Covenant: A *binding* treaty or agreement.

Declaration: A serious expression of opinion and intent, not binding. A Declaration is usually agreed as a preparation for a Convention.

Denunciation: A Government declares it will no longer be bound by a treaty, Convention, etc.

Derogation: A Government declares that it intends to suspend temporarily some provision(s) of a treaty or Convention *provided* the Treaty permits this and under the circumstances the treaty provides.

Domestic law: The law of a State on *all* or *any* topic.

Entry into force: A Treaty enters into force binding all States which have ratified it, when the number of States specified in the treaty have ratified it and any other conditions specified have been satisfied.

Negotiation and adoption: Governments negotiate the text of a treaty, Declaration or Convention (or Covenant); this is usually a long and difficult process because they have to agree on the exact words as well as the general sense and their laws, traditions, interests and experiences differ widely, so that the same words do not mean the same things in all countries. When they agree, the text is adopted and opened for signature.

* Sieghart, 1983: 33-38, explains these terms more fully.

Observations, recommendations, reports: These are terms used by monitoring bodies for their findings whether on individual cases or on the reports made by Governments.

Protocol: A binding addition to a Treaty, coming into force subject to the conditions set out in the Protocol.

Ratify: This means that a Government has made the Convention binding in law upon itself. In most countries, the Convention can then be applied by the national Courts, but this is not the case in the UK. Only the Government is bound.

Recommendations: Governments are expected to comply with Recommendations which they have signed and international bodies may monitor how far they have complied, but Recommendations are less binding than Conventions.

Reservation, interpretation: These terms mean that a Government generally agrees with the provision to which it has attached the reservation or interpretation, but wants the provision to be binding in a specific way or subject to specific conditions.

Sign: When a Government signs a treaty, it expresses its general approval of it, and intends to ratify it. Delay may be necessary because it has to change its own laws.

Treaty: A Convention, treaty or other binding agreement. The text specifies the conditions for entry into force.

Appendix 3

Simplified diagrams of Human Rights organs: Council of Europe and UN

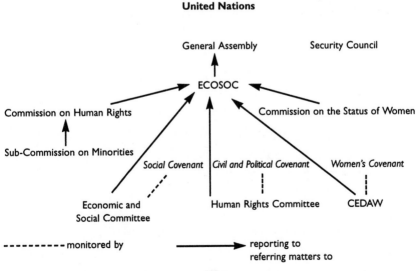

Council of Europe

European Convention

Social Charter

Commission on Human Rights Chambers

Committee of Independent Experts

Directorates

Committees

Governmental Committee

Court of Human Rights Chambers

Committee of Ministers

Parliamentary Assembly

United Nations

General Assembly

Security Council

ECOSOC

Commission on Human Rights

Commission on the Status of Women

Sub-Commission on Minorities

Social Covenant

Civil and Political Covenant

Women's Covenant

Economic and Social Committee

Human Rights Committee

CEDAW

- - - - - - - - - monitored by

————▶ reporting to
referring matters to

TABLE OF BRITISH LEGISLATION and CIRCULARS

Statutes

Statutory Instruments

Circulars

TABLE OF DECLARATIONS, CONVENTIONS AND RESOLUTIONS

International Labour Organisation

UNESCO

1960 Convention Against Discrimination in Education · 81, 83, 90, 94n.4/6/7, 114

1978 Decision 3.3, 104 Executive Board, Doc.104 EX/Decision · 114-5

1974 Recommendation concerning Education for International Understanding, Co-operation and Peace and Education Relating to Human Rights and Fundamental Freedoms · 93, 165

Council of Europe

1950 European Convention on Human Rights and Fundamental Freedoms · 14, 16, 29, 43, 81, 89, 94n.4, 95, 97, 103, 127, 129, 132, 135, 142, 149, 164, 168-171

[Eleven] Protocols · 43, 81, 83, 127, 128, 129, 130, 131, 139, 169-170

1961 European Social Charter · 82, 85, 87, 89, 94n.4, 95, 136, 137, 138, 140

1988 Additional Protocol · 136

1991 Protocol of Turin · 137

1978 Resolution (78) 41 on *The Teaching of Human Rights* · 93

1985 Recommendation No.R (85)7 of the Committee of Ministers to Member States on Teaching and Learning about Human Rights in Schools · 93, 94n.9, 165

1987 European Convention Against Torture · 29

European Common Market/Communities/Union

1957 Treaty of Rome · 141

1975 Directive of 10 February on Equal Pay (75/117/EEC) · 20n.19, 141

1976 Directive of 9 February on Equal Treatment (76/207/EEC) · 141, 143, 144

1978 Directive of 19 December on Equal Treatment in Social Security (79/7/EEC) · 141, 142

1982 Resolution of the European Parliament on the Teaching of Human Rights in the European Community (OJ. No.C 304/255) · 93, 94n

1992 Treaty of Maastricht · 96, 138, 141, 179

1992 Pregnancy and Maternity Directive (92/85/EEC) · 141, 142-143

1996 Parental Leave and Leave for Family Reasons Directive (94/34/EC) · 179

Conference/Organisation on Security and Co-operation in Europe

1975 Final Act of the Helsinki Conference · 81, 82, 85, 86, 87, 91, 93

1990 Charter of Paris · 81, 82, 85, 86, 87, 91

TABLE OF CASES

British Cases

United States

Permanent Court of International Justice

UN Human Rights Committee

European Commission and Court of Human Rights

(The Commission makes Decisions and the Court makes Judgements)

Belgian Linguistic Cases, Judgements, Series A, 5 and 6; 11 Yearbook 832
   Stocktaking 1984:97 • **83, 168, 171**

Berrehab v. *Netherlands*, Judgement of 21 June 1988, *Information Sheet No.
   23*, pp. 22-23 • **139**

Buckley v. *UK*, Application No. 20348/92, *Information Sheet No. 36*, p. 57 • **135**

Campbell and Cosans v. *UK*, Judgement of 25 February 1982, 3 EHRR 531; 3
   Human Rights Law Review (1982), Nos 1-4, pp. 231-136 • **170, 171**

Costello-Roberts v. *UK*, Application No. 13134/87, Judgement of 25 March
   1993, *Information Sheet No. 32*, pp. 31-33 • **131**

Glasenapp and Kosiek v. *Federal Republic of Germany*, Nos 9228/80 and
   9704/82, Judgements of 28 August 1982, *Stocktaking* (1984) pp. 296-298;
   Information Sheet No. 20, pp. 28-32 • **124**

Graeme v. *UK*, Case No. 13887/88, Decision of the Commission of 5 February
   1990 • **169**

Hoffman v. *Austria*, Application No. 12875/87, *Information Sheet No. 32*, p. 51
   • **131**

J. N. C. James and others [Trustees of the Duke of Westminster] v. *UK*,
   Application No. 8793/79, *Stocktaking* (1984) pp. 305-306; *Yearbook 1986*:
   151, Judgement 21 February 1986 • **41**

Karnell and Hardt v. *Sweden*, *X* v. *Sweden* Application 4733/71, Decisions of
   19 July and 13 December 1971, 14 *Yearbook* 664 and 676 • **171**

Keegan v. *Ireland*, Judgement of 26 May 1994, *Information Sheet No. 34*, pp.
   43-47 134

Kjeldsen, Busk Madsen and Pedersen v. *Denmark*, Judgement of 7 December
   1976, 19 *Yearbook* 502; Series A, No. 23; 1 EHRR 711 • **170, 171**

Kroon, Zerouk and Samir v. *Netherlands*, Application No. 18535/91,
   Information Sheet No. 35, p. 31 • **134**

Lavisse v. *France*, Application No. 14233/88, *Information Note No. 97*, p. 21 •
   133

Lithgow and others v. *UK*, Judgement of 6 May 1985, *Information Sheet No. 20*,
   p. 18 • **41**

López Ostra v. *Spain*, Application No. 16798/90, Judgement of 9 December
   1994, *Information Sheet No. 35*, p. 53 • **134**

Mellacher and others v. *Austria*, Judgement of 19 December 1989, *Information
   Sheet No. 26*, p. 19 • **41**

Minniti v. *Italy*, Resolution of the Committee of Ministers DH (92) 50,
   Information Sheet No. 31, pp. 61 and 118 • **128**

Nortier v. *Netherlands*, Application No.13924/88 *Information Note* No. 100,
   p.11 • **159**

European Court of Justice

Inter-American Court of Human Rights

Botswana

Tanzania

SELECT BIBLIOGRAPHY

OFFICIAL PUBLICATIONS

United Kingdom

Commission for Local Administration in England, *Annual Reports*, London

_____ *Report on Investigation No.94/A/0015 into a Complaint Against the London Borough of Enfield*, 22 March 1995, London

_____ *Report on Investigation No.94/B/0524 Against Leicester County Council*, 8 December 1994, Coventry

Commission for Racial Equality (1988) *Medical School Admissions: Report of a Formal Investigation into St George's Hospital Medical School*, London

Committee on Higher Education (1961-1963), Chairman: Lord Robbins, *Report*, Cmnd 2154, London: HMSO

Department for Education (1994) *Our Children's Education: The Updated Parent's Charter*, London

Equal Opportunities Commission (1979/83) *Do You Provide Equal Opportunities?* Manchester

Hansard, *Parliamentary Debates*, House of Commons, London

National Curriculum Council (1990) *Curriculum Guidance 8: Education for Citizenship,* London

United Nations

Beijing Declaration and the Platform for Action (1996) A/CONF.177/20, New York

Centre for Human Rights, *Human Rights Newsletter*, Geneva

Commission on the Status of Women, *Minutes*, etc. E.CB.6/1995/5/Add.4 of 6 January 1995; E/CN.6.1995.2 of 27 February 1995

Committee on the Elimination of Discrimination Against Women (CEDAW), *Minutes, Reports*, etc.; CEDAW/C/SR/257 of 4 February 1994; CEDAW/C/LIB/1/Add.1 of 4 October 1994; CEDAW/C/1995/2 of 31 October 1994; CEDAW/C/7/Rev.1 of 3 February 1995; CEDAW/C/TUN/1-2 of 12 April 1994; GA Res.48/104

Economic and Social Council (ECOSOC), E/1994/INF/6

Human Rights Committee, *Minutes, Reports,* etc.; A/36/40 (1981); A/38/40 (1983); A/39/40 (1984); A/40/40 (1985); A/45/40 (1990)

_____ *Reports to the General Assembly:* (1981) Supp.No.40, A/36/40, 36th sess.; (1990) Supp.No.40, A/45/40 (2 vols) 45th sess.; (1991) Supp.No.40, A/46/40, 46th sess., (UK Report, pp.87-103)

_____ (1994) *Yearbook of the Human Rights Committee 1985-86,* CCPR/5/Add.1; Doc.A/40/40, Ninth Annual Report of the Human Rights Committee to the General Assembly, p.323ff.; Report on the UK and General Observations pp.379-389; Doc.CCPR/C/32/Add.5, p.162, Report by the UK, New York and Geneva

Vienna Declaration and Programme of Action (1993) Doc.A/CONF.157/23 (Basic Text) reprinted in *The Review,* No.50

International Labour Organisation

Committee of Experts, *Reports,* Geneva

Constitution, Geneva

ILO at Work, A4 folder with 65 leaflets, London

World of Work, Quarterly, Geneva

UNESCO

Director-General, *Reports,* Paris

General Conference, *Comptes-Rendus,* Paris

Council of Europe

Case-Law on the European Social Charter, Supplement No.3 (1993) Strasbourg

Human Rights in International Law, 1992, Strasbourg, Council of Europe Press

Directorate of Human Rights, *Information Sheets: No.20* May-October 1986; *No.23* May-October 1988; *No.26* November 1989-April 1990; *No.31* July-December 1992; *No.32* January-June 1993; *No.34* January-June 1994; *No.35* July-December 1994; *No.36* January-June 1995, *No.37* July-December 1995, Strasbourg

_____ *Stocktaking* (1984) Strasbourg

European Commission of Human Rights, *Human Rights News,* 262(91) 17.6.91

_____ *Information Notes: No.97,* 27 May-7 June 1991 (17 June 1991); *No.100,* 7-18 October 1991 (12 November 1991) Strasbourg

_____ (1995) *Survey of Activities and Statistics,* Strasbourg

European Court of Human Rights, Registry of the Court (1994) *Aperçus, Survey of Activities 1993*, Strasbourg: Carl Heymanns Verlag
_____ Press releases

European Commission
Charter of Fundamental Social Rights for Workers (1990) Brussels
_____ *The Week in Europe*, weekly, London

Organization of American States
Inter-American Commission on Human Rights, *Annual Reports*, Washington D.C.
_____ *Report on the Situation of Human Rights in Haiti* (1995), OEA/Ser. L/V/II.88, Doc.10 rev., 9 February, Washington D.C.
Inter-American Commission of Women, *Final Acts of Assemblies*, Washington D.C.
_____ *Studies*, Washington D.C.
Inter-American Court of Human Rights, Advisory Opinions, Judgements, San José,   Costa Rica
_____ *Annual Reports*, Washington D.C.

BOOKS AND ARTICLES

Aaron, Jane and Sylvia Walby (eds), (1991) *Out of the Margins*, London: The Falmer Press.

Advisory Group of Commonwealth NGOs (1991) *Put Our World To Rights: Towards a Commonwealth Human Rights Policy*. London: Commonwealth Human Rights Institute

Alston, Philip, (1980) Unesco's Procedures for dealing with Human Rights Violations, *Santa Clara Law Review*, Vol. 20, pp. 665-696.

Alston, Philip, (ed.) (1992) *The United Nations and Human Rights: A Critical Appraisal*, Oxford: Clarendon Press.

_____Critical Appraisal of the UN Human Rights Regime, in Alston (1992) pp. 1-21.

_____The Commission on Human Rights, in Alston (1992) pp. 126-210.

Aristotle, *Politics*, Trans. T. A. Sinclair (1962) Harmondsworth: Penguin, Book V, chapter 2.

Arnot, Madeleine, Miriam David and Gaby Weiner (1996) *Educational Reforms and Gender Equality in Schools*, Manchester: EOC

Arnot, Madeleine and Gaby Weiner (eds) (1987) *Gender and the Politics of Schooling*, London: Hutchinson in association with the Open University

Association of County Councils and Association of Metropolitan Councils, (1996) Report on Capital Expenditure on Schools, London: mimeo.

Azzan, Fateh (1993) Non-Governmental Organisations and the UN World Conference on Human Rights. *The Review*, No. 50, pp. 89-100

Banks, J. A. and Olive (1965) *Feminism and Family Planning in Victorian England*. Liverpool: Liverpool University Press

Barnard, Catherine (1992) The Maastricht Agreement and Education, *Education and the Law*, Vol. 4(3), pp. 123-134

Barnard, H. C. (1961) *A History of English Education from 1760*. London: University of London Press

Beck, Ulrich (1986) *Risk Society: Towards a New Modernity*, translated by Mark Ritter. London: Sage Publications (1992)

Beyani, Chaloka (1994) Toward a More Effective Guarantee of Women's Rights in the African Human Rights System, in Cook, pp. 285-306

Bossuyt, Marc (1993) International Human Rights Systems: Strengths and Weaknesses, in Mahoney and Mahoney, pp. 47-55

Boutros-Ghali, B. (1982) The League of Arab States, in Vasak, pp. 575-582

van Boven, Theo (1993) Prevention of Human Rights Violations, in Mahoney and Mahoney, pp. 937-949

Brett, Rachel (1995) The Role and Limits of Human Rights NGOs at the United Nations, *Political Studies*, Special Issue, pp. 96-110

Brown, L. Neville and Francis G. Jacobs (1977) *The Court of Justice of the European Communities*, London: Sweet and Maxwell

Brownlie, Ian (1981) *Basic Documents on Human Rights*. Oxford: Oxford University Press, 2nd ed.

Butegwa, Florence (1994) Using the African Charter on Human and Peoples' Rights to Secure Women's Access to Land in Africa, in Cook, pp. 495-514

Byrnes, Andrew (1994) Toward More Effective Enforcement of Women's Human Rights through the Use of International Human Rights Law and Procedures, in Cook, pp. 189-227

Chafee, Zechariah (1963) *Documents on Fundamental Human Rights*. New York: Atheneum, 2 vols

Christie, Kenneth (1995) Regime Security and Human Rights in Southeast Asia, *Political Studies*, Special Issue, pp. 204-218

Coard, Bernard (1971) *How the West Indian Child is Made Educationally Sub-normal in the British School System*, London: New Beacon Books for Caribbean Education and Workers Association

Cohn, Cindy (1991) The Early Harvest: Domestic Legal Changes Related to the Human Rights Committee and the International Covenant on Civil and Political Rights, *Human Rights Quarterly,* Vol. 13: pp.295-321

Coliver, Sandra (1989) United Nations Machineries on Women's Rights: How Might They Better Help Women Whose Rights Are Being Violated? in Lutz pp. 25-49

Collins, Randall (1977) Functional and Conflict Theories of Educational Stratification, in Karabel and Halsey (eds), pp. 118-136

Cook, Rebecca J. (1990) International Human Rights Law Concerning Women: Case Notes and Comments, *Vanderbilt Journal of Transnational Law*, Vol. 23, pp. 779-813

Cook, Rebecca J. (ed.) (1994) *Human Rights of Women: National and International Perspectives.* Philadelphia: University of Philadelphia Press

Cranston, Maurice (1967) Human Rights, Real and Supposed, in D. D. Raphael (ed.) *Political Theory and the Rights of Man.* London, Macmillan

Croll, Elisabeth, (1978) *Feminism and Socialism in China.* London: Routledge and Kegan Paul.

David, Miriam (1980) *The State, the Family and Education.* London: Routledge and Kegan Paul

_____(1995) Parental Wishes versus Parental Choice, *History of Education*, Vol 24(3) pp. 267-276

Davies, Peter (ed.) (1988) *Human Rights.* London: Routledge

Davin, Anna (1978) Imperialism and Motherhood, *History Workshop*, Issue 5, Spring, pp. 9-65

_____(1979) 'Mind that you do as you are told': reading books for Board School girls, *Feminist Review*, No. 3, pp. 89-98

Delamont, Sara (1978a) The Contradiction in Ladies' Education, in Delamont and Duffin, pp. 134-163

_____(1978b) The Domestic Ideology and Women's Education, in Delamont and Duffin, pp. 164-187

Delamont, Sara and Lorna Duffin (eds) (1978) *The Nineteenth Century Woman: Her Cultural and Physical World.* London: Croom Helm

Devlin, Richard (1993) Solidarity or Solipsistic Tunnel Vision? Reminiscences of ʑ Renegade Rapporteur, in Mahoney and Mahoney, pp. 991-1003

Donnelly, Jack (1989) *Universal Human Rights in Theory and Practice.* Ithaca and London: Cornell University Press

Dugard, John (1985) Towards Racial Justice in South Africa: Can the American Constitutional Experience Help? Paper to Bicentenary Conference on the American Constitution organised by Columbia University in Dallas, Texas, 21-22 November

Dyhouse, Carol (1981) *Girls Growing up in Late Victorian and Edwardian England.* London: Routledge

Eggleston, John *et al.* (1986) *Education for Some: A Summary of the Eggleston Report on the Educational and Vocational Experiences of Young Black People,* London: The Runnymede Trust

El-Sanabary, Nagat (1994) Female Education in Saudi Arabia and the Reproduction of Gender Division, *Gender and Education,* Vol. 6(2) pp. 141-150

Entwistle, Harold (1979) *Antonio Gramsci: Conservative Schooling for Radical Politics.* London: Routledge and Kegan Paul

European Community Law – An Overview (1990) London: HLT Publications

Evans, Richard J. (1977) *The Feminists.* London: Croom Helm

Feldman, David (1993) *Civil Liberties and Human Rights in England and Wales.* Oxford: Clarendon Press

Fenwick, Helen and Tamara K. Hervey (1995) Sex Equality in the Single Market: New Directions for the European Court of Justice, *Common Market Law Review,* Vol. 32, pp. 443-470

Galtung, Johann (1994) *Human Rights in Another Key.* Cambridge and Oxford: Polity Press in association with Blackwell Publishers

Gillborn, David (1990) *'Race', Ethnicity and Education: Teaching and Learning in Multi-Ethnic Schools.* London: Unwin Hyman

Glass, David (1959) Education, in Morris Ginsberg (ed.) *Law and Opinion in England in the Twentieth Century.* London: Stevens

Gramsci, Antonio (1971) *Selections from the Prison Notebooks,* edited and translated by Quintin Hoare and Geoffrey Nowell Smith. London: Lawrence and Wishart

The Guardian, newspaper, London and Manchester

Halliday, Fred (1995) Relativism and Universalism in Human Rights: the Case of the Islamic Middle East, *Political Studies,* Vol XLIII Special issue, pp. 152-167

Hammond, J. L. and Barbara Hammond (1948) *The Village Labourer.* London: Guild Books, Longmans Green (1911, 1st ed.)

Harlow, Carol and Richard Rawlings (1984) *Law and Administration,* London: Weidenfeld and Nicolson.

Harris, David (1984) *The European Social Charter.* Charlottesville, Va.: University of Virginia Press

Harris, Neville (1993) *Law and Education: Regulation, Consumerism and the Education System.* London: Sweet and Maxwell

Hoggart, Richard (1957) *The Uses of Literacy: Aspects of Working Class Life with special reference to publiations and entertainments.* London: Chatto and Windus

Hopper, Earl I. (1977) A Typology of Classification of Educational Systems, in Karabel and Halsey

Human Rights Internet Reporter, Ottawa

Ilumoka, Adetoun (1994) African Women's Economic, Social and Cultural Rights – Toward a Relevant Theory and Practice, in Cook, pp. 307-325

Jackson, Roberta (1992) The Committee on the Elimination of Discrimination Against Women, in Alston, pp. 444-472

Justice (1995) Human Rights – The UK's Record, *Bulletin,* August, London, pp. 1-2

Kaballo, Sidgi (1995) Human Rights and Democratisation in Africa, *Political Studies,* Special Issue, pp. 189-203

Karabel, Jerome and A. H. Halsey (1977) *Power and Ideology in Education.* New York: Oxford University Press

Kartashkin, Vladimir (1982) The Socialist Countries and Human Rights, in Vasak, pp. 631-650

Kuenyehia, Akua (1994) The Impact of Structural Adjustment Programs on Women's International Human Rights: the Example of Ghana, in Cook, pp. 422-436

Law, Cheryl and Margherita Rendel (1992) Human Rights Materials in British Schools. Strasbourg: Council of Europe, Council for Cultural Co-operation, S:\II\EDECSSE1. 92

Leary, Virginia (1992) Lessons from the Experience of the International Labour Organisation, in Alston, pp. 580-619

Luckhaus, Linda (1986) Payment for Caring: A European Solution? *Public Law,* pp. 526-537

Lutz, Ellen L., Hurst Hannum and Kathryn J. Burke (eds) (1989) *New Directions in Human Rights.* Philadelphia: University of Pennsylvania Press

McGoldrick, Dominic (1991) *The Human Rights Committee: Its Role in the Development of the International Covenant on Civil and Political Rights.* Oxford: Clarendon Press

MacKinnon, Catherine A. (1993) On Torture: A Feminist Perspective on Human Rights, in Mahoney and Mahoney, pp. 21-31

Madiot, Yves, (1991) *Droits de l'homme,* Paris: Masson, 2nd ed.

Mahoney, Kathleen E. and Paul Mahoney (1993) *Human Rights in the Twenty-First Century: A Global Challenge.* Netherlands: Martinus Nijhoff

Marsh, Norman S. (1973) *Interpretation in a National and International Context.* Heule, Belgium: UGA

Martindale, Hilda, (1938) *Women Servants of the State, 1870-1938,* London: Allen and Unwin.

Medina, Cecilia (1994) Toward a More Effective Guarantee of the Enjoyment of Human Rights by Women in the Inter-American System, in Cook, pp. 257-284

Meron, Theodor (1982) Norm-making and Supervision in International Human Rights: Reflections on Institutional Order, *American Journal of International Law*, Vol. 76, pp. 754-778

Meron, Theodor (ed.) (1984) *Human Rights in International Law: Legal and Policy Issues.* Oxford: Clarendon Press

Mertus, Julie and Pamela Goldberg (1994) A Perspective on Women and International Human Rights after the Vienna Declaration: The Inside/Outside Construct, *New York University Journal of International Law*, Vol. 26: 201-234

Mirza, Heidi Safia (1992) *Young, Female and Black.* London: Routledge

Mowbray, Alistair R. (1994) A New European Court of Human Rights, *Public Law*, pp. 540-552

Norman, Sara (1991) Reports of the 8th and 9th Sessions of the African Commission on Human and Peoples' Rights, *Human Rights Internet Reporter*, Vol. 14(1), pp. 95-96

O'Neill, Onora (1986) *Faces of Hunger: An Essay on Poverty. Justice and Development.* London: Allen and Unwin

Opsahl, Torkel (1989) Instruments of Implementation of Human Rights, *Human Rights Law Journal*, Vol. 10(1-2), pp. 13-34

_____(1992) The Human Rights Committee, in Alston, pp. 369-443

Paine, Thomas, (1791/2) *Rights of Man.* Harmondsworth: Pelican (1969).

Palmer, Camilla and Kate Poulton (1987) *Sex and Race Discrimination in Legislation.* London: Legal Action Group

Partsch, Karl Josef (1990) La Mise en Oeuvre des Droits de l'Homme par l'Unesco, *Annuaire française de Droit International*, Vol. XXXVI, pp. 482-506

Political Studies (1995) Special Issue on Politics and Human Rights, edited by David Beetham, No. XLIII

Ramcharan, Bertrand (1989) in *Universality of Human Rights in a Pluralistic World*, Proceedings of the Colloquy organised by the Council of Europe in Co-operation with the International Institute of Human Rights, Strasbourg, 17-19 April 1989 Kehl am Rhein: N. P. Engel

Rampton, Anthony (1981) *West Indian Children in Our Schools, Interim Report of the Committee of Inquiry into the Education of Children from Ethnic Minority Groups*. London: HMSO

Reanda, Laura (1992) The Commission on the Status of Women, in Alston, pp. 265-303

Rendall, Jane (1985) *The Origins of Modern Feminism: Women in Britain, France and the United States, 1780-1860*, London: Macmillan

Rendel, Margherita, (1977) The Contribution of Labour Women to the Winning of the Franchise, in *Women in the Labour Movement*, Lucy Middleton (ed.), London: Croom Helm.

_____(1991) Abortion and Human Rights, *New Law Journal*, Vol. 141, 20 September, pp. 1270-1271

Rendel, Margherita (ed.) (1981) *Women, Power and Political Systems*. London: Croom Helm

The Review, Geneva: International Commission of Jurists

Robertson, A. H. (1982) *Human Rights in the World: An Introduction to the Study of the International Protection of Human Rights*. Manchester: Manchester University Press

Rosenthal, Robert and Lenore Jacobsen (1971) Pygmalion in the Classroom, in Melvin Silberman (ed.) *The Experience of Schooling*. New York: Rinehart and Winston, pp. 107-120

Ruskin, John (1864) *Sesame and Lilies*, three lectures delivered in Dublin first printed in 1871. London: Geo. Allen, 9th complete ed. 1894

Schwelb, Egon and Philip Alston (1982) The Principal Institutions and Other Bodies Founded under the Charter, in Vasak, pp. 231-301

Seck, Moustapha (1990) A Plea for Human Rights Education in Africa, *Human Rights Law Journal*, Vol. 11(3-4), pp. 283-299

Sen, Amartya (1981) *Poverty and Famines: An Essay on Entitlement and Deprivation*. Oxford: Clarendon Press

Sharpe, R. J. (1976) *The Law of Habeas Corpus*. Oxford: Clarendon Press.

Sieghart, Paul (1983) *International Law of Human Rights*. Oxford: Clarendon Press

_____(1985) *The Lawful Rights of Mankind: An Introduction to the International Legal Code of Human Rights*. Oxford: Oxford University Press

Simon, Brian (1960) *The Two Nations and the Educational Structure, 1780-1870*. London: Lawrence and Wishart

_____(1974) *Education and the Labour Movement, 1870-1920*, London: Lawrence and Wishart

Spender, Dale (ed.) (1981) *Men's Studies Modified: The Impact of Feminism on the Academic Disciplines*. Oxford: Pergamon Press

Stone, Maureen (1981) *The Education of the Black Child in Britain*. London: Fontana

Strachey, Ray (1928) *The Cause*. London: Virago (1978).

Strohal, Christian (1993) The United Nations Responses to Human Rights Violations, in Mahoney and Mahoney, pp. 347-360

Tabak, Fanny (1981) Women's Role in the Formulation of Public Policies in Brazil, in Rendel (ed.), pp.66-80

Tardu, M. E. (1988) International Complaint Procedures for Violations of Human Rights, *Indian Journal of International Law*, Vol. 28(2), April-June, pp. 171-187

Tawney, R. H. (1931) *Equality*. London: Unwin Books (1964).

Thompson, E. P. (1963) *The Making of the English Working Class*, Harmondsworth: Pelican (1968)

Tomlinson, Sally (1983) *Ethnic Minorities in British Schools: A Review of the literature, 1960-1982*. Policy Studies Institute. London: Heinemann Educational Books

Trubeck, David M. (1984) Economic, Cultural and Social Rights in the Third World: Human Rights Law and Human Needs Programs, in Meron, pp. 205-271

Tyagi, Yogesh K. (1983) Cooperation between the Human Rights Committee and Non-governmental Organisations: Permissibility and Propositions, *Texas International Law Journal,* Vol. 18: 273-290

Unger, Roberto Mangabeira, (1976) *Law in Modern Society*, New York: The Free Press.

Vallat, Sir Francis, (ed.) (1971) *An Introduction to the Study of Human Rights*, London: Europa.

Vasak, Karel (1979) *Pour une 'troisième génération' des droits de l'homme: les droits de solidarité*, Inaugural lecture at the Tenth Study Session of the International Institute of Human Rights. Strasbourg, mimeo

Vasak, Karel (ed.) (1982) *The International Dimensions of Human Rights*, revised and edited for the English edition by Philip Alston, 2 vols. Westport, Connecticut: Greenwood Press and Paris: UNESCO

Wade, H.E.W. (1994) *Administrative Law*. Oxford: Clarendon Press, 7th ed.

Walkerdine, Valerie (1992) Progressive Pedagogy and Political Struggle, in Carmen Luke and Jennifer Gore (eds), *Feminisms and Critical Pedagogy*. New York: Routledge

Weiner, Gaby (ed.) (1985) *Just a Bunch of Girls*. Milton Keynes: Open University Press

Weiner, Gaby and Madeleine Arnot (eds) (1987) *Gender under Scrutiny: New Enquiries in Education.* London: Hutchinson in association with the Open University

Weiss, Edith Brown (1984) The Planetary Trust: conservation and intergenerational equality, *Ecology Law Quarterly,* Vol. 11, pp. 495-581

_____(1988) *In Fairness to Future Generations: International Law, Common Patrimony and Intergenerational Equity.* Dobbs Ferry, New York: The United Nations University, Tokyo and Transnational Publishers Inc.

Weiss, Edith Brown (ed.) (1992) *Environmental Change and International Law: New Challenges and Dimensions.* Tokyo: United Nations University Press

Weissbrodt, David and Rose Farley (1994) The UNESCO Human Rights Procedure: An Evaluation, *Human Rights Quarterly,* Vol. 16, pp. 391-414

Whyte, Judith, Rosemary Deem, Lesley Kant and Maureen Cruickshank (eds.) (1985) *Girl-Friendly Schooling.* London: Methuen

Wolf, Francis (1984) Human Rights in the International Labour Organisation, in Meron, pp.273-304

Wollstonecraft, Mary, (1792) *Vindication of the Rights of Woman,* Harmondsworth: Penguin (1975) London: Walter Scott (1891)

Woodham-Smith, Cecil (1951) *Florence Nightingale.* Harmondsworth: Penguin (1955)

Yamane, Hiroko (1982) Asia and Human Rights, in Vasak, pp. 651-670

Youssoufi, A. (1987) Human Rights in Arab Countries, *The Review,* No. 39, pp. 33-35

_____(1994) Report of the Workshop in Amman, January 1994, *The Review,* No. 52, June, pp. 92-95

INDEX

See also Tables of British Legislation, of Declarations and Conventions, and of Cases

Abortion 12, 15, 77, 132, 151

Administration, bureaucracy 1-3, 13, 46, 78, 102, 105, 138, 146, 154n.6, 163. *See also* public servants

Admissibility 97, 115-118

Adult, continuing education 51, 59-61, 65-67, 69, 75n.13, 92, 155, 178, 180

Advisory services, programmes, technical assistance 100-101, 119, 120, 124-5, 182

Affirmative, positive action, 17, 105

Africa 46, 78, 119, 150, 151, 153; North Africans in France 130; Institutes of Human Rights 180

Africa, individual States 3, 42, 46, 112, 119, 123, 151, 152

African Commission on Human and People's Rights 149-53

Age, elderly persons 82, 136, 181, 183

Agriculture 28, 109-10, 125, 152

America, Central 44; Latin 44, 78; North-East 44; *See also* Canada, Brazil, Caribbean, United States

America, Central, individual States 146, 147, 148, 149

America, South, individual States 78, 106, 119, 125, 146, 147

Animals 8, 10, 43

Arab 45, 78, 79-80, 119, 180

Arab, individual States 25, 57, 110, 112

Asia 45, 78, 79, 119, 135; Asia-Pacific 45, 78; Central Asia 29; South-East 45, 125. *See also* India

Asia, individual States 6, 24, 28, 39, 57, 104, 110.

Assembly, right of 6, 10, 32, 34, 36, 116

Association, freedom of, right of 27, 32, 34, 36, 116, 122-3, 132, 133

Australasia, individual States 44, 78, 112, 122, 123

Berufsverbot 124, 132

'Bias' in legal processes 17, 19

Boys 53, 63, 70, 73, 94, 160, 163, 166. *See also* Men

Brazil 39, 78, 104, 119, 122, 149

Britain, Government and education 52, 63; DES, DFE, DfEE, Secretary of State for 1, 156-159, 162, 164, Ch.3, Ch.6 *passim*; inspection of schools 59. *See also* Education, Examinations, Higher Education, Northern Ireland, Schools.

Britain, Governments 9-11, 25, 28, 33-36, 77, 124, 128-30, 135, 138-40, 142-144, 154n.4; criticised 103-4, 121, 123,125; Departments 1-5, 15, 16, 19nn.1-6, 57, 172; Opt-outs 96, 179. *See also* English law; Local government

British Parliament 3, 9, 18

Canada 81, 149

Caribbean, individual States 122, 149, 184

Case-law, jurisprudence, litigation 16, 19, 108, 113, 130, 144-5, 153, 156

Children; abuse 133; claims to rights 8, 34, 43, 83, 85, 89, 94; education 32, 33, 58-9, 64, 74n.11, 83, 85, 89, 131, Ch.6 *passim*; and parents 94, 130, 151, 152; welfare 27, 91, 120, 124, 131,181, 183